'*1973 and Me is a vital account of the spirit,
dynamism and cultural transformation of cricket
brought about by West Indian cricketers. It is told
with verve and brio by Colin Babb and along the
way gives the reader plenty of fun*'.

Colin Grant, historian, author and broadcaster

'*Colin Babb has a rare and beautiful talent for
immersing the reader into history, allowing them
to feel and share the journey of our pasts*'.

Karen Hunte, Chair, Caribbean Politics, British Political
Studies Association

'*A warm and captivating read with a legendary
cast of characters*'.

Lainy Malkani, Director of the Social History Hub, author
and journalist

'*A treasure trove of fascinating historical details
and personal stories*'.

John Stevenson, broadcaster and journalist

1973 *and* Me

The England v West Indies Test Series
and a Memorable Childhood Year

COLIN BABB

Foreword by Simon Lister

Features
Author Q&As with Dickie Bird
Deryck Murray on Inshan Ali
and
Colin Grant on The Wailers in Britain 1973

HANSIB

H
HANSIB
*Celebrating
50 years of
publishing
1970–2020*

First published in Great Britain by Hansib Publications in 2020

Hansib Publications Limited
P.O. Box 226, Hertford, SG14 3WY

info@hansibpublications.com
www.hansibpublications.com

ISBN 978-1-912662-12-8

A CIP catalogue record for this book
is available from the British Library

Design & Production by Hansib Publications Ltd

Printed in Great Britain

Dedication

For my great-grandmother, Lea 'Baba' Osborne also known as Baba Short. Born in Plaisance, East Coast Demerara, Guyana, 1901 and died in London, England, 1987.

Contents

Foreword

by Simon Lister

E veryone nowadays is going on a journey. You can't turn on the TV without hearing a celebrity or an athlete or a member of the public telling you about the journey they've been on. Emotional journeys, journeys of self-discovery, journeys to hell and back.

Ding-ding, all fares please!

They're not alone, these folks. I'm here to tell you, slightly sheepishly, that I'm a fellow traveller – but in my defence, the journey I went on was fairly specific. I was a kid, but as far as I can recall it was on a 133 London bus from Streatham to Kennington with my dad in August 1976. On the top deck of the bus near the stairs on the left. We were going to The Oval for my first Test match. England versus the West Indies.

And that was that. Life, really, was never quite the same again. I had witnessed excellence from West Indian cricketers at an early enough age to let them seep good and proper right down into my inner core. Greenidge, Fredericks, Lloyd, Richards, Murray, Holding – all there marinating in my marrow as I grew up. There was little resistance; they all entered my young consciousness swiftly and decisively. They're still there today.

Many years later I tried to make sense of this invasion by writing *Supercat*, a book about Clive Lloyd – and *Fire in Babylon*, a book about the West Indies from the mid-70s to the mid-90s. It was during this time that I first met Colin. He kindly gave me an excellent interview. And it struck me, while reading this fine book of his, that I was now actually enjoying a much longer and enticing version of that interview. The full-fat version. Actually, 'longer' is the wrong word. More like richer, heavy with explanation, scented with nuance and full of unexpected turns. And always there, in the living room, was the sound of a 1970s TV on in the background.

1973 articulates, with a vivid authority, the journey made from West Indian boyhood to British manhood. And the guiding light on this twisting and sometimes uncertain road is cricket. Caribbean cricket. Colin sets out with humour and deep understanding how the game informed his identity. The result is an articulate exposition of how he has changed, how Britain has changed, how West Indian cricket has changed, since he first saw Sobers and Kanhai on his telly more than four decades ago. Just as

Simon Lister, senior BBC TV news producer, journalist and author of *Supercat: The Authorised Biography of Clive Lloyd* and *Fire in Babylon: How the West Indies Cricket Team Brought a People to its Feet.*

the summer of 1976 was the jumping-off point for me, Colin took his running leap three years earlier.

But this is not a mere autobiography. This is valuable social history. Articulate insight from a collection of guests – some of whom played the game at the highest level and others who never lifted a bat – who riff around the successes of a team that should never have been as outrageously brilliant as they were. Given the constraints of their history, their geography, their politics and their disparate societies.

1973 was probably the year that everything began to fall into place for West Indian cricket. The prime movers that awakened the extraordinary achievements of the next two decades were all there. The best cricket team that has ever played the game was getting ready.

'Here we are', the fast bowler Andy Roberts once said. 'We end up having one of the greatest teams in the history of sport – several dots on the map dominating the world'.

That 1973 tour of England showed what West Indians could do together, and to do it in England was all the sweeter. We should be grateful too that it was the spark that ignited a desire in Colin to write this book.

Ding-ding! Have your tickets ready please. This is a fascinating journey. Enjoy the ride.

The West Indies cricket team was so powerful for me. I tell people this all the time, and I really appreciated all those guys and what they did. Because once I saw them doing well, it made me step up and feel that I could do well too.

CLYDE BEST

* * *

Boycey was also a top fielder, up close or in the deep, and was very popular at Essex because he was the absolute of what every spectator should love. He was a fast bowler and an exciting batsman who could hit the ball out of the ground.

KEITH FLETCHER on Keith Boyce

* * *

That left foot qualifies him for the magic circle.

DAVID COLEMAN, BBC television match commentator, on Norman Hunter – Leeds United v Sunderland 1973 FA Cup final

* * *

The Wailers realised that if they came to England, they would have a chance to meet Chris Blackwell. They heard a lot about Chris Blackwell in Jamaica and really wanted to meet him.

COLIN GRANT on The Wailers in Britain 1973

* * *

There were still black and white programmes being made during the early 70s but by 1973 they were all in colour. So, 1973 was a very typical year for many people in Britain to get their first colour television.

PROFESSOR JOE MORAN

Introduction

In June 1973, the ninth West Indies Test cricket tour of England began with a match against Essex at the County Ground, Chelmsford. For many in the Caribbean diaspora in Britain, the three Test matches and two one-day internationals (ODIs) v England were keenly anticipated events. From 1968 to 1973, the West Indies did not win a Test series. In 1969, the previous West Indies tour to England ended in a 2-0 series defeat for the tourists.

In the summer of 1973, could the West Indies erase the disappointment of 1969, and produce a rewarding experience for the many thousands of Caribbean migrants in Britain, and their British-born descendants? *1973* outlines the significance of this tour for the Caribbean diaspora and others in Britain, whether they were passionate cricket supporters or not.

In 1948, the HMT *Empire Windrush* ship sailed from Jamaica to Britain. The ship carried just over 1,000 passengers with over 700 of them from the Caribbean, including Jamaicans, Trinidadians and Guyanese. This was the symbolic arrival and starting point for substantial post Second World War migration to Britain from the Caribbean.

Many of the Caribbean passengers on board the *Windrush* brought a wide range of ambitions and expectations to create new lives for themselves in Britain, the 'mother country'. Twenty-five years after the *Windrush's* landmark arrival, the 1973 West Indies tour of England was packed with incident and thousands of West Indian supporters who made their presence felt at The Oval, Edgbaston and Lord's.

The drama and spectacle during the 1973 England v West Indies series included a bomb scare, crowd invasions, tensions between players and umpires, players receiving kisses from spectators on the

13

field, an English batsman scoring a century on debut, Garry Sobers and Rohan Kanhai playing their final Test matches in England, Ron Headley – son of the legendary George Headley, making his Test debut, Harold 'Dickie' Bird's entry into the Test arena as an umpire, and the first England v West Indies ODI match at Headingley.

It was also the year of the inaugural Women's Cricket World Cup tournament in England, and Viv Richards' first competitive match in England for the Lansdown Cricket Club in the Somerset seaside town of Weston-super-Mare.

From a Guyanese perspective, the 1973 tour has another enduring legacy. Rohan Kanhai became the first Guyanese cricketer to captain the West Indies team for an entire series. He was also the first West Indian of Indian-Caribbean heritage to hold the post. Lance Gibbs was vice-captain. Four other Guyanese players were selected for the tour.

1973 shares the experiences and memories of the players and umpires who took part in the England v West Indies series action on the field, and the spectators, writers and broadcasters who witnessed these events from beyond the boundary. Alongside the compelling story and legacy of the series, underpinned by historical, political and social perspectives, my memories and observations of growing up as a British-born Caribbean schoolboy in London are a pivotal feature of *1973*.

1973 was the year that I 'discovered' cricket through the West Indies tour that year, the John Player League competition, and the evocative commentary voice of John Arlott. Four years later, I was one of the youngest members of an under-18s team playing in a cricket cup final at The Oval.

1973 was a memorable childhood year for me. I was settling into my street, neighbours, friends and primary school in south London and beyond, with an increasing devotion to Leeds United, the pioneering presence of black players in English football, and the shared family experience of watching television. In 1973, a colour television arrived in our home during the Test series, the mighty Leeds United played Sunderland in one of the most memorable FA Cup finals, Cliff Richard represented the UK for the second time in the Eurovision Song Contest, Peters and Lee were one of the groups who had a *Top of the Pops* number one chart hit, and The Wailers arrived from Jamaica for their first UK tour.

The far-right National Front achieved its highest UK parliamentary election vote, Edward Heath was the British Prime Minister, Britain joined the European Economic Community (EEC), the Caribbean Community (CARICOM) was created, and Guyana experienced its second national election following independence from British colonial rule.

1973 recalls how some of my family, friends, acquaintances, the wider Caribbean diaspora and non-Caribbean people in Britain, felt the impact of these events and more.

The book also features extended author Q&As with Dickie Bird, Deryck Murray on Inshan Ali, and Colin Grant on The Wailers in Britain 1973.

Colin Babb

2018 marked the 90th anniversary of West Indies Test cricket, the 70th anniversary of the Empire Windrush's landmark voyage from the Caribbean, the 70th anniversary of the Leeds Caribbean cricket club – one of the oldest West Indian clubs in Britain, and the 45th anniversary of the 1973 West Indies tour of England. Alvin Kallicharan was awarded a British Empire Medal (BEM) in the Queen's 2018 New Year Honours list. 2019 marked the 40th anniversary of the second West Indies World Cup win in 1979.

CHAPTER 1

My street, my family, my school, politics and cricket

As 1972 Old Year's Night slowly slipped away and New Year's Day 1973 began, I was an eight-year-old primary schoolboy looking forward to being nine years old later in the year. I had settled quite comfortably into our first-floor housing association maisonette flat in Streatham, south London, where we had lived for the last two years. I lived there with my Guyanese mother, my Guyanese great-grandmother (mother's grandmother) and my father from Barbados. It was noticeably more spacious than our previous accommodation in Norbury, which was about two miles away.

Our flat was in an unremarkable south London street with a mixture of working-class and lower-middle-class families from a wide range of backgrounds. Our street was a mixture of owner-occupiers and private, housing association and council flat renters. In the flat downstairs lived the Hines-Hibbert family from Jamaica who, eventually, moved to another part of south London before some of the family migrated to the United States. When they moved out, the flat downstairs was occupied by a woman from Guyana called Miss Glasgow.

The house to our left was occupied by the English-Irish Kelly family. We weren't particularly close to them. But we said hello and goodbye in the way of common courtesy whenever our paths crossed. The youngest child in the family was called Mike. We sometimes played together in our front yards and talked about cricket and football.

Mike supported Kent County Cricket Club and Leeds United. He scrawled Kent CCC and Leeds slogans in chalk on his front yard concrete pathway for our amusement. There was also an older lad with long hair in the house next door who played the drums. I presumed it was one of Mike's brothers. We occasionally heard rhythmic drum noises cascading through the walls that separated our buildings.

A few years later, the Kelly family were replaced by the Harrison family from Jamaica. One of the Harrison boys followed my path and joined the local battalion of the Boys' Brigade, which met in a Methodist church hall at one end of our street. The house to our right was derelict and empty for years. Some of the children in the street called it the 'Haunted House'. This was a building surrounded by intrigue and mystery. In 1973, as in the previous year's school summer holidays, some of the more adventurous (and older) children would creep alongside the house, then crawl through gaps in the wall, or the partially open back door, to look inside. From time to time, curiosity would get the better of me. I would also jump over the fence from our shared back yard and look inside. There were numerous holes in the floorboards and we would, collectively, shriek if we saw a dead rat in the backyard. This only happened once or twice.

A few years later, the Haunted House was renovated and converted into flats. One of the flats was soon occupied by a Jewish family. The children were called Rachel and Jonathan and, for some reason, which I still can't recall, they both called me Jimmy. We'd often have 'round the block' bike races (on the pavement only as instructed by our families). I'd usually win these races because I was older, much more competitive and, in my opinion, had a bigger and better bike.

Denise was one of the children in our street who helped me to ride a bike, which was a major milestone in my young life. Denise was an English girl who lived on the opposite side of the street at number five, in a house with a red door. She was slightly older than me, had a generous soul, and briefly took a few of us younger children under her wing. Denise owned a big red bike and, if she was in the mood, some of us were granted permission to ride it. During the summer of 1973, for part of the school summer holidays when I wasn't watching ball-by-ball coverage of an England v West Indies Test on television, I struggled to learn how to ride Denise's bike. I crashed into front garden hedges and collected bruises on my knees from falling off the bike on the pavement.

A few doors down from us, lived a woman who we all called Fusspot. I don't know how she earned this nickname. But I think it had something to do with her horn-rimmed glasses, permanent stern expression and, for a variety of reasons, she would appear in her front garden and give some of the children on the street a stern telling off. Perhaps, some of us deserved it.

Fusspot's house was targeted by some of the older children on the street during knock down ginger sessions. The knock down ginger game involved one of the older children ringing Fusspot's front door bell, while a group of spectators, including me, watched. We all quickly disappeared just before Fusspot angrily opened her front door.

The families on the opposite side of the street, near the busy adjoining main road, included the Sunich family who lived at number 27 and the Cort family at number 21. The Sunich and Cort families were both from Guyana. The Sunich family moved into our street a few years ahead of us in the late 1960s. They lived in a housing association flat with Irish families living in adjoining flats, the Foxes and the Sullivans. In 1961, Stanley Sunich was the first member of their family to arrive in Britain. His motivation to migrate from Guyana was to speculate with the aim to accumulate.

> The only reason I came to England was to speculate. I came on a whim. One day, my uncle came into the shop where I worked in Georgetown and said to me, 'Let's go to England and do something different, something better'. I had to borrow some money for the flight, but I thought to myself, OK, and so I followed my uncle to London.

Stanley was born in Berbice and grew up in Georgetown. As a schoolboy, he was a keen cricketer and captained his Central High School class cricket team. Basil Butcher, Rohan Kanhai and Jo Solomon lived near his family home in Berbice. Butcher lived near his aunt's house and his father was a close friend of the Madray family, including Ivan Madray. All these players went on to represent Guyana and the West Indies.

Stanley worked as bus conductor based in Streatham Bus Garage for 18 and a half years. Alongside his working life, Stanley developed his passion for cricket from Guyana by playing for the Old Castletonians Cricket Club. The club had a mix of cricketers from across the Caribbean, including Barbadians, Guyanese and Trinidadians, and a few English players. Basil Butcher is one of the club's joint presidents.

One of Stanley's close friends at the Old Castletonians was Neville Carberry, his fellow Guyanese opening batsman. Neville has been the club's chairman for over the last 20 years. Neville, who migrated to England in 1960, is the father of Michael Carberry. Michael is one of the last British-born players of Caribbean heritage to play Test cricket for England. He played six Tests for England from 2010 to 2014. Michael regularly came along with his father to watch the Old Castletonians play. He developed some of his early cricket skills while playing for the club.

Mr Cort also migrated from Guyana to Britain in the 1960s. He played for a cricket team in Guyana and, after a few years, many of his friends – including some whom he played cricket with in Guyana, also arrived in Britain. Mr Cort became the team captain of the Old Castletonians and some of Mr Cort's friends from Guyana also joined the club.

Mr Cort was a central figure in running the Old Castletonians and one of the main organisers of the social events, including the dances. He also acted as the club secretary. Mr Sunich and Mr Cort were close friends and drinking buddies. They regularly visited each other to eat, drink, reminisce about growing up in Guyana and, of course, to talk cricket. In 1973, both Mr Sunich and Mr Cort were looking forward to the West Indies tour of England.

Other families on the opposite side of the road included the Sinclair family from Jamaica, Veronica and her family from the Seychelles and the McElwees from Scotland. The McElwee family were one of the organisers of our street party to celebrate the Queen's Silver Jubilee in 1977. The party was a memorable event for me. I won the children's sprint road race, trying to imitate the running style of David Jenkins, the Trinidadian-born Scottish sprinter. I received a Ladybird hardback book as a reward.

The book told the story of Bonnie Prince Charlie, grandson of the exiled King James II. Bonnie Prince Charlie led an invasion of England in 1745 to regain the English throne, which his grandfather had forfeited in 1688. I still have this book on a bookshelf in my office at home.

Most of the time, there was very little tension between the families from the various social and cultural backgrounds on our street. However, not all the families on our street were especially friendly towards each other. There were situations when conflicts occurred, but we co-existed comfortably enough on a day-to-day basis. One of the houses around the corner from our street was owned by the Prentis family.

They were a large, English family with a couple of menacing dogs. During the school summer holidays, their front door was always open, with various members of the family leaving and arriving. Whenever we walked past their house, there was always the risk of slightly heated words being exchanged between us and them. There was also the threat of their dogs barking aggressively at passers-by for no apparent reason.

On one occasion, words were exchanged between a small group of us, all black children, and a few members of the Prentis family who watched us walk by. The dogs began to bark loudly as usual. I was partly to blame for this, as I gently teased the dogs as I walked by. I felt relatively safe in the knowledge that their front garden fence and entrance gate were too high for the dogs to jump over. Despite this, we quickly walked around the corner to get back to our homes. Within an hour or two, some members of the Prentis family appeared outside our flat hoping for a verbal showdown. Without question, there was racial tension in the air. A few passing residents on the street observed the ongoing spectacle at a safe distance.

My great-grandmother stood her ground outside our front door. I just stood, watched and waited alongside her with the Jamaican children who lived in the flat downstairs. Words were exchanged. Within ten minutes, the Prentis family all turned around and sauntered off back home. Years later, I struck up a friendship with Grant Prentis, one of the younger members of the Prentis clan. We occasionally reflected on that incident and nervously attempted to laugh it off.

The Show Off boys were another group of people who we were wary of. They lived on the opposite side of the street and a few doors down from Veronica and family. The Show Off boys (I think Melanie, one of Jamaican children downstairs, gave them this name and it stuck with me) were a gang of lads who all lived in the same house. The Show Off boys would always leave their house as a group and saunter down the street with an air of confidence blended with a 'don't mess with us' body language display. They were a group of six or seven lads with an age range from late teens to mid-20s.

Two of the Show Off boys were black and the rest were white. The black lads had mini-Afros and the white lads had longish straggly hair or skinhead haircuts. The Show Off boys wore slightly flared jeans or trousers, Monkey boots or Doctor Marten (DM) boots, wide lapel shirts, tank tops and blazer, denim or leather jackets. This was 1973 and that was generally the fashion at the time for many young lads in Britain.

At home, my life before 1973 and for many years afterwards was underpinned by my evolving sense of being a British-born black Caribbean child in Britain. Many years later, I borrowed a term which was introduced to me in London by Karen, an Australian-born Chinese-Malaysian colleague at the BBC. Karen talked about some of her Chinese friends in Britain who described themselves as British Born Chinese (BBC). I borrowed and re-interpreted the term and now consider myself to be British Born Caribbean (BBC).

The British Nationality Act in 1948 made thousands of people living in the British-ruled Caribbean, and millions of people from countries across the globe, citizens of the United Kingdom and Colonies. This act of parliamentary legislation permitted thousands of people from the Caribbean, including my family, with an opportunity to create a new life for themselves in Britain.

For many people in the Caribbean, especially due to its much closer geographical location, the US was a more desirable place to migrate to than Britain. This pattern of migration from the Caribbean changed during the 1950s. In 1952, the McCarren – Walter Immigration and Nationality Act passed through the US Congress. This act limited the number of Caribbean people who could migrate to the US to a small quota of 100 per island, per year. In turn, this block on Caribbean migration to the US made Britain, over 4,000 miles from the English-speaking Caribbean, a more desirable option.

Migrants from the Caribbean travelled to settle in Britain for variety of reasons. For many, the main objective was to secure work as soon as possible. Working in the mother country was a realistic alternative to the high levels of unemployment and steadily declining economies in the Caribbean. In turn, this was a response to the post-Second World War demand for labour to help rebuild Britain. This was a significant motivational tool for many people in the Caribbean who had struggled to find opportunities, which were often limited and had worsened, during the period before and after the Second World War.

Some cricketers from the Caribbean, who played club cricket in England in the 1950s and 1960s, were part of this tide of post-war migration to Britain. Therefore, they completely understood the reasons for it. Conrad Hunte, who played 44 Tests for the West Indies, arrived in England in 1956. He travelled on a ship with about 200 people from the Caribbean. Most of them were recruited from Barbados to work for London Transport and the National Health Service (NHS). Hunte worked in an axle shop for Leyland Motors in Lancashire, before playing for Enfield as a professional cricketer in the Lancashire League.

> The difference in wages between Britain and the West Indies seemed to open dazzling prospects. The average pay for a sugar worker in Barbados was four pounds a week during the 'crop' season, but only two pounds a week during the other eight months of the year. Even teachers and civil servants, though maintaining the trappings of an elite, started at a salary of ten pounds a month. And thousands of young people came out of the grammar schools each year with only hundreds of Government jobs available for them. The openings in commercial firms were still limited to applicants with white or light skins. So, with the promise of better pay and greater opportunity for self-advancement in Britain, hundreds of teachers, civil servants and skilled workers threw up their jobs and joined the queue for Britain. Some came under a labour scheme, and some without it. Some came out of economic necessity. Others, like myself, through restlessness or the desire to climb.[1]

Some people in the Caribbean responded to targeted campaigns aimed at recruiting workers for Britain's bus and rail transport systems, including London Transport and British Rail. From the late 1940s to the 1960s, thousands of people arrived from the Caribbean to work for the NHS which was launched in 1948. Many of them were recruited to work as doctors, nurses, administrators, cooks, porters and cleaners. In 1959 to 1960 some 5,850 trainee nurses and midwives arrived in Britain from overseas. In 1966 to 1967 the figure was 16,745. Of these, nearly 75% were from the Caribbean.[2]

Clive Lloyd met Waveney, his former wife from Guyana, in the late 1960s in London. Waveney was working as a nurse in a psychiatric hospital in Kent. Two of Lance Gibbs' sisters from Guyana were nurses in London in the 1960s. One of them worked in Essex and the other sister worked in West London.

My cousin Pauline arrived in Britain from Guyana in the early 1960s and worked as a paediatric nurse. As her nursing career progressed she became a ward sister. One of my great-aunts from Guyana worked as a nurse in a mental hospital in Surrey. Jean, another one of my great-aunts, trained as a nurse at the St Joseph Mercy Hospital in Georgetown. In Britain, Jean pursued a career path as a medical secretary in the NHS as an alternative to additional training. In 1973, Desree, Jean's daughter and my cousin, started working in the NHS as a student nurse at Hammersmith Hospital in West London. Desree worked in the NHS for over 40 years, which included working as a midwife and a health visitor in south London.

Thelma, a close friend of our family from Georgetown, trained as a nurse with my great-aunt Jean at the St Joseph Mercy Hospital in Georgetown and arrived in Britain in 1955. Thelma continued her training in London as a Medical Laboratory Scientific Officer (MLSO) and worked in the NHS for over 40 years. In 2003, Thelma was awarded a Guyana High Commission Certificate of Achievement which recognised her service to Guyana and the Guyanese community in Britain. In 2005, Thelma received an MBE for helping to improve the health and quality of life for people in Guyana and Britain.

In the mid- to late-1980s, I briefly worked in administrative roles in three NHS hospitals in London and Surrey with nurses from Barbados and Jamaica. I also became a member of the Confederation of Health Service Employees (COHSE) trade union.

As part of a series of programmes produced to celebrate and reflect on 70 years of the NHS, a BBC television documentary called *Black Nurses: The Women Who Saved The NHS*, told the story of the thousands of women from the Caribbean who arrived in post-war Britain to help establish the NHS. The documentary revealed that many of these women were teenagers. They were determined to leave the Caribbean for the first time to create a better future for themselves in Britain.

Many post-war migrants from the Caribbean were motivated to leave by a sense of adventure. For them, this impulse could only be satisfied by searching for better opportunities in Britain. Some Caribbean people arrived in Britain with ambitions to further their education by attending schools, training courses, colleges and universities. Many of them joined family or friends who could help them cope with the challenges and uncertainties of migrant life. Some, like Sam King, served in the UK with the British Armed Forces during the Second World War. After returning to the Caribbean and struggling to settle, some of these ex-servicemen travelled back to Britain.

For others, there was a strong reluctance, despite the hardships and uncertainties they experienced in Britain, to return to the Caribbean unless they achieved their ambition of self-improvement or/and earned enough money to send back to their families. There was also the incentive for some to work hard, save money and return to the Caribbean after a temporary stay in Britain. For many migrants from the Caribbean, once they had settled into the routine of work, raising children, and striving to earn enough money to pay rent or get a foothold on the property ladder, the prospects of returning home permanently to the Caribbean slowly evaporated, or became delayed for many years until retirement.

Most of my family who migrated to Britain in the 1950s and 1960s were from Guyana. The first family member to arrive in Britain from Guyana was Rupert Hunte, a great-uncle, in 1951. Uncle Rupert arrived in Britain three years after 44 Guyanese passengers arrived in Britain on the *Windrush*.

Rupert played the saxophone and sang with the Militia Band in Georgetown. During his life in Britain, Rupert continued to play music in bands across London. He played the saxophone, the piano and sang. Rupert also worked for many years as a store keeper in a prison in south London. He shared his passion for music by teaching some of the prisoners to play instruments and read music.

A year later, the second family member to arrive in Britain was my great-uncle Ivan Hunte, Rupert's brother. Ivan was another accomplished musician who played piano for Nello Lucky's band in Guyana. Lucky's band specialised in jazz, Nat King Cole standards, Latin American music and calypsos, and played in tours across the

Caribbean. During the 1940s and 1950s, some of the countries the Lucky's band visited included Guadeloupe, Martinique and Surinam.

My maternal grandfather, Byron Hunte, brother of Rupert and Ivan, was a pianist in the popular Tom Charles and the Syncopators band in Guyana. Byron settled in Guadeloupe during the 1970s. I mentioned this during a chat with Alvin Kallicharan. Alvin told me that he remembered hearing about Tom Charles and the Syncopators playing at the Belvedere Hotel in Georgetown.

Eight months after Ivan arrived in Britain, my great-aunt Muriel, Ivan's wife, travelled to join him in Britain. Muriel's route to Britain was similar to many Guyanese migrants who travelled to Britain in the 1950s and 1960s. A plane from Guyana to Trinidad followed by a boat from Trinidad to Britain. Muriel's boat arrived in Plymouth on the English south-west coast in 1953. Muriel then boarded a train from Plymouth to re-unite with Ivan in London.

During conversations I've had with Muriel about her early days in England, she clearly remembers having to use ration books to cope with the shortage of food supplies. Muriel also has fond memories of being in central London to watch Queen Elizabeth II's coronation parade. As more of my relatives migrated to Britain from Guyana, Muriel gradually became a matriarchal figurehead for our family in Britain from her north London home with Ivan and their four children. Three of their children were born in Guyana and one was born in Britain.

If we wanted to connect with members of my family from other parts of the Caribbean, we travelled to see my father's family in Barbados, my grandfather's family in Guadeloupe, or various other relatives who had migrated from the Caribbean to North America. Some of my family in Britain also completed another familiar Caribbean migrant route. Settling in Britain before moving to pursue the promise of a bigger and brighter future in the US and Canada. Some family living in the Caribbean and North America travelled to stay for long and short-term periods with our family in Britain.

Some of my family who migrated from Guyana to Britain in the 1960s, returned 'home' in the 1970s. Then, for various reasons – including dissatisfaction with the political and economic situation in Guyana, came back to live in Britain. Consequently, as a schoolboy in 1970s Britain, I grew up with an evolving sense of my Caribbean heritage, and an uneasy personal journey coming to terms with being British, combined with a strong sense of being Guyanese above all.

Guyana, despite its location on the northern mainland of South America, sharing land borders with Portuguese-speaking Brazil, Spanish-speaking Venezuela, and Surinam – a former Dutch colony, has a long and deep cultural, economic, historic, and political connection with the English-speaking Caribbean islands. Guyana is usually identified as being part of the English-speaking Caribbean island region rather than with its immediate South American neighbours. In 1973, Guyana became one of the founder member nation states of the Caribbean Community (CARICOM). The CARICOM Secretariat, the main administrative centre of the organisation, has its headquarters in Turkeyen, Guyana.

In 1831, after 200 years of Dutch rule, with interruptions of French and British colonial control, the colony of British Guiana was created. Therefore, British Guiana became the only English-speaking British colony in South America. Guyana's colonial history exists in stark contrast to Barbados which was settled by the British in 1627. Barbados had uninterrupted British colonial rule until it became independent in 1966.

The Amerindians are the indigenous people of Guyana, and there are nine main indigenous tribal groups including the Arawak, Carib and Warrau. The legacy of the original people of Guyana, and the period of Dutch and British colonial rule, is clearly revealed in the names of the cities, towns, villages and regions across Guyana. The name Guyana derives from the Amerindian word meaning 'Land of Many Waters'. The name describes the many rivers, waterfalls and creeks in Guyana – one of the country's most characteristic geological features.

Beterverwagting, New Amsterdam and Soesdyke reveal Guyana's Dutch colonial past. In 1812, the Dutch named town of Stabroek was renamed Georgetown by the British in honour of King George III, the ruling British monarch. Georgetown eventually became the capital city of British Guiana when the colony was fully under British control.

As European colonial power expanded throughout the Caribbean from the 17th century onwards, the process of colonisation and the emerging plantation economy began to utilise slave labour from Africa. Africans were captured and forcibly transported to the Caribbean colonies in brutal conditions. Those who survived the journey were sold at auctions, and prepared for unrelenting toil on the sugar plantations.

African slaves and their descendants became the purchased or inherited property of plantation owners and installed as a permanent labour force. Slaves supplied the workforce for the sugar plantations in Guyana, which satisfied the demand for sugar consumption in Europe, and were largely owned and managed by Dutch and British colonisers. The product known as Demerara sugar was named after the county in Demerara, Guyana, where it was first produced.

In 1834, following the abolition of slavery in the British-ruled Caribbean, indentured labourers were transported from India to Guyana to provide a cheap, continuous and controllable labour supply. The Indian workforce replaced the freed Africans and assumed their tasks on the sugar plantations. This was considered by plantation owners as the solution to save their sugar industry and decreasing post-emancipation incomes. Smaller amounts of indentured labourers also arrived in Guyana from China – mainly from China's southern provinces, and from Portugal – mainly from the Portuguese island of Madeira situated on the north-west coast of Africa.

From 1838 to the end of indenture in 1917, 240,000 Indians arrived in Guyana, 143,000 in Trinidad and 36,000 in Jamaica.[3] Smaller numbers of Indians arrived in Grenada, St Lucia and St Vincent. Very few Indians were brought to Barbados. In 1866 a ship called *Countess of Ripon* with indentured Indians aboard destined for Grenada and St Vincent was wrecked off the coast of Barbados. All the passengers were saved but none of them stayed on in Barbados. The ship continued its journey to Grenada and St Vincent.

By 1973, as an eight to nine-year-old schoolboy in England, I was completely aware of the diverse nature of the societies across the Caribbean. I understood that it was a cosmopolitan region of multiple ethnicities, which included a population of diverse heritage in Guyana. In 1973, Forbes Burnham, a Guyanese of African descent was Prime Minister of Guyana. Arthur Chung, a Guyanese of Chinese descent, was President of Guyana. I was aware of the social and political tensions between the developing nation states and identities in the Caribbean. I was also aware of the internal tensions which existed between different social, economic and ethnic groups in the Caribbean.

In Guyana and Trinidad, ethnic rivalry would embed itself at the core of national politics.

The diverse nature of Guyana's social and cultural heritage was also reflected in the food I ate at home. I ate chow mein brought to Guyana by the Chinese, and metemgee, channa and cook-up rice. I ate soup with meat, pig tails, potatoes, yam and cassava. My favourite meal, which we usually ate on Sundays, was curried meat and roti brought to Guyana by the Indians.

Later that year, as always, we ate garlic pork (another personal favourite) for Christmas morning breakfast with homemade bread, sliced oranges and coffee. Garlic pork was brought to Guyana by the Portuguese. Growing up in south London, I do not remember a Christmas morning without the smell of fried garlic pork wafting through our flat.

On Christmas Day or on Boxing Day we ate pepperpot – a dish with its roots in the food culture of the Amerindian people, the indigenous people of Guyana. Each year, we had to obtain some cassareep. An essential seasoning and preservative syrupy residue used for pepperpot produced from cassava juice. At Christmas we sometimes drank sorrel. We occasionally drank mauby leading up to the Christmas period.

In 1970s Britain, the ingredients required to prepare the food and drink we wanted were not always available in our local (or not so local) shops or markets. Therefore, we would have to wait in hope (and sometimes in vain) for a friend or relative from the Caribbean, or from Britain on a trip to the Caribbean, to arrive in Britain with, for example, cassareep, mauby tree bark, and a bottle or more of rum.

If I wanted to eat English food, well, there was plenty of it available during dinner breaks at school. I had a large appetite and ate everything on offer. Including shepherd's pie with gravy, sausages and mashed potato, bread and butter pudding, and anything with custard. I always quickly joined the queue when I heard the call for second helpings of food. When curry meals became available on my primary school's dinner menu, I was astonished to discover that the curry was cooked with raisins. Curry with raisins? Really?! I shared my amazement and disappointment about this with my family when I returned home from school later that afternoon.

At home during the summer holidays, I would make mild requests to my great-grandmother to eat some 'English food'. On one occasion, she grilled some beef burgers with bread and butter on the side, which I thoroughly enjoyed as it briefly altered my daily food routine. I also increased my familiarity with English food after visits to our local fish and chip shop and to Nick's house. Nick was one of my best friends at primary school.

During one weekend day trip to Nick's house, I shared a meal with him and his family. The main course was toad-in-the-hole, a traditional British sausage dish which I had not heard of or eaten. Back home my great-grandmother was genuinely bewildered by the name of this meal, which she had not heard of. Toad? Hole? What?!

Whatever food I ate during the year, my body had to endure an annual summer 'wash out'. During the summer of 1973, as in the years which preceded it and immediately followed, I spent at least one day suffering after a dose of senna. This was another tradition which arrived in Britain with my family from the Caribbean. Utilising the senna plant as a laxative. After drinking a cup of water with soaked senna plant leaves, I would soon feel regular churning stomach pains and rush to the toilet.

There was no point in playing with my friends on the street. There was always the fear of being caught due to bowel movements in my body, followed by an urgent visit to the toilet. While watching cricket matches on television, I would be upset if I missed a crucial wicket or scoring shot because of an emergency dash to the toilet.

At home during the 1970s, we regularly enjoyed gatherings of people from a variety of social, ethnic and cultural backgrounds in the Caribbean. These gatherings, usually on Friday evenings, included the sharing of challenges and experiences as Caribbean migrants in Britain, family news from the Caribbean, nostalgic memories and opinions on political and social developments 'back home' and in the UK, and humorous tales about the mysterious world of 'English people'.

Why didn't they put seasoning in their food when they cooked? Why couldn't they enjoy themselves unless they were completely drunk? What was this 'tea' that English people ate and didn't drink? The one I always thought was hilarious was the advice to 'eat before you leave' if you were invited to an English wedding. As the food on offer wouldn't be enough to fill your belly! Added to this was the often heard complaint by some of the non-Jamaicans - in our group and in many other social situations I found myself in. Why did English (and other non-Caribbean) people still think that all West Indian people in Britain were Jamaicans? Many of these conversations, debates and stories were fuelled by noisy games of dominoes, complemented by Caribbean rum and snacks. Rum was the most popular drink among the people who gathered in our flat. All of whom had grown up in Caribbean societies with a history of manufacturing rum – as a by-product of the once dominant sugar industry. This tradition of drinking rum, which much of the social life in the Caribbean revolved around, arrived with some West Indian people when they migrated to Britain. During the 1970s, most of the rum in our flat came from family and friends who brought bottles back from Barbados. Usually Cockspur and Mount Gay. There were also some good-natured exchanges about where the best rum came from in the Caribbean. For example, the Guyanese talked about El Dorado and Trinidadians sang the praises of Angostura.

One of my main tasks during these gatherings was to manage the plastic pineapple ice bucket. The ice bucket sat on our brown double-decker platform drinks trolley, complete with gold colour trimmings. I would, on request, drop a few ice cubes into a drink belonging to one of the 'big people'. This was before or after they had poured some rum, whisky, Martini or Babycham into their glass. After a while, when the ice cubes had been used or melted into water, I trotted downstairs to the fridge in the kitchen, and broke some more ice into the bucket.

My other, more enjoyable task, when the television's volume was turned down, was to help arrange the music. I carefully selected the vinyl I wanted to play on our turntable as background music throughout the evening. My favourite selections included the *Get on the Good Foot* LP by James Brown, and *Hard to Handle* by Otis Redding and *Skinny Legs and All* by Joe Tex from our *HIT68* funk and soul compilation album.

My collection of rewards for these duties included a bottle of ginger ale to drink, more channa to eat, and staying up late to watch and laugh along to a Marx Brothers film on television. I'd try and follow the antics of the Marx Brothers surrounded by the merriment and noise created by my family and our guests. Lenny Henry's early passion for comedy began after watching a run of Friday night Marx Brothers films on BBC television. He watched these films as a young school boy in the 1970s living with his Jamaican family in Dudley,

West Midlands. Henry was seriously interested in the way Groucho Marx walked, talked, and sang, and the unique way Chico Marx played the piano – including using an apple in his right hand.

All of our Friday evening social gatherings happened in our living room. The living room was the epicentre of all entertainment and social activity in our flat. By the early 80s, we had moved out of social housing and progressed to a neat three-bedroom, owner-occupied, house in semi-suburban south London. The house had a living room and a front room. Our traditional West Indian-in-Britain front room included a very comfortable and pristine sofa, a glass cabinet, music centre, a generous array of ornaments, family photographs and special possessions on display. The front room was typically used only for specific occasions, including special visits by family and friends.

During the 1970s, one of the main Friday evening living room topics of conversation and concern was, of course, the current state of West Indies cricket. Who should be in the team? Why did one Caribbean nation have more players than another Caribbean nation in the team? This partly reflected the regional bickering, rivalries and tensions which existed amongst the Caribbean diaspora in Britain. Who should be the captain? Why did that captain make this or that decision? Why did this or that batsman play this or that shot to get out? What player should never play for the West Indies again and, of course, frustration at West Indian selectors and how cricket in the Caribbean was managed and organised.

All of this was interspersed with nostalgic memories of playing cricket in the Caribbean. Stories were often shared about the process of organising cricket matches as children. A typical tale, as recalled by my Barbadian father, would describe using a small stone with cloth, and string and cord tightly wrapped around it to make a ball.

The bat was made from a coconut tree limb with the branches cut off and shaped. If you were fortunate enough to have a saw, you could get a branch, saw it down the centre, and then cut the handle out in a round shape. The stumps would usually be two stones used to form the imaginary width of a set of stumps. A batsman would be out if a bowler breached the batsman's defences and the ball went through the two stones.

In later years, I read and heard similar stories told by current and former West Indian cricketers. As a young boy in Barbados, Garry

Sobers organised cricket matches with his friends at weekends and during school holidays. They made their own bats and balls. Some of the balls Sobers made with his friends were knitted. On other days they would find a shovel, or something similar, to dig the tar off the road. The tar melted when the weather was extremely hot. Sobers and his friends would then dig up the tar and use it to make tar cricket balls.

I consciously and subconsciously absorbed elements of these debates, stories and nostalgic memories, which helped to further my inherited interest in West Indies cricket.

Some of the players mentioned – both past and present – including Ramadhin and Valentine, Weekes, Worrell and Walcott, Hall and Griffith, and Kanhai and Sobers, were often talked about with a deep sense of sincerity and reverence. This increasingly fascinated me. So, as I got older, I wanted to find out more about them. Debates about the state of West Indian cricket would blend in seamlessly with robust reflections on recent political developments in the Caribbean.

All this talk about politics and cricket, or the politics of cricket, which I consciously and subconsciously tuned in to, was my informal way of learning more about events and situations. Usually beyond my immediate concerns and interests as a young schoolboy in Britain. In many ways, this contributed to my deep interest in all matters West Indian, including cricket, during my primary school years and beyond. Regular trips to the Caribbean also helped to cement this connection.

Whenever I was among a group of older Guyanese people in Britain, there was a constant stream of economic, political and social developments and tensions 'back home' to reflect and focus on. A few years after the end of the Second World War, the People's Progressive Party (PPP) was formed in what was then British Guiana. The leading figures in the PPP were Dr Cheddi Jagan – an Indian-Guyanese from Berbice, Forbes Burnham – an African-Guyanese from Georgetown, and Dr. Jagan's wife, Janet Jagan (nee Rosenberg) – a Jewish-American from Chicago.

Of course, as a nine-year-old in 1973, I didn't understand the detailed nuances of parliamentary party politics. However, I was aware of the dominant figures in post-independence Guyanese politics as I was with the dominant figures in politics in Britain. In 1973, Edward

33

Heath was Britain's Conservative party Prime Minister and Harold Wilson was the leader of the main opposition Labour party.

In 1953, the PPP won the first popular national elections in British Guiana. However, there was very little time for the party to reflect on their electoral success and prepare for the future. Led by the Prime Minister, Winston Churchill, the British government's response to PPP victory was to dismiss the election results. They suspended the British Guiana constitution after 133 days. Therefore, the PPP were prevented from being able to control the colony's political and economic affairs. The PPP victory was perceived by the British government as a threat.

The party was suspected of supporting communist policies, with ambitions to subvert the colony and move British Guiana towards an alliance with the Soviet Union. British troops – both military and naval forces – were sent to British Guiana to protect the colony against the British government's fear of civil disturbances. My great-grandmother always kept a photograph of Burnham and Jagan on a dressing-table in her bedroom. The picture showed Burnham and Jagan in 1953. Both are immaculately dressed in suits, and waving to photographers and onlookers, as they board a plane for a flight to Surinam. From Surinam, they continued their journey to London to meet the British government to discuss the suspension of the constitution in British Guiana. My great-grandmother gave me this photograph shortly before she passed away.

Under a restored constitution, the PPP enjoyed further national electoral successes in 1957 and 1961. Between these two elections, the political relationship between Cheddi Jagan and Forbes Burnham changed from being allies to fierce rivals. Internal turbulence within the ranks of the PPP resulted in the party being divided along the lines of ethnicity. Burnham's new political party was called the People's National Congress (PNC) and attracted most of its support from the African-Guyanese population. The PNC won the national elections in 1964. Jagan continued to lead the PPP, which continued to develop as the party supported by most of the Indian-Guyanese population.

In 1966, British Guiana had a new name, Guyana, as it achieved full independence from Britain with Burnham as the Prime Minister. Burnham consolidated his political power in Guyana with victories in the 1968 and 1973 national elections. Jagan remained as the PPP leader of the main opposition party following both elections.

The *World in Action* current affairs team produced a documentary for British television, which investigated alleged electoral irregularities linked to Burnham's election victory in 1973. The documentary primarily focussed on the alleged irregularities which appeared to involve Guyanese residents in Britain, all of whom were registered to vote in the 1973 elections.

The rapidly evolving cycle of bitter ethnic and social suspicion and polarisation between Guyana's two largest communities, African and Indian, continued to dominate many areas of political and economic life. In response to the relentless instability, economy turmoil and racial disunity, increasing numbers of Guyanese from across the ethnic and social spectrum left to seek a better future for themselves and their families – to Britain, Canada, the US and other countries in the Caribbean.

In Britain, the main political event at the beginning of 1973 was the country joining the European Economic Community (EEC) also known as the Common Market. Britain was now a member of an organisation of nine European nation states. Ireland and Denmark also joined in 1973 as new members. To emphasise the celebratory and cultural aspects of British's new membership of the Common Market, there was a 'Fanfare for Europe' gala opening night at Covent Garden. The performances featured drama, music and poetry and was attended by the Queen, the Duke of Edinburgh and other members of the royal family.

According to Edward Heath, the British Prime Minister, there were enormous benefits to be gained by Britain being a member of the Common Market. As Heath recalled in his autobiography, published 25 years after the start of Britain's membership, 'I saw this as a wonderful new beginning and a tremendous opportunity for the British people'.[4] The BBC estimated that 'more than 1,000 Britons will relocate to Brussels over the coming months to take up their places as civil servants of the community'.[5] In Britain's first national referendum in 1975, with Harold Wilson as the Labour party British Prime Minister, voters backed Britain's continued membership of the Common Market.

In the English-speaking Caribbean, there was a major attempt at regional political and economic self-government from 1958, which disintegrated four years later. The West Indies Federation was created as a pan-Caribbean institution independent from British colonial rule.

The Federation united 10 colonial territories, including Antigua, Barbados, Dominica, Grenada, Jamaica, Montserrat, St. Kitts-Nevis-Anguilla, St. Lucia, St. Vincent and Trinidad and Tobago. Grantley Adams from Barbados became the Prime Minister of the Federation and Port of Spain became the Federation's capital city. In 1958, Princess Margaret visited Trinidad to offer British royal approval of the West Indies Federation, and to inaugurate the first federal legislature of the West Indies in Port of Spain.

In 1961, following a referendum, Jamaicans voted to take their island out of the West Indian Federation. 54.1% voted 'no' and 45.9% voted 'yes' with just over 60% of the registered electorate turning out to vote. After Jamaica's withdrawal, Trinidad also decided to cut itself adrift from the Federation. The unwillingness of Jamaica and Trinidad, the two Caribbean territories with the largest economies and populations, to pursue the federal route led to the Federation's eventual collapse.

After the Federation fell apart, Frank Worrell, as the first full-time black captain of the West Indies, emerged as an alternative symbol of Caribbean regional leadership. Despite the territorial rivalries, disputes, and the threat of long-term fragmentation, the West Indies Cricket Board continued to exist as the oldest established Caribbean regional institution. West Indies cricket continued to progress as the only international team representing a collection of individual nation states and colonial territories.

Frank Worrell insisted that West Indies cricket should represent a symbol of regional togetherness for the Caribbean diaspora in Britain. Perhaps, Worrell's personal experience of being born and raised in Barbados before relocating to Trinidad and Jamaica – the island he played much of his first-class cricket for, influenced his lack of patience for inter-island pettiness and rivalries. After leading the West Indies team in Australia during the 1960/1961 tour, Worrell returned to Jamaica and was appointed warden at the Mona Campus of the University of the West Indies. He was later appointed as a senator by Sir Alexander Bustamante, the Jamaican Prime Minister.

As captain, Worrell stressed the importance and principles of self and team discipline and mental toughness. This was added to his team's abundance of skill, flair and flamboyance. These were the foundations of a new West Indian cricket spirit which was further developed by the captaincy and leadership of Rohan Kanhai, Clive Lloyd and Vivian Richards in the 1970s and 1980s. Deryck Murray credits Worrell's leadership skills for instilling the values of Caribbean regional unity and excellence during the 1963 tour of England.

> He (Frank Worrell) saw the West Indies as almost one place. And we, as players, were representing the West Indies and asserting the independence of each of our territories as we were breaking away from colonialism. And it was so easy under Frank Worrell to unite under that kind of banner that we were totally West Indian and totally committed to the fans (in England).

After the West Indies Federation collapsed, political leaders in the English-speaking Caribbean gradually worked towards strengthening ties between each other. The Dickenson Bay agreement, signed in 1965 between Antigua, Barbados and Guyana, established the Caribbean Free Trade Association (CARIFTA). This was a crucial stepping stone towards the Treaty of Chaguaramas, signed in Trinidad, which established CARICOM in 1973. Just over a decade after the end of the Federation and in the same year that Britain joined the EEC.

The original members of CARICOM were Barbados, Guyana, Jamaica and Trinidad. In the following year, eight other territories – Antigua, British Honduras (Belize), Dominica, Grenada, St Lucia, Montserrat, St Kitts-Nevis-Anguilla and St Vincent were welcomed into the CARICOM group as the journey towards regional integration continued.

By 1973, all four original member nation states of CARICOM had achieved full independence from British rule. Jamaica and Trinidad became independent in 1962. Barbados and Guyana, which as British Guiana had stood outside the West Indian Federation by holding the status as an observer, achieved independence in 1966. After Guyana and Barbados gained independence, the two new nation states shared a High Commission office in London and, represented by Sir Lionel Luckhoo from Guyana, they also shared a High Commissioner. All four of these countries were led by Prime Ministers who were dominant political figures in the Caribbean – Errol Barrow in Barbados, Forbes Burnham in Guyana, Michael Manley in Jamaica and Eric Williams in Trinidad.

As a student in London in the 1940s, Barrow served as Chairman of the Council of Colonial Students where his contemporaries included Burnham and Manley. Barrow also developed lifelong friendships with other contemporaries during this period, including Pierre Trudeau and Lee Kwan Yew, who were also destined to become political leaders in their home countries of Canada and Singapore respectively.

By 1973, whenever I was in the company of groups of older West Indian people in Britain, I would casually overhear all four of these influential political leaders – Barrow, Burnham, Manley and Williams – referred to with either sky-high levels of admiration, positivity, loyalty and support. Or vitriolic levels of criticism and negativity with disparaging remarks made about their character, personalities and politics.

When I was in the company of older Guyanese or Jamaican people, similar levels of response and reaction, both positive and negative, were offered with reference to Cheddi Jagan and Edward Seaga. Jagan was the main political opposition leader in Guyana. In 1974, Edward Seaga became leader of the Jamaica Labour Party, the island's main opposition political organisation.

As 1973 continued to be a year of significant political and social change in the Caribbean and Britain, I had settled, after a couple of years, into my second south London primary school. The school was a 15-minute walk from our flat. I now had a new group of close friends and many of them lived nearby. These included classmates who, like me, had Caribbean heritage. Arnold's parents were from Georgetown, Guyana and had the same surname as my mother's maiden name – Hunte. We would, jokingly, speculate about our families in Guyana being related to each other. Dharmesh's parents were from Berbice, Guyana. Barry's parents were Jamaican. Simon's father was Jamaican and his mother was English.

A few weeks after I joined the school, I became friends with Irshad. He was another boy in our class with parents from Guyana. A few months later, Irshad announced that his family were going back to live in Guyana. A couple of days after his announcement, Irshad left our school and I haven't seen or heard from him since! My other close friends included Nick, Christopher J, Ian L and Ian I, who had a Nigerian father and an English mother.

I have vivid memories of running in and around the block of flats and garages on our street with Christopher J. We loved to act out the comic-drama, buddy, crime-solving adventures of *The Persuaders*. Danny Wilde was a charismatic, millionaire thrill-seeker from New York with a rough diamond personality played by Tony Curtis. Brett Sinclair was a suave, stylish, but slightly aloof, English upper-class gentleman played by Roger Moore. *The Persuaders* was one of our favourite TV programmes. Sadly, for me, at the end of the 1973 summer term, Christopher J announced that he was leaving our school. His family had decided to move away from our neighbourhood.

Simona was the first girl in my class who I remember becoming friends with. Simona had Italian heritage and her family owned the nearby hairdressing salon which was a five-minute walk from our school. A year later, Shakil, a recent arrival in Britain from Kenya, became a new boy at our school. We quickly became close friends with a shared interest in cricket and Leeds United.

Next door to our primary school was a factory complex. One of the companies in the complex produced rubber products. The pungent smell of rubber would often waft over the wall, which separated our school from the factory, and drift across our small playground. Some of the factory workers would throw balls and animal shapes (the mice were very popular), made of solid rubber, over the wall for us to play with. The balls were about the size of a cricket ball and usually dark blue, green or red. They caused serious pain and bruises if they hit your body at high speed.

Although they made excellent cricket balls, we used them to play football. I played football with my friends at virtually every opportunity, wherever we could find space in our small school playground. Until the spring/summer of 1973, I still considered watching or playing cricket as more of an occasional pastime.

CHAPTER 2

The origins of cricket in the Caribbean

The game of cricket emerged and developed in the British-ruled Caribbean from the early 19th century. The introduction of cricket evolved to provide an additional leisure pursuit for the ruling European colonial planter class, senior civil servants managing the colonies and the garrisons of British soldiers stationed across the Caribbean.

Alongside being prepared to combat slave rebellions, the main occupation of the military was to defend British territories in the Caribbean from external forces. The wealth and trade, largely generated by the sugar industry and slave labour, had to be protected from being seized by other European powers.

Very few of the islands in the British-ruled Caribbean were safe from attack. For example, there was the constant threat of military conflict with the French. British soldiers were on constant military alert. Therefore, for some of the British military in the Caribbean, cricket was a welcome form of recreation, release and distraction. Cricket would also become steadily institutionalised throughout the English-speaking Caribbean colonial education system.

During its years of colonial expansion and Empire, the passion for sport quickly followed wherever the British flag was planted. For British colonial societies in the Caribbean and beyond, organised sport was not just about the pleasurable pursuit of physical activity and glory. It was about character building, how the game was played, team spirit and, most importantly, part of the British Empire's civilising mission.

The European colonial elite in the Caribbean attempted to widely utilise cricket, through its assumed high values as a social activity, rituals of fair play and respect for rules and codes of conduct, as an additional tool to culturally and socially distinguish itself from the rest of society. For many of the colonial elite, the importation of cricket also maintained cultural ties with their British 'home' and the imperial centre of colonial rule.

Throughout the Caribbean, while the colonial elite played the game, black people were usually required to undertake peripheral tasks such as the preparation of the playing area. This included 'the weeding or scything of the ground, retrieving the ball from the ubiquitous cane field, and performing a range of chores connected with the entertainment of guests'.[1]

As Scyld Berry, cricket journalist, author and former editor of *Wisden Cricketers' Almanack*, persuasively suggests, being a non-contact sport was essential to cricket's growth around the British Empire. A bowler from Barbados in the Caribbean or the North West Frontier Province in India could bowl as fast as they liked, but they could not come closer than a few feet to the batsmen representing the Raj, and certainly could not touch him. According to Berry, if there had been physical contact – as in football, rugby and other sports, it was unlikely that the British colonial establishment would have taken the field with their native colonial subjects.

Towards the end of the 19th century, cricket developed into an activity taken up by all social groups in Caribbean. The planter elite, merchants and colonial administrators continued to administer and play cricket as a superior cultural pursuit. However, this did not deter people from the perceived lower social orders and other ethnic groups, including the descendants of African slaves, mixed-race descendants of Europeans and Africans, and indentured labourers from China, India and Portugal from playing the game.

Clubs were established across the British-ruled Caribbean to satisfy the need for the various social groups to play cricket. These groups, with distinct class, race and social identities, established their own cricket clubs and associations. They directly appealed to members who possessed their specific class, race and social characteristics.

In *Beyond a Boundary*, C.L.R James, the Trinidadian historian, journalist and writer, clearly outlined how cricket clubs represented the different social strata in Trinidad in the early 20th century. At the top of the social scale was the Queen's Park club, whose members were mainly white and wealthy; Shamrock was the club of the old Catholic families; Stingo members were black with no status; Maple was the club of the brown-skinned middle class, and Shannon was the club of the Trinidadian black lower middle class.[2]

In British Guiana, the Georgetown Cricket Club (GCC) was established for those from the higher echelons of white Guyanese colonial society, including sugar estate managers and government officials. The Catholic Guild was a predominantly Portuguese club which played competitive cricket and some of its players were called for trials for the British Guiana team. The Demerara Cricket Club (DCC) was created to serve the Portuguese community in Georgetown. The DCC gradually evolved into an organisation where the majority of its members were from Georgetown's black lower middle-class population. Maurice Fernandes, a Guyanese cricketer with Portuguese heritage, who played with distinction for the DCC, captained West Indies to their first Test victory against England at Bourda, Georgetown in 1930.

The Churchmen's Union Cricket Club (CUCC) was a black lower middle class organisation whose members predominantly worked at the junior levels of the civil service. The Georgetown East Indian community's passion for cricket was channelled through the East Indian Cricket Club, which later became known as the Everest Cricket Club. After the Second World War there was a steady increase in players and members from outside Georgetown, including Berbice, who contributed to the development of the club. The Chinese Sports Club in Georgetown, which later became known as the Cosmos Sports Club, provided a home for the Chinese community in British Guiana to participate in a wide range of sports. The Chinese in British Guiana were dominant in hockey and squash but also played cricket.

By the first decade of the 20th century, cricket continued to be a growing social and cultural force in the English-speaking Caribbean. All social groups played the game with varying degrees of enthusiasm, seriousness and skill. However, strict social codes and divisions continued to be enforced in the cricket clubs throughout the region.

Cricket also provided an arena for the majority non-white Caribbean population to witness significant levels of achievement and celebrate sporting triumphs and heroes. In 1899, the Spartan Cricket Club, consisting of the Barbadian coloured middle-class, won the Challenge Cup in Barbados by defeating teams with all-white members. According to Hilary Beckles, the cricket historian and academic,

Spartan's victory served to undermine the ideology of white supremacy in the cricket culture within Barbados.[3]

Despite the development of cricket within each colonial territory, regular competitive fixtures between the territories, and progress towards creating a pan-Caribbean representative team, provided serious logistical and organisational challenges. Until the age of commercial inter-island air travel and more developed telecommunications, the inconvenience of travel from one territory to another was a major obstacle.

Jamaica was less actively involved than Barbados, British Guiana and Trinidad during the early period of inter-colonial cricket in the Caribbean. As Michael Manley explains in his comprehensive work, *A History of West Indian Cricket*, it was not because of an absence of interest and enthusiasm by cricketers in Jamaica – an island 90 miles south of Cuba. This was more of a serious question of logistics. Mainly due to Jamaica's geographical location in the Caribbean, which is about 1,000 miles away from the other three territories that were within a day's sail of each other by steamship.[4]

The first competitive inter-colonial cricket match was played in 1865, when Barbados hosted British Guiana at the Garrison Savannah in Bridgetown. All the players who represented the British Guiana team were members of the Georgetown Cricket Club. This was the colony's premier cricket institution. This was the beginning of first-class cricket in the Caribbean.

Barbados won the match by 138 runs and a return fixture was arranged in British Guiana later in 1865. In both matches, all the players from Barbados and British Guiana were white. The majority of them were born in the Caribbean. This early period, and for many years afterwards, of competitive inter-colonial cricket in the Caribbean was the strict preserve of white West Indian players and colonial administrators.

The British Guiana v Barbados match was played at The Parade Ground in Middle Street, Georgetown. The spectators included a significant number of black Barbadian supporters who enthusiastically backed the all-white Barbadian team. Between 1835 and 1893, an estimated number of 40,656 Barbadians arrived to settle in British Guiana.[5] For many of the Barbadians resident in British Guiana, and although black cricketers were excluded from the Barbados team, the pride and status of Barbadians in British Guiana was at stake. However, British Guiana gained revenge for their defeat in Barbados earlier on in 1865 and won the match in Georgetown by two wickets.

As cricket continued to develop in the region, a representative regional team was finally selected to tour in 1886. The first West Indies team, led by George Wyatt from the Georgetown Cricket Club in British Guiana, was an all-white side that toured America and Canada with mixed fortunes in terms of results. The West Indies played 13 matches, won six, lost five and two were drawn. The next chapter in the development of cricket in the Caribbean was to send a team to challenge the 'mother country' on English soil.

CHAPTER 3

West Indies cricket tours in England 1900 to 1969

From 1900 to 1927, a combined West Indies team completed three tours of England. In 1900, their inaugural tour to England, the West Indies won five matches, lost eight and drew four. Twelve of the 17 matches were recorded as first-class. The outstanding West Indies player during the 1900 tour was Charles Ollivierre from St.Vincent.

Ollivierre, a Vincentian who represented Trinidad, became a pioneering black Caribbean migrant and professional cricketer in Britain. He finished the 1900 tour with the best batting average of 32.70 from 883 runs. Ollivierre's impressive performances for the West Indies in England, in completely unfamiliar playing and weather conditions, alerted the attention of Derbyshire County Cricket Club. Derbyshire encouraged Ollivierre to stay on in Britain after the tour to qualify and play for the county. In 1901, Ollivierre created history when he made his debut for Derbyshire and, in turn, became the first West Indian to play cricket for an English county.

Nineteen matches were completed during the following West Indies tour of England in 1906. The tourists won six matches, lost 10 matches and one match was drawn. Thirteen fixtures on this tour were confirmed as first-class. In 1923, the West Indies played 20 first-class matches and many of them were against English county teams. As in 1906, six matches ended in West Indian victories. Seven matches were lost and seven were drawn. The West Indies avoided defeat in 13 first-class matches during the 1923 tour. This suggests an improved overall performance compared to their two previous pre-Test match tours in England.

George Challenor, who was born into a wealthy white family in Barbados, was the star West Indian batsman during the 1923 England tour. His scored a tour total of 1,895 runs with an average of just over

52, including eight centuries. Challenor's performances in England contributed to him being the first Caribbean batsman to receive international cricket recognition.

By 1928, as the West Indies prepared to tour England, their unique status as an international Test cricket team had been confirmed. The West Indies team was established as the first official federal Caribbean institution with an identifiable regional identity. The team was a collection of British-ruled Caribbean colonial territories which combined to form a representative team.

The representative spectrum of the team was, as before, restricted to players from Britain's four major sources of wealth from the Caribbean, plantation agriculture in Barbados, British Guiana, Jamaica and Trinidad. The West Indies Cricket Board of Control was established 17 months before the first West Indies Test match v England at Lord's in June 1928.

Although the 1928 West Indies team in England featured a mixture of white and black players, as in the previous three tours to England, the firmly established Caribbean colonial system of white leadership and control continued. The 1928 West Indians were led by Karl Nunes, the team captain and opening batsman. Nunes was a white Jamaican who was largely educated in England. He was also a former British army officer and a founder member of the Jamaican Board of Control, the organisation which managed cricket in his home island.

The continuing cricket and social relationship between Barbados and British Guiana was personified by Cyril 'Snuffy' Browne who became a stalwart of cricket in British Guiana during the 1920s. Browne was a black lawyer who migrated to British Guiana from Barbados and became a magistrate. As an all-rounder, he had played first-class cricket for Barbados before representing British Guiana after his arrival in the colony. Browne made his debut for the West Indies, the first of his four Test matches, in the first Test of their 1928 tour of England.

In 1928, the series of three (three-day) Test matches were scheduled at Lord's in London, Old Trafford in Manchester and back down to London for the final Test at The Oval. After Percy Chapman, England's captain, won the toss at Lord's and decided to bat first. The first ball in West Indies Test cricket was bowled by George Francis, the Barbadian pace-bowler. The West Indies suffered a defeat by an innings in each of the three matches in the series. Their heaviest defeat was in the third and last match at The Oval where they were comprehensively beaten by an innings and 71 runs.

One West Indian player who enhanced his reputation during the 1928 tour, despite the three Test defeats, was Learie Constantine from Trinidad. Constantine, who also toured England with the West Indies in 1923, was the son of Lebrun Constantine. Lebrun was the only specialist black batsman selected for the 1906 tour of England. Learie's all-round flamboyance and panache as a batsman, bowler and fielder embraced a black Caribbean style of cricket which many English spectators had not seen.

Constantine's first wicket in the 1928 series was at Lord's. Constantine dismissed Charlie Hallows, one of the English opening batsmen, who was caught by Herman Griffith. This was an historic dismissal. It was the first wicket taken by the West Indies in Test cricket. After the 1928 tour, Constantine consolidated his position, with George Headley to soon follow, as a black West Indian cricketer with a global reputation who became an international sports star.

Constantine's performances for the West Indies helped him to secure a contract to play for Nelson in the Lancashire Cricket League in the north of England. As a result of his agreed contractual arrangements, Constantine became one of the highest-paid sportsmen in Britain. In many ways, Constantine was a pioneering Caribbean migrant in 1920s Britain, as well as a well-known sports star, in a new and uncomfortable environment. He was a figure of intense curiosity for spectators who were unfamiliar with the sight of a black person.

Many people in Nelson offered Constantine a warm welcome. However, there were also people who disliked the presence of a black man in and around their town and cricket club. Constantine seriously considered the prospect of going back to Trinidad after his first year in Nelson but Norma, his wife, eventually convinced him to stay.

Constantine's performances, with bat, ball and in the field, continued to draw crowds. He significantly contributed to Nelson's seven Lancashire League titles during his nine seasons at the club. One of Constantine's most memorable individual performances was finishing, after one particular league fixture v Accrington, with the remarkable bowling figures of 10 wickets for 10 runs. Constantine had dismissed all the opposition batsmen with only 10 runs registered against his bowling.

Constantine was joined for a period in Nelson by C.L.R James, who also made an important personal journey from Trinidad to Britain. Constantine and James worked together to deliver talks and take part in public meetings and events in and around Nelson, to audiences who knew very little about life and cricket in the Caribbean. What also inspired their work was to share and promote knowledge about the existence and location of the Caribbean, the region's importance to the development of the British colonial empire, the case for political and social reform in the Caribbean and the desire for self-government. James published his book, *The Case for West Indian Self-Government* in England. Constantine provided James with much needed financial assistance and moral support during his stay in Nelson.

The West Indies next arrived on tour in 1933. They played three Test matches at the same venues as in 1928 and in the same order: The Oval, Old Trafford and Lord's. The West Indies were defeated by England in the first Test match at The Oval, and the final Test match at Lord's. The Old Trafford match was significant as it ended in a draw. Therefore, the West Indies had avoided defeat in England for the first time in a Test match. Another milestone was recorded for pan-Caribbean progress and recognition in the arena of Test cricket.

Another important feature of the 1933 tour was the opportunity for George Headley to demonstrate his batting skills in front of curious crowds across England. George Headley's father was one of the many thousands of workers who left Barbados to work on the construction of the Panama Canal. In the English-speaking Caribbean, the colonial governments were reluctant to encourage the recruitment of workers for Panama. At the end of the French period of the canal's construction, many labourers from the Caribbean were stranded in Panama and had to be repatriated at their governments' expense.

The Barbados government was one of the Caribbean territories which agreed to release significant levels of migrant labour to travel to Panama. Eventually, there were up to around 19,900 Barbadian labourers working on the canal project. This was reportedly some 10% of the island's population of Barbados and nearly 40% of the island's adult men[1], including George Headley's father. The construction of the Panama Canal was completed in 1914.

George Headley was born in Panama in 1909 and Spanish was his first language. Due to the Americanisation of Panamanian social and cultural life, baseball was the first sport that Headley played as a young schoolboy. At the age of 14 Headley was taken to Jamaica, the home of his mother, to live with an aunt and improve his English. When Headley watched some young boys in Jamaica playing cricket for the first time, he carefully observed how the boys held their cricket bats. He compared the width of a cricket bat with the regular size of a baseball bat, which he was more familiar with. Headley had played and watched baseball in Panama. He immediately thought to himself, that if he played with the boys and had a cricket bat, 'They will never get me out!'

In 1930, Headley announced his arrival in Test cricket by scoring a century on his debut for the West Indies v England in Barbados. Headley's emergence as a premier class batsman challenged the idea that a black batsman could not represent the West Indies at the top of the batting order. In 1931, the West Indies won their first Test match outside the Caribbean in Australia. The West Indies lost the series 4-1 to Australia. However, Headley and Freddie Martin, a black opening batsman from Jamaica, both scored centuries in the West Indies first innings in the fifth and final Test of the series in Sydney to secure a landmark victory. This also signalled evidence of further progress for a team in its early years of playing Test cricket.

In 1933, Headley's score of 169 helped to secure the draw for the West Indies v England in the second Test at Old Trafford. Headley's performance at Old Trafford alerted Haslingden Cricket Club in the Lancashire League. Haslingden offered Headley a contract which he accepted. The 1933 tour was Headley's first tour in England with the West Indies. He arrived in England with a growing reputation as a batsman who was, at least, equal in his abilities with Australia's Donald Bradman. This led to Headley being tagged outside the Caribbean as 'the black Bradman'. Many West Indians across the Caribbean responded by insisting that Donald Bradman was, indeed, 'the white Headley'. A huge amount of mutual admiration existed between Headley and Bradman, and they occasionally corresponded by letter.

Two years later in the Caribbean, in front of his home crowd in Jamaica, Headley demonstrated his skill and technique by scoring an unbeaten 270 v England. Headley's innings powered the West Indies towards victory in the fourth and final Test in the 1935 series by an innings and 161 runs. West Indies victory in Jamaica clinched their first Test series win, 2-1 v England.

In 1939, the West Indies played three Test matches in England at Lord's, Old Trafford and The Oval. Once again, the West Indies lost the Tests v England at Lord's and The Oval but avoided defeat at Old Trafford with a draw. Headley scored a century in each innings in the first Test at Lord's, but he couldn't prevent the West Indies losing by eight wickets. Once again, Headley had demonstrated to the British public why he was often referred to as 'Atlas' in the Caribbean. Atlas was the Titan god whose burden was to carry the world, the sky and the heavens on his shoulders. Headley was considered as the number one world-class batting star in the Caribbean. Therefore, he had the daunting sole responsibility of carrying the hopes and dreams of West Indies cricket on his back.

By 1939, with the outbreak of the Second World War, the West Indies had played nine Test matches in England. They had drawn two Tests and lost seven with no victories. In 1950, two years after Headley became the first black West Indies captain v England in Barbados, and the *Empire Windrush* arrived at Tilbury Docks, an historic West Indies cricket success story in England was celebrated by the small Caribbean population in Britain.

After suffering a heavy defeat in the first Test of the 1950 series at Old Trafford by 202 runs, the West Indies beat England in the second Test at Lord's by an impressive margin of 326 runs. After 22 years of playing Test cricket, the first West Indies Test victory in England was achieved at the spiritual headquarters of English cricket. Lord's was also the headquarters of the Imperial Cricket Conference, international cricket's governing body.

This symbolic West Indian triumph over British colonial power was also witnessed at Lord's by King George VI, the reigning British monarch. John Goddard, the West Indies captain, presented his players to the King as they lined-up on the hallowed Lord's turf before the start of the Test. The West Indies also won the remaining two Tests at Trent Bridge and The Oval to secure a 3-1 series victory.

At Lord's, the spin bowling performances of Sonny Ramadhin from Trinidad and Alf Valentine from Jamaica combined to dismiss 18 English batsmen and produced a vibrant display of young Indian-Caribbean and African-Caribbean collaborative effort. Ramadhin, a

20-year-old off and leg-spin bowler, who by 1950 had only played two first-class matches, was the first cricketer of Indian descent to represent the West Indies.

'The three Ws' middle-order batting force of Everton Weekes, Frank Worrell and Clyde Walcott, who made a commanding score of 168 not out in the West Indies second innings at Lord's, made significant contributions with the bat throughout the series. Everton Weekes scored five consecutive Test centuries for the West Indies during their previous tour in India in 1948/1949. He was run out on 90 in his next innings v India in Madras. So, Weekes was only 10 runs short of achieving a sixth consecutive Test century. His five centuries in a row is still (at the time this book was published) a Test record.

Weekes, Worrell and Walcott were the core members of an exciting new generation of black cricketers who dominated West Indies cricket throughout the 1950s and 1960s. The three Ws were all born within 18 months of each other in Barbados and born within a square mile of the Kensington Oval cricket ground in Bridgetown. Walcott, the youngest of the three, believed that he was delivered by the same midwife who also delivered Weekes and Worrell!

The performances of the three Ws, building on the foundations and legacy created in England by Learie Constantine, George Headley and others, gradually erased the belief that batting was a craft that white Caribbean batsmen were better disposed to. In the Caribbean, batting was largely perceived as a refined art form compared to the muscular activity of fast bowling. This was viewed by many of the European elite in the Caribbean as a laborious activity, traditionally undertaken by black cricketers. This was also rooted in the social legacy from plantation hierarchies. Where white employers increased their batting skills by having their black workers bowl at them for long periods of time.

The 1950 win at Lord's and the 3-1 Test series victory provided the slowly emerging post-war Caribbean diaspora in Britain, whether they were cricket fans or not, with a symbol of arrival and success. Sam King was part of the small group of delighted West Indian spectators at Lord's. Four years into the Second World War, King was one of the many young people in Jamaica and across the Caribbean, who enthusiastically responded to the call to volunteer for the war effort and fight for the mother country.

In 1944, King replied to an advertisement in *The Gleaner* newspaper in Jamaica for people to enlist in active service in Britain. Months later, King travelled from Jamaica to Britain on the *SS Cuba*, a French troop ship with a French crew, which dropped anchor in Greenock on the River Clyde near Glasgow. This was followed by a train journey with other volunteers. Accompanied with a combination of kind words of support and much appreciated hot cups of tea and buns provided by the Salvation Army. King finally arrived at a military camp in Filey, Yorkshire, where he began training.

King served with the Royal Air Force (RAF) in England and returned to Jamaica after the war in 1947. According to King, the Jamaican economy had still not recovered from the effects of a hurricane in August 1944. The hurricane destroyed large swathes of the island's bananas, coconut, coffee, and pimento crops. Many of King's friends in Jamaica were also unemployed. These were some of the reasons why King and many others in Jamaica were determined to take a chance and seek work opportunities in post-war Britain.

King's fare for the journey to Britain on the *Windrush* was £28.10s. His family had to sell three cows to raise the money for his passage. King re-joined the RAF soon after arriving back in Britain. Two years later, King organised leave from his RAF duties to attend the last two days of the 1950 Test at Lord's. 'I went to the match in my Royal Air Force uniform. So I had to behave!' King told me with a chuckle in his family's living room in Brixton, south London.

About a week before the match there was an article in a newspaper which said that the West Indians were jolly. They played good cricket but they didn't know the finer points of field placing and other things, so England would beat them easily. They actually believed that! So when the West Indies beat England at Lord's we were very, very happy. The English fans thought we were just jolly (cricketers). So they were really shocked and disgruntled when we beat them, but there were some English people who came to the match just to see the West Indies play. I sat in an area of the ground with a couple of West Indians and next to us were two people from Somerset who wanted to see the West Indies because we (the West Indies) could really play cricket. We could now stand up and be counted in this country, and the English really couldn't say anything about it because the facts were there for all to see.[2]

King also met Alf Valentine, his fellow Jamaican, at the fourth Test match at The Oval. During their meeting, King offered Valentine some tips on spin bowling and how to take wickets against English batsmen in unfamiliar English conditions! The small band of West Indian supporters at Lord's certainly made themselves heard during the Test. According to King, there were 'no more than 20 or 30' West Indians in the crowd. The final wicket of the match in England's second innings was claimed by Frank Worrell. Johnny Wardle attempted to play a sweep shot at a delivery by Worrell which struck his pads. An appeal for leg before wicket (LBW) was upheld by the umpire. Wardle snatched a stump and sprinted across the field. Rex Alston commentated on the Test for BBC radio and described the scene of jubilant West Indian 'characters' celebrating victory.

Here come the ground staff to prevent an encroachment of the wicket. But they are one or two West Indian characters running out on the field waving their hats as the West Indies players walk quietly off the field. Yes, there are several West Indian players running from the far end and they're going to escort their team off the field. The score is 274. Goddard running in with his stump being chased harum-scarum by lots of West Indian players. Such a sight never been seen before at Lord's!

Two of the West Indians at Lord's that day were Egbert 'Lord Beginner' Moore and Aldwyn 'Lord Kitchener' Roberts. Beginner and Kitchener were Trinidadian calypso musicians who both travelled to Britain on *The Windrush* in 1948. For Beginner and Kitchener, who were both established and well-known performers in Trinidad and across the Caribbean, Britain was a country where they could develop their careers as musicians and fulfil a sense of adventure. There was also the potential to earn reasonable sums of money by performing live to new audiences. A core element of this audience included the slowly increasing numbers of Caribbean migrants who had settled in Britain.

In his book, *Sounds Like London*, Lloyd Bradley, a black music author, journalist, broadcaster and lecturer who was born in London to parents from Jamaica, describes how Beginner and Kitchener (Kitch) survived and flourished as musicians in London in the 1950s.

> By the time *The Windrush* docked, calypso was popular enough in London to offer all sorts of opportunities. For Kitch and Beginner, it was more a case of how soon would a gig find them than how soon would they find a gig. They were celebrated artists all over the Caribbean, who were happy to front an orchestra playing big-band arrangements, but could also hold their own interacting with boisterous audiences in small clubs, backed by local players, or accompany themselves on guitar on a variety bill in music halls or between orchestra sets in a ballroom. It was not unusual for a star of Kitch's calibre to dash around the West End playing sets in three or four clubs in a single night.[3]

After witnessing the triumph of West Indies victory, Kitchener and Beginner led a theatrical procession of West Indian supporters around the perimeter of Lord's. The spontaneous victory procession continued outside Lord's and through central London. This was a collective public display of black Caribbean confidence, success and exuberance that had not been seen before on London's streets.

Lord Kitchener celebrated the occasion by composing the *Victory Test Match* calypso song. According to Sam King, Kitchener felt inspired to create a calypso, and a few of the other jubilant West Indians at Lord's volunteered a word or two to help develop the tune. After it was recorded and performed by Lord Beginner, *Cricket Lovely Cricket,* the memorable first line in *Victory Test Match*, continued to have an honoured place in West Indian calypso and cricket folklore.

The 1950 West Indies team, as with other teams from the Caribbean who toured England in future years, also left a permanent impression on some English cricket supporters who saw them play. In 1950, Brian Osborne, who was then a 13-year-old schoolboy, attended the second Test match at Lord's. Brian's interest in watching the West Indies sharply increased after seeing Everton Weekes hit a triple century during a Cambridge University v West Indies tour match at the Fenner's ground, Cambridge. The West Indies scored over 700 runs in their innings and Robert Christiani and Frank Worrell also scored centuries. One of Brian's main sources of knowledge about cricket came from some West Indians who arrived near his home town of Baldock, Hertfordshire, during the early 1950s. After the Second World War, a prisoner of war camp in Baldock was converted into a workers' hostel. The hostel housed some of the employees at the local hosiery factory. Some of the workers included a group of West Indians who played in a local cricket team managed by Brian's father. Brian was the team's scorer and, occasionally, the West Indian players put Brian in the nets and gave him some informal coaching sessions. Brian attended the first day of the 1950 Lord's Test with a friend. They were both keen to see the West Indies players who were always talked about in reverential tones by the West Indian workers in Baldock.

When the West Indies arrived in 1957 for their fifth Test tour in England, their allocation of Test matches had increased from three to five. Edgbaston, Birmingham, the home of Warwickshire Cricket Club, Headingley, Leeds, the home of Yorkshire Cricket Club and Trent Bridge, Nottingham, the home of Nottinghamshire Cricket Club were the new Test venues added to the West Indies tour schedule.

In 1957, Rohan Kanhai and Garry Sobers, who would become two of the pivotal West Indian figures during the 1973 series in England, completed their first tour of England. The West Indies were beaten at The Oval, Headingley and Lord's. The heaviest loss endured by the West Indies was the innings and 237 runs defeat at The Oval. The matches at Trent Bridge and Edgbaston were both drawn. The West Indies suffered a disappointing 3-0 series defeat. There was very little to celebrate for West Indians in Britain expecting more success following the tour of 1950.

The West Indies Cricket Board (WICB) finally overcame their reluctance to appoint a full-time black captain when Frank Worrell was appointed captain for the 1960/1961 tour of Australia. George Headley was given the captaincy for just one Test in 1948. However, Worrell was the first black player appointed for an entire Test series. White captaincy was an expected feature of West Indian cricket. It reflected colonial Caribbean society's social and political values, and a general distrust of non-white leadership and self-rule. Despite losing the series 2-1 in Australia, including the drama of the first Test match in Brisbane which ended as a tie, the West Indies brand of attractive and aggressive cricket contributed to a thrilling series of rich entertainment.

After the 1962 Commonwealth Immigration Act, migration figures for Caribbean migrants to Britain decreased due to the restrictions of the voucher system. Despite this, dependants of migrants from the Caribbean who had put down more permanent roots could settle in Britain without vouchers. Between 1962 and 1967, 55,310 dependants of settled Caribbean migrants arrived in Britain.[4]

Therefore, when the West Indies arrived for their sixth Test tour of England in 1963, the Caribbean diaspora had significantly increased in numbers since the last West Indies tour in 1957. West Indian players could now expect more support from Caribbean migrants and their immediate descendants in Britain. Cricket continued to provide some Caribbean migrants with a sense of connection to Britain, now as residents in the country which transported cricket to the Caribbean territories they had left behind.

West Indies cricket, and especially West Indies tours in England, also helped Caribbean migrants in Britain to renew their sense of connection with the territories they came from. For many Caribbean migrants who arrived in Britain in the early 1960s, including some members of my family, the 1963 tour offered them their first opportunity to watch the West Indies play in England.

From 1928 to 1957, the white captains who led West Indies teams on tour in England were Karl Nunes from Jamaica in 1928, Jackie Grant from Trinidad in 1933, Rolph Grant from Trinidad in 1939 (brother of Jackie Grant), and John Goddard from Barbados in 1950 and 1957. In 1963, following the 1960/1961 tour of Australia and the convincing 1962 5-0 series victory v India in the Caribbean, Frank Worrell retained the captaincy. Worrell then became the first black cricketer to captain the West Indies in England.

Some of the Caribbean diaspora in Britain could now be inspired by Worrell's appointment as captain. It offered a sense of social and political fulfilment and a blow against some deeply held colonial values. By the 1963 West Indies tour of England, two countries in the Caribbean, Jamaica and Trinidad (in 1962), had achieved independence from British rule.

'For a number of years, especially for the first and second generation of West Indians, how the West Indies team performed was very important. They were extremely demoralised in 1957 when the West Indies came to England and lost the series', says Professor Clem Seecharan, cricket author, academic, and Emeritus Professor of History at London Metropolitan University.

By then, the whole anti-colonial movement had developed significantly, and the Caribbean was on the threshold of independence. There was a heightened sense of national consciousness and I think that is why, when Frank Worrell became captain, he became such an important aspect of the whole anti-colonialist movement. Largely pioneered by (C.L.R) James during the time he was editor of *The Nation* newspaper in Trinidad. So, in 1963 and 1966, which were the years of consolidation for many West Indian families in Britain, this was the icing on the cake. That we (Caribbean people in Britain) were somebody and our great cricketers could come to England, and carry themselves with great dignity and pride, within the boundary and beyond the boundary. Frank Worrell was not just a great cricket captain, but he was also a great statesman and spokesman for West Indian people. So, all these things were interlinked.

For Tony Cozier, the cricket journalist, author and broadcaster from Barbados, the 1963 series was his first West Indies tour assignment in England. Cozier knew some of West Indian players personally, having played club cricket with and against them in Barbados. During the 1963 tour, Cozier stayed in the same hotels as the players and travelled around the country on tour in the team van, or in a car driven by Roy Lawrence, the West Indian BBC radio commentator from Jamaica. Cozier was able to observe, at close quarters, the rapidly developing connection between West Indies cricket and some of the Caribbean diaspora in Britain.

There were quite a few people in England who I had gone to school with in Barbados, who I knew had immigrated to England, and some of them had moved to England to study. I knew that as the West Indies were winning (in 1963) it meant a hell of a lot to them. They could boast about the West Indies team beating England. And with Frank Worrell as the captain, and Sobers, they could boast about having the best team with the best players and that was a tremendous boost to them.

In 1963, Deryck Murray made a major impact on his first tour of England. Murray claimed a record-breaking 24 dismissals – a combination of 22 catches and two stumpings during the five Test series. This record still stands as the most dismissals claimed by a West Indian wicketkeeper in a Test series. As the tour progressed, Murray quickly realised how important it was, as a West Indies player on tour in England, to recognise and represent the hopes and aspirations of the Caribbean diaspora in Britain.

When you met West Indians in the street you quickly realised how much you, as cricketers, meant to the diaspora in England, particularly in the 60s and the 70s. In those days, there was still an element of having to prove yourself as a West Indian in Britain. There was still the feeling that as a West Indian you weren't getting a fair deal. For example, getting jobs suitable to your capabilities and that you were always feeling like second class citizens. Even though some of that generation was born in Britain or had recently arrived from the Caribbean – with the promise of the mother country being able to provide you with the good things in life. So, there was a sense of disappointment for many Caribbean people when they went to Britain. And, I think, it was only through cricket that Caribbean people could feel that they were equal.

So much then depended on us as cricketers from the West Indies to produce the goods in England. So that we could show we could beat our old colonial masters at their own game. So, on a Monday morning, as a West Indian in England, you could go into work on the underground, in the office, or whatever, and hold your head up. That was such a strong feeling and it really inspired us as cricketers. There was also the feeling amongst us as West Indian players that we wanted to prove ourselves as cricketers, and there was pride in simply trying to be the best cricketers in the world. In those days, it was expected that if you were an English or Australian cricketer you were better than anyone else. Although, people were starting to notice the West Indies as a team, and in the 1920s, 1930s and up to 1950s great players from the Caribbean like Constantine, Headley, Ramadhin and Valentine did well very in England. But it was not until later into the 1950s and 60s that people started recognising individual West Indian cricketers as being amongst the best in the world.

In 1963, the West Indies team that toured England also left a long-lasting impression on Mark Cripps, now a cricket and football blogger and memorabilia dealer. After witnessing his enthusiasm for cricket in the family back garden, inspired by watching the 1963 West Indies team on TV, Mark's father encouraged him to join the Finchley Cricket Club colts. Finchley was then a top north London club in the days just before the formation of the Middlesex League. This was a competition that Finchley would dominate for many years.

'The West Indies were always the starting point for me' says Mark as he fondly recalls the moment his passion for cricket began.

I was a seven-year-old at the time just playing in the sun in our garden in North West London. Up to that point, I wasn't a cricket fan, but I came into the house one day and there was this thing on the television called cricket. Wes Hall and Charlie Griffith were bowling for the West Indies and after watching them I went back out in the garden and started bowling. I found three bits of wood and banged them into three holes to make some stumps and found a plastic ball and started copying Wes Hall.

I tried to mimic Wes Hall and his long run-up. It was just a case of me trying to do what these men on the telly were doing, and it just seemed a fun thing to do. I loved watching the cartwheeling bowling action of Wes Hall and I remember thinking: Wow! And the guys at the other end, (John) Edrich and (Micky) Stewart, were trying to get out the way! I didn't understand it all but as each year went by I really did understand it and that's how my understanding of cricket evolved. It was all about the feeling, imagery and the aesthetic appeal of these two West Indian fast bowlers in 1963 on television that first drew me into the game.

Frank Worrell led the 1963 West Indies team in England to a 3-1 Test series win. The West Indies victories were at Old Trafford, Headingley and The Oval. England's only victory in the series was at Edgbaston. Worrell retired from professional cricket after the 1963 tour and the West Indies captaincy was taken over by Garry Sobers.

One of the most memorable England v West Indies Test matches was the ebb and flow of the 1963 Test at Lord's, which ended in a dramatic climax. The match got off to an explosive start when Conrad Hunte, opening the West Indies first innings with Easton McMorris, hit Fred Trueman's first three deliveries for four runs each. On day two, during England's first innings, Ted Dexter fought an individual contest with the fearsome Barbadian fast-bowling combination of Hall and Griffith at each end. Hall was arguably the fastest pace bowler in international cricket. Dexter scored a defiant innings of 70 before he was trapped LBW by Sobers.

By the tea interval on day three, West Indies were 104 for 5 during their second innings and struggling against the serious prospect of defeat. The stage was now set for Basil Butcher to produce, which he later described as, his best innings for the West Indies. As the main pillar of resistance, he scored 133 runs in over four hours in a second innings total of 229. Butcher considered this innings at Lord's in 1963 more valuable to him, and the team, than the unbeaten double century he scored three years later (out of a second innings total of 482 for five declared) to help West Indies beat England at Trent Bridge by 139 runs.

England now required 234 to win but got off to a poor start. At one stage in their second innings they were 31 for three. Colin Cowdrey, the England captain, continued to face-up to Hall and Griffith with Ken Barrington. Both batsmen were forced to fend off a series of fierce short-pitched deliveries. Cowdrey received a blow on his left arm from a Hall delivery and retired hurt. Ten years later Cowdrey remembered.

There were a number of bouncers flying but it was a good length ball which flew, quite unaccountably, and broke my arm just above the wrist. It made the most awful noise and must have been quite unnerving for the next batsman, not to mention poor Ken Barrington at the other end.[5]

During the final over on the last day, as the conditions at Lord's slowly became gloomier, any one of four results were still possible. A win for either team, a draw or a tie. The West Indies needed just one more wicket for victory. England required six runs for what would have been a remarkable win and a halt on West Indian progress in winning the series. Cowdrey, with only two balls left in the match to be bowled by Wes Hall, strolled out from the Lord's pavilion to bat with his injured left arm in a bandage. Fortunately for Cowdrey, he wasn't required to face any of Hall's deliveries.

Cowdrey looked in relief at the non-striker's end as David Allen, England's off-break spin bowler, survived the last two balls from Hall, prevented England from losing their final wicket and saved the game by securing a draw. The West Indies avoided defeat and maintained their 1-0 lead in the series. This provided increased momentum for the West Indies to progress and win the series 3-1.

Three years later in 1966, the Caribbean diaspora in Britain had another opportunity to celebrate West Indian cricket domination in England. According to the 1966 UK census, an estimated 454,100 black West Indians were now resident in Britain.[6] These included children born in Britain to families who had migrated from the Caribbean. In 1966, the West Indies were led by Garry Sobers on his first tour in England as captain. The 1966 West Indies team was dominated by players from Barbados. Sobers and Hunte, his vice-captain, were two of the nine Barbadian players selected for the team that beat England to win the series 3-1. As in 1963, the West Indies won three Test matches, lost one and drew one.

Sobers had a magnificent series in 1966 and delivered a collection of inspirational individual performances. Sobers scored 722 runs including three centuries, a 94 and an 81, at an average of 103.14, took 20 wickets at 27.25, 10 catches, and won all five tosses![7] One of his centuries was a 163 not out during the second Test at Lord's which was drawn. David Holford, a cousin of Sobers, also hit a not out century in only his second Test. Sobers and Holford produced an enthralling second innings 274 run match-saving partnership.

The West Indies started the 1966 tour by comfortably winning the first Test at Old Trafford in three days by an innings and 40 runs. The second Test at Lord's, as in 1963, finished in a draw but with no final session drama on the last day. Their two other victories were at

Trent Bridge and Headingley. At Trent Bridge, Geoffrey Boycott was dismissed for 0 in England's first innings by a ball by Sobers which Boycott claims, 'swung prodigiously – the best delivery I have ever faced in cricket'.[8] England won the final Test, much to the disappointment of the large groups of expectant West Indian spectators at The Oval. By the mid-1960s, there was a firmly established Caribbean community resident in nearby Brixton, a short bus ride or a walk from The Oval.

The West Indies arrived in Britain in 1969 for their third and final tour of the 1960s. The team now appeared as a side entering a transitionary phase. The 1969 tour of England was Basil Butcher's last series for the West Indies and Garry Sobers' last series as team captain. There was no Hall and Griffith who had both retired from international cricket. Rohan Kanhai was injured. Seymour Nurse had also retired, partly to spend more time with his young family. A few months earlier, Nurse signed off his international career in outstanding style with his highest Test score of 258 in Christchurch v New Zealand. Of the 16 West Indian players selected to tour England in 1966, 11 of the team had very little or no experience of playing in English conditions.

Philbert Blair from Guyana was considered by some to be the quickest and most promising bowler in the West Indies team. The 1969 tour was Blair's first West Indies tour, but he did not play in any of the three Tests. In 2014, I spoke to Basil Butcher about Blair's absence from the 1969 Test team during a visit to his house in Watooka, Guyana. Butcher suggested that questions about Blair's bowling action had contributed to him being passed over for selection in the Tests.

For the Caribbean diaspora in Britain, who demanded continued West Indies success in England, 1969 was a frustrating tour in terms of performances and results. The tour was reduced, in comparison to the 1963 and 1966 tours, to three Tests. West Indies were soundly beaten in the first Test at Old Trafford by 10 wickets. As in 1963 and 1966, the match at Lord's ended in a draw.

The final Test at Headingley was a much closer affair, which England eventually won by 30 runs. During the West Indies second innings run chase, Sobers was bowled for a duck by Barry Knight, England's fast-medium pace all-rounder, which helped England to close in on victory. England won the 1969 series 2-0. Sobers conceded that the West Indies were beaten fair and square by the better team in Ray Illingworth's first series as England captain.

'In 1969, we lost the series but we still played quite well. It's just that we weren't quite good enough', insists Vanburn Holder. He made his debut for the West Indies in the first Test match at Old Trafford. Holder claimed his first Test wicket at Old Trafford by bowling Tom Graveney, his captain at Worcestershire, who had scouted him in Barbados during the previous year.

We came over to England before New Zealand and we came quite early in April when it was still fairly cold. Most of the lads on the 1969 tour were not used to the conditions in England and just couldn't cope. For some of us it was quite tough, especially the younger players. We had a fairly young side and I had only had a season playing for Worcestershire up to then. We had some lads in the West Indies team who were playing county cricket but, like myself, had only played a season before the tour. So, I think that inexperience had a lot to do with it. But we got more experience after a few more years playing county cricket, and that helped us to master the game, become more professional, and from 1973 we started to get a bit more respect from England.

In 1969, the West Indies suffered their first series defeat in England since 1957. The next opportunity for the West Indies to provide a rewarding experience for their supporters in Britain would take place during the tour of England in 1973.

CHAPTER 4

The mighty Leeds United, Best from Bermuda, black football pioneers and more

Until the spring/summer of 1973, football was still my number one sporting passion. This was also fuelled by reading the 7p (soon to be increased to 8p) weekly edition of *Shoot!* magazine. By then, many of my friends at primary school had committed themselves to the lifelong emotional rollercoaster ride associated with supporting a football club. Alan, Daniel, Nigel and Simon supported Arsenal. Barry and Ian I supported Crystal Palace. Ian L supported Liverpool and Nick supported Norwich City.

Mr Walker, a teacher who passed on his passion for chess to our class, was a loyal supporter of Liverpool Football Club. At any given opportunity, Mr Walker entertained us with tales of his upbringing in Merseyside and burst with pride when talking about his favourite Liverpool players, including Emlyn Hughes, Kevin Keegan and John Toshack.

Mr Sweeney, another one of our teachers, was also from Merseyside and supported Everton. But he very rarely expressed his passion for football and sport in general. Compared with Mr Walker, Mr Sweeney was a more no-nonsense character with a pirate-style beard and a bristling personality. Mr Sweeney was also less inclined to get involved in small talk with any of us pupils.

The team I supported, and still do, was Leeds United. Don Revie was the manager who masterminded the progress of Leeds United towards being one of the dominant teams in English and European football during the 1960s and 1970s. In *The Unforgiven: The Story of Don Revie's Leeds United*, Rob Bagchi and Paul Rogerson describe Revie's arrival as Leeds manager in 1961 at a time when the club 'were unfashionable and provincial in outlook'.[1] Leeds were a football club who had 'spent forty years skipping between the top two divisions to little effect'.[2]

As a statement of ambition and intent, Revie changed the Leeds kit colours from dark blue shirts with gold collars, white shorts, and blue and gold hooped socks to an all-white kit. Revie was influenced to change the club's kit colours in order to emulate Real Madrid. From 1956 to 1960, Real Madrid won the European Cup for five seasons in a row. During this period, they were widely considered to be Europe's most dominant and glamorous football club.

Under Don Revie's leadership, Leeds were crowned Second Division champions in 1964 and promoted to the First Division. Leeds had an impressive first season in the First Division, but it also featured a sequence of near-misses. At the end of the 1964/1965 season, Leeds finished as runners-up to Manchester United in the First Division on goal average. Leeds also narrowly lost 2-1 to Liverpool, after extra time, in their first FA Cup final at Wembley.

The club's ground-breaking year was in 1968 when they won their first top-flight major trophies. The League Cup final v Arsenal at Wembley and the European-wide Inter-Cities Fairs Cup final played over two legs v Ferencváros from Hungary. After the intense frustration of finishing as runners-up in 1965 and 1966, Leeds eventually reached the summit of English football when they became First Division champions in 1969. My support for Leeds was confirmed after the first football match I can remember watching on television. The 1970 FA Cup final replay between Leeds and Chelsea at Old Trafford, the home of Manchester United.

The first final in 1970 was played, as usual, at Wembley with a Saturday 3pm kick-off. This was Leeds United's second FA Cup final and, once again, as in their 2-1 defeat in 1965 v Liverpool, extra time was played. On this occasion, Leeds avoided defeat as the match ended in a 2-2 draw after extra time. It was the first FA Cup final to finish as a draw and require a replay. I have cloudy memories of the first Leeds v Chelsea FA Cup final at Wembley, but more vivid memories of the replay two weeks later.

The match was played on a Wednesday evening at Old Trafford with a 7.30pm kick-off time. I can't recall whether it was played during a school week, or whether it was during a term break from school. However, I was allowed by my family to stay up and watch the match from start to finish. None of my family were deeply interested in watching football and, especially, anything to do with Leeds United.

As with many of the live matches I watched as a child, I watched the 1970 FA Cup final replay on our small black and white television by myself. During the match various family members drifted in and out of the living room.

Leeds opened the scoring in the first-half with a goal by Mick Jones but Chelsea equalised in the second half through Peter Osgood. Then, disaster struck in the Leeds penalty area. Jack Charlton, from a trademark Ian Hutchinson Chelsea throw-in, back-headed the ball in a struggle to clear it away from danger. The ball kindly floated in the air across to David Webb. He easily nodded the ball into the Leeds net from a few yards out to win the FA Cup for Chelsea. All I could remember thinking, as an upset five-year-old boy, was why did Jack Charlton head the ball backwards, instead of forwards, across the Leeds penalty area?

Despite the crushing emotions of defeat, I became attached to this team who wore a gleaming all-white kit which was, visually, quite striking as seen through our black and white TV set. My commitment to Leeds United was confirmed.

During the 1970s, the FA Cup final at Wembley, whether Leeds were in the final or not, quickly became one of my major television events of the year. The FA Cup final was one of the few football matches, alongside European-wide club competition matches featuring English teams, and the England v Scotland home international clash, which was shown live each year on British television. By 1973, the FA Cup final was a unique annual occasion for all football supporters in my class at primary school, and a strangely surreal day. We all woke up bright and early on FA Cup final day and watched the television coverage from late morning onwards.

The sun always seemed to shine on a Saturday FA Cup final day at Wembley Stadium. The pitch always looked much bigger than any other pitch we saw on television. The playing surface always looked in immaculate condition, except for the 1970 final. In 1970, the poor state of the pitch was blamed on an equestrian event held at Wembley a week before the match. Celebrity fans of each club would be interviewed, and we'd hear from fans travelling from different parts of England on trains and coaches taking them to Wembley.

The team buses were followed by the television cameras from their hotels to the stadium. Television studio pundits would often speculate on the mythical nature of the Wembley pitch, which was often described as having 'wide open spaces' with the potential to 'sap the energy' of the players. A military band in immaculate uniforms would march up and down in straight lines across the pitch to entertain the crowd. The crowd would indulge in some community singing including the FA Cup final hymn/anthem, *Abide with Me*, which is still a Cup final tradition at Wembley. Alongside these pre-match rituals, the television cameras scanned the crowd for humorous slogans written on banners by supporters.

In 1972, Leeds progressed to their third FA Cup final v Arsenal. The match was a historic event as it was the 100th year of the FA Cup competition. Arsenal were defending the FA Cup trophy they won the previous year after beating Liverpool 2-1 during their FA Cup and First Division double winning season.

As the television cameras scanned the crowd for humorous slogans before the 1972 Cup final kick-off, one banner stood out for its humour and impact. A group of Leeds fans held a banner which read 'Norman Bites Yer Legs' in recognition of Norman Hunter's abrasive and uncompromising approach to defending. The 'Bites Yer Legs' banner captured the attention of the television cameras and was screened on several occasions. The 'Bites Yer Legs' nickname became associated with Hunter throughout his career.

In the second half of the 1972 Cup final, Mick Jones crossed from the right and Allan Clarke met the cross with a spectacular diving header in the penalty area. The ball flew past Geoff Barnett, the Arsenal goalkeeper, and hit the back of the net. David Coleman, a year on from being confirmed as the BBC's senior football commentator, cried, 'One nil!' Mick Jones landed awkwardly after crossing the ball for Clarke and injured his left arm. Leeds held on to their 1-0 lead until the final whistle to win the FA Cup for the first time. Clarke's diving-header and Jones with a heavily bandaged arm and shoulder, climbing the steps with Hunter's help to collect his medal, are two of the most memorable moments I have experienced watching sport on television.

There was no time for extended celebrations by Revie and the players after Cup final victory at Wembley. On a Monday night in the West Midlands, 48 hours after winning the FA Cup, Leeds were required to play their final First Division fixture of the 1971/1972 season away v Wolverhampton Wanderers at Molineux. Leeds lost 2-1 and missed out on clinching the domestic league and cup double which Arsenal had achieved the season before.

In 1973, Leeds returned to Wembley during the famous old stadium's jubilee year, to defend the FA Cup and play their fourth final (including the 1970 FA Cup final replay v Chelsea) in three years. Their opponents were Sunderland. Bob Stokoe, a long-term adversary of Don Revie, was the manager who masterminded Sunderland's progress to Wembley. Leeds were the overwhelming favourites to win and I was confident of victory. Sunderland were in the Second Division. A Second Division club had not won the FA Cup for 42 years. Sunderland's last FA Cup final victory was in 1937. The last two numbers were a reverse of 1973. Thirty-six years later, would this be a lucky omen for Sunderland at Wembley?

Ten Leeds players had represented their countries at full international level. Billy Bremner, Eddie Gray, David Harvey and Peter Lorimer for Scotland. Allan Clarke, Norman Hunter, Mick Jones, Paul Madeley and Paul Reaney for England. Johnny Giles for Ireland and substitute Terry Yorath (father of Gabby Logan, the television sports presenter) for Wales. Hunter was also a member of the 1966 England squad which won the World Cup. Trevor Cherry was the only non-international player on the Leeds team sheet in the 1973 FA Cup final. Cherry made his full international debut for England three years later.

I was excited about the prospect of my team winning the FA Cup for the second year in a row. What could possibly go wrong? For many of us at primary school who were football fans, the prestige of winning the FA Cup was as important, if not more important, as seeing your club win the First Division championship. Of course, as with all the televised FA Cup finals that I watched, I had to watch the game on the BBC. So, I could listen to David Coleman's magnificent match commentary.

A year later, Coleman delivered one of my favourite match commentator responses to a goal scored on British television. After Kevin Keegan scored Liverpool's first goal in the second half during their convincing 3-0 1974 FA Cup final victory v Newcastle United, which was the first final I saw on television in colour, Coleman proclaimed, 'Goals pay the rent and Keegan does his share!' There was a short pause while the noise of Liverpool supporters celebrating Keegan's goal streamed out of our television's audio speaker. Coleman then continued, 'The fans celebrate and so they might!'

Back in 1973, most football supporters across England were hopeful of a Sunderland victory. This was due to a combination of factors. Sunderland had received an avalanche of praise and affection for their exploits in reaching the FA Cup final. This included plaudits for their 2-1 semi-final victory v Arsenal at Hillsborough, the home of Sheffield Wednesday Football Club. The first Sunderland goal scored by Vic Halom was a result of a calamitous mix-up between Jeff Blockley, one of the Arsenal centre-halves, and Bob Wilson, the Arsenal goalkeeper. There was also the long-established English tradition of having sympathy for the underdogs battling against all the odds.

By 1973, despite their dominant position in English football, which included a combination of successes as well as near misses, Don Revie and Leeds United had become a club who were widely disliked. Leeds were viewed by many football fans across the country, and many casual observers of the game, as a team who employed cynical methods and an uncompromising, physical approach to win matches. Hence, their 'Dirty Leeds' tag. For me, their widespread unpopularity among other supporters increased their appeal. No one liked them but I didn't care. The day before the 1973 final, *The Times* newspaper described the contest as a battle between 'inspiration' (Sunderland) v 'hardened skill' (Leeds United).

> Tomorrow's FA Cup final at Wembley brings together Leeds United from the first division and Sunderland from the second. The difference in status is not the only contrast. This can also be seen as a final between the unloved and the loved, between the experienced and the inexperienced; and between the old master and the new Messiah.[3]

As Roger Hermiston – a writer, journalist and broadcaster, noted in his combined biography of Don Revie and Brian Clough, two successful football managers and rivals from Middlesbrough in the North East, Leeds v Sunderland fixtures often took place against a backdrop of bitter rivalry.

In the 1960s and early 1970s, clashes between Sunderland and Leeds United were invariably bitter in spirit and often violent in deed. Take the fierce, highly personal rivalries between Don Revie, Alan Brown and Bob Stokoe, add the natural contention between two Northern sides with partisan, committed sets of supporters, and the concoction was a witches' brew that would often poison the encounters.[4]

To add a twist to this historical rivalry, Don Revie first arrived at Leeds in November 1958 as a player from Sunderland for a transfer fee of £12,000. Leeds would be Revie's last club as a professional footballer. Revie was appointed as player-manager of Leeds in March 1961.

Back to Wembley Stadium, 1973. As the first half of the Cup final progressed, Sunderland repelled early attempts from Leeds to get a dominant foothold in the game. Sunderland then gradually increased in confidence and made positive strides into the Leeds half. David Coleman quickly eased into his commentary stride. During the first half, and with his trusted left-foot, Norman Hunter brought the ball out across the edge of the Leeds penalty area. Hunter then skilfully glided past two Sunderland players who attempted to tackle him. Coleman, impressed by Hunter's skill and technique, told BBC viewers, 'That left foot qualifies him for the magic circle'.

As the first half continued, many of the Sunderland supporters, who were also beginning to gain in confidence and expectation, joined in with a clearly audible chant of 'What a load of rubbish' aimed at the Leeds players and supporters. Coleman was quick to highlight this chorus of derision by Sunderland supporters, who were unimpressed by the lack of threat posed by Leeds.

After 31 minutes in the first half, Sunderland took the lead with a goal from Ian Porterfield. I was in a state of shock, but I still thought there was plenty of time for a Leeds equaliser. My *1973 Football Champions* book, which was a highly desired annual Christmas Day gift, reported that after Porterfield's goal, 'Leeds were strangely bewitched. Nothing was going right for them. They were a bothered, almost bewitched side as Sunderland assumed total control'.[5]

Leeds slightly improved and created more chances to score in the second half. Twenty minutes into the second half, Trevor Cherry's diving header was saved by Jim Montgomery, the Sunderland goalkeeper and their longest serving player. Montgomery pushed the ball away into the path of Peter 'Lash' Lorimer. By 1973, most of the football supporters at school knew that Lorimer was a Scottish international player with the hardest shot in British football. Lorimer's right foot shot from close range was miraculously saved by Montgomery who tipped the ball onto the crossbar. The ball came down from the crossbar, and bounced on the goal line and away, before being cleared by a Sunderland player in the penalty area.

Just over 20 years later, Norman Hunter, who was Revie's second signing for Leeds after Albert Johanneson, reflected on the anguish he experienced during and after the 1973 FA Cup final. In his autobiography, *Biting Talk*, Hunter vividly recalls how he jumped up to celebrate Lorimer's shot at goal. Hunter was certain the ball was going to hit the back of the net. He was convinced that if Montgomery had not pulled off that brilliant double save, Leeds would have continued to dominate the game and win the cup. Hunter was also desperate for a Leeds victory v Sunderland as he was a lifelong fan of Newcastle United. In the North East of England, Newcastle and Sunderland have always experienced an intense regional football rivalry.

Months before the 1973 FA Cup final, I received a combined Leeds United-themed present from my family. A Leeds jigsaw puzzle and a pair of Leeds number 11 football sock tags. Number 11 was Eddie Gray's shirt and sock tag number. Thirty years later, *The Guardian* newspaper included Leeds United sock tags as one of the top 10 coolest items of sportswear ever![6] Another item included in the top 10 was Jack Russell's distinctive floppy hat. From 1988 to 1998, Russell played 54 Test matches as a wicket-keeper for England.

By 1973, Allan Clarke and Eddie Gray were two of my favourite Leeds players. When I represented my primary school football team as a centre forward, I always wanted to wear the number eight shirt. This was because Clarke always wore the number eight shirt for Leeds. Clarke is in action for Leeds v Wolves on the cover of one of my archived 1973 *Shoot!* magazines. My cricket and football annuals and magazines from the 1970s have provided a valuable source of research for this book.

Clarke, described as the 'Leeds and England goal ace', is closely marked in the picture by Derek Parkin, a Wolves defender. A poster of Clarke was one of the first to adorn my bedroom wall. Clarke's pride of place on my bedroom wall was followed years later by various other Leeds players, West Indian cricketers, Laurie Cunningham, Cyrille Regis, Annabella Lwin from Bow Wow Wow, Orange Juice, Sade, The Specials, and Martin Luther King.

Clarke had arrived at Leeds from Leicester City in preparation for the 1969/1970 season. He was signed for a British domestic record fee of £165,000. Clarke was nicknamed and known as 'Sniffer' because of his ability to sniff out and identify half-chance goal-scoring opportunities in and around the penalty area. Unfortunately, for Leeds supporters at Wembley in 1973, Clarke, Gray and many of their team mates failed to make an impact in the FA Cup final.

Revie suggested on the day before the final that Gray could make a major impact and be the match winner. Despite Revie's pre-match remarks, Gray was substituted in the second half and replaced by Terry Yorath. Despite the pressure Leeds put on the Sunderland defence in the second half, and I was still convinced that a Leeds goal would eventually arrive, Sunderland held on to win the match 1-0. It was one of the biggest shocks in the history of the FA Cup and I chocked back the tears.

A few years later, when I had left primary school to begin secondary school in London, Mike, one of my new classmates, gave me a well-worn Leeds United rosette. Mike's brother wore this rosette to the 1973 FA Cup final and, after the bitter disappointment of defeat, gave it to Mike. Soon after he discovered that I supported Leeds, Mike (who supported Liverpool) passed on the rosette to me.

The defeat by Sunderland at Wembley was followed 11 days later by further cup final misery. Leeds lost 1-0 to AC Milan in the European Cup Winners' Cup final in Salonika, Greece. Leeds took the field without Jack Charlton, who had retired at the end of the domestic football season. Their creative and destructive midfield partnership of captain Billy Bremner and Johnny Giles was also absent. Bremner was suspended and Giles was withdrawn due to an injury.

Mick Bates replaced Bremner and Paul Reaney was handed the captaincy by Don Revie in Bremner's absence. Allan Clarke, another notable absentee due to suspension, was replaced by Joe Jordan. The 1973 Cup Winners' Cup final was played against a backdrop of rumour and speculation surrounding the managerial future of Don Revie. Was Revie preparing to leave Leeds and become the new manager of Everton?

Leeds conceded a goal after only three minutes in first-half following an AC Milan free kick. Despite a batch of decent opportunities throughout the game, Leeds were unable to force an equaliser. Towards the end of the match, Norman Hunter was sent off after retaliating to a crude foul from behind by AC Milan's Gianni Rivera. Hunter had responded angrily by jumping into the back of Rivera who tumbled down to the ground. All hell broke loose on the pitch as players from both sides squared up to each other. After the mayhem ended, Riccardo Sogliano from AC Milan was also sent-off by Christos Michas, the Greek referee. Michas made a series of bewildering refereeing decisions during the match, which all appeared to go against Leeds.

After the trophy and medals were awarded, the Leeds players received a sympathetic response by the home crowd in Salonika during their lap of honour. Hunter recalls that they stood and applauded the Leeds team. Only muted acknowledgment was offered to the Italian side. Perhaps, they also noticed something which disappointed them in the way the game was refereed.

Christos Michas was later investigated by the Greece Football Association over allegations that he was offered and accepted a bribe from AC Milan officials. Michas was later banned from officiating football matches by UEFA.

From the start of Revie's reign as manager in 1961 to the end of the 1973 season, Leeds United and their supporters had celebrated a haul of five trophies. The First Division championship, one FA Cup win and one League Cup win (both victories were 1-0 v Arsenal at Wembley), and two Fairs Cup wins. In 1973, Leeds were now forced to reflect on yet another season of setbacks and near-misses which, since 1961, had included five First Division runners-up finishes, three FA Cup final defeats, and a Cup Winners' Cup final loss.

There was one significant personal milestone achieved by Norman Hunter in 1973. He was awarded a silver tray on the pitch at Elland Road by Manny Cussins, the Leeds Chairman, to mark his 700th appearance for the club. For Hunter, despite this personal accolade for his years of loyal service, 1973 was also a year racked with bitter disappointment. The FA Cup final defeat v Sunderland and the Cup Winners Cup final defeat v AC Milan – which included Hunter being sent-off, was followed by further upset on international duty for England v Poland at Wembley in October.

England needed to win the game to ensure qualification for the 1974 World Cup tournament in West Germany. It was the first England match I can remember us children at school getting excited about. It was also the first and last game, for many years, that I was genuinely interested in seeing England win. Looking back, during the 1970s, my attitude towards the England football team was, partly, influenced by my family. At home there was no tradition of supporting England at anything, football or otherwise. My family, and many Caribbean people I knew, were either disinterested in supporting England at football, took some pleasure in seeing England lose, or adopted the default position of ABE (Anyone but England).

If there was a major domestic or international football match played that evening, Mr Burns, our head teacher, would pass by the school dinner table that I sat around with my friends. He would then briefly canvass opinion on what we thought the score would be. I predicted a 1-0 win with Allan Clarke, my Leeds United centre forward hero, scoring the winner for England. Well, in the end, I was partly correct. Clarke managed to get his name on the score sheet. The two other Leeds players on duty for England were Norman Hunter and Paul Madeley.

The score was 0-0 at half-time, but a costly defensive error by Hunter in the second-half led to Poland scoring an equaliser. Hunter mistimed an interception on the half-way line to clear the ball away from the advancing Gregor Lato. Lato continued to progress dangerously down the left flank and cut inside to feed the ball to Jan Domarski. He slid the ball under and away from the grasp of Peter Shilton, the England goalkeeper. Gregor Lato is a name I will never forget.

The other Polish player whose name will always remain lodged in my memory from that match is Jan Tomaszewski, the Polish goalkeeper. Tomaszewski, whose abilities as a goalkeeper were mistakenly doubted by Brian Clough – who described him on TV as a clown, produced a dynamic performance to repel the constant waves of England attacks. Tomaszewski produced a collection of brilliant saves. His goalkeeping performance, combined with a defensive barrier of last-ditch blocks by some desperate but brave Polish defending, ensured that Poland only conceded one goal, a penalty converted by Allan Clarke, which earned them a 1-1 draw.

Hunter described the mistake that led to Poland's equaliser as the lowest point of his career. He was inconsolable and convinced his international career was over. Bobby Moore, who was not selected for the match, attempted to console Hunter as he left the pitch. I had to admit my prediction was wrong when we saw Mr Burns in the school dinner hall the following day. Poland qualified for the World Cup in West Germany the following year. England failed to qualify for the tournament and Sir Alf Ramsay, who led England to World Cup success in 1966, was removed from his post as manager the following year.

Another factor which influenced my lack of interest in supporting England was that England failed to qualify for the 1974 World Cup in West Germany and the 1978 World Cup in Argentina. So there was no England team to support. England did not qualify for a World Cup tournament until 1982 in Spain.

In 1973, Ajax from Amsterdam won the European Cup, which was always viewed by supporters and pundits alike as the premier European-wide club knock-out competition. Ajax were the dominant side in European football in the early 1970s. When Ajax beat Juventus 1-0 in the 1973 final in Yugoslavia, it was their third European Cup triumph in a row. I was fascinated by Ajax and their group of youthful looking and exciting players, especially Johan Cruyff, Johan Neeskens and Johnny Rep – who scored the winning goal for Ajax in the 1973 final.

A year later, I travelled with my mother and great-grandmother to Holland on a ferry from Harwich, Essex. This was my first trip to a country on the European mainland. We visited a family friend from Guyana who lived in Holland with her Dutch husband. During our stay, I was driven past the Ajax Football Club stadium in Amsterdam. I was very excited to catch a brief glimpse of the stadium from a back-passenger seat. Whenever I met any Dutch grown-ups during the trip, all I wanted to talk about with them was Ajax, Johan Cruyff, Johan Neeskens and Johnny Rep. All three of these Ajax players played for the Dutch team in the 1974 World Cup tournament in West Germany a couple of weeks before we travelled to Amsterdam. West Germany beat Holland 2-1 in the World Cup final in Munich.

In 1973, the other major domestic trophies in England were won by Liverpool and Tottenham Hotspurs (Spurs). Liverpool won the First Division championship; Leeds finished third, seven points behind the champions, and Spurs won the League Cup final at Wembley. Spurs reclaimed the trophy they won two years before in 1971 and kept their proud unbeaten run in Wembley cup finals.

1972/1973 was a history-making season for Norwich City. This was their first season in the First Division. The 1973 League Cup final v Spurs was Norwich's first major domestic cup final at Wembley. Previously to 1973, Nick, one of my best friends at primary school, had been an Arsenal supporter. This was in response to Arsenal's 1971 First Division and FA Cup double winning season. The 1971 Arsenal 2 Liverpool 1 FA Cup final, with Charlie George's extra time winning goal followed by his memorable 'lying flat on the back' celebration, was the first Cup final Nick remembers watching.

In 1973, Nick's uncle and grandfather travelled in his uncle's MG sports car from Norwich, where his family lived, to Wembley. The car broke down around the halfway point of the trip on the motorway. Nick's uncle and grandfather were now forced to make a decision. Should they stay in the car and wait for help, or hitch a lift to the game? Still determined to watch Norwich in a Cup final for the first time, they successfully hitched rides to Wembley and watched the match. This family story is what influenced Nick to transfer his support from Arsenal to Norwich City in 1973. Nick's grandmother also looked after some of the football club's young trainees and apprentices in her house in Norwich.

Spurs beat Norwich City 1-0 and Ralph Coates scored their winning goal after 72 minutes in the second-half. Coates came on as a substitute to replace the injured John Pratt midway through the first-half. Coates also received the Man of the Match award for his winning goal and overall contribution to Spurs' victory. I will always have fond memories of Ralph Coates for two specific reasons.

Firstly, his match winning goal in the 1973 League Cup final which Brian 'the voice of football' Moore, the ITV match commentator, described as a 'beautiful shot'. Secondly, his comb over hairstyle from left to right which was designed to cover up his bald head. This was in a style and fashion similar to Andy Lochhead at Aston Villa and Bobby Charlton at Manchester United.

Ralph Coates, alongside and closely followed by Martin Dobson, Leighton James and Steve Kindon, emerged through the ranks at Burnley as a player through the club's youth development system. By

1973, Burnley was a football club that I didn't have a lot of knowledge about. But I do recall that they had a nationally acknowledged tradition of producing talented young players. Coates signed for Spurs from Burnley after the club was relegated from the First to the Second Division. Dobson and James both played influential roles in Burnley's successful campaign which saw the club promoted back to the First Division in 1973 after winning the Second Division championship.

Back to the 1973 League Cup final. Although Spurs supporters were thrilled to see their team win another Wembley final, the match itself was a rather uninspiring contest. According to my *1973 Football Champions* annual, this was one of the worst Wembley finals for many years. However, my *Football Champions* annual enthusiastically reported the move which led to the Spurs winning goal scored by Ralph Coates.

Coates, who cost the club £190,000 from Burnley, brought this dull affair to the boil in the 72nd minute. The move to goal began with a long throw from Martin Chivers. Martin Peters touched the ball across goal, Mike England went up for a header and the ball fell for Ralph Coates to shoot hard for the far post. Norwich keeper Kevin Keelan, whose great ability had kept Spurs at bay for so long, could do nothing to prevent that Coates cracker from going into the net. [7]

Len, a friend whose family knew our family in Guyana, was also pleased that Spurs won. Martin Chivers was one of his favourite players. I always admired the Spurs forward partnership of Martin Chivers and Alan Gilzean, and my young schoolboy imagination was also captured by other striking partnerships in English football. For example, Allan Clarke and Mick Jones at Leeds, Ray Kennedy and John Radford at Arsenal, Malcolm MacDonald and John Tudor at Newcastle United, and John Toshack and Kevin Keegan at Liverpool. Striking partnerships were far more common in the 1970s. Especially when compared with the current tactical preference of teams in the English Premier League to play with one forward alone up front.

By 1973, in the few photographs of the Leeds United squad I had seen in football annuals and magazines, I was always pleasantly surprised and intrigued to see a black player pictured alongside Jack

Charlton, Allan Clarke, Eddie Gray, Peter Lorimer and the rest of the squad I admired. Unsurprisingly, I wanted to find out more about who this player was. I eventually discovered that this player was Albert Johanneson, who I had not yet seen play for Leeds on television.

The post Second World War tide of migration to Britain from the British-ruled Caribbean and Africa had not yet produced a significant flow of black professional footballers into the British leagues. So, the only black players in the English leagues I was fully aware of by 1973, and in the immediate years that followed, were Clyde Best and Ade Coker at West Ham, and Trevor Lee and Phil Walker at Millwall. Paul Reaney at Leeds United sometimes appeared to look mixed-race to me. But, then, sometimes he didn't.

Albert Johanneson was born and raised in Germiston, a suburb of Johannesburg in South Africa. Johanneson's first sporting love was running but he quickly developed a passion for football and became a supporter of Manchester United. He also developed some impressive ball control skills by teaching himself some neat tricks and flicks with tennis balls on the streets of Germiston.

Johanneson's football talent was spotted by Barney Gaffney, a black South African schoolteacher and football scout. In 1961, Johanneson followed a path to Leeds United that had previously been trodden by Gerry Francis, who was the first black player to play for Leeds in 1959. Johanneson was full of envy when Gerry, a friend of his from South Africa, was offered an opportunity to join Leeds. Before the end of a three-month trial, Don Revie was satisfied with what he saw and also offered Johanneson a contract. Johanneson was Revie's first signing as Leeds manager.

Johanneson's performances, mainly as a left-sided winger, helped to promote Leeds as champions from the Second Division to the First Division in 1964. He finished that season as the club's joint top scorer with 13 goals. Johanneson played an influential role in the club's early development and progress from Second Division champions to winning domestic and European trophies. Leeds supporters quickly began to admire Johanneson's talent and he soon became affectionately known by many of them as 'The Black Flash'.

Back home in South Africa, Johanneson's daily life was dominated by the apartheid system of state-enforced racial segregation and discrimination. As a black migrant in 1960s Britain, Johanneson was often viewed as an object of curiosity, but he also had to face the bitter reality of racist confrontation on and off the football pitch. As one of the very few black professional footballers in English football, Johanneson had to confront racist abuse from opposition players and supporters throughout his career.

In 1965, Johanneson created history when he became the first black African footballer to play in an FA Cup final. He played for Leeds in their 2-1 defeat, after extra time, by Liverpool at Wembley. Johanneson couldn't produce the skill, guile and style which confirmed him as a favourite with the Leeds supporters. Years later, Johanneson revealed how intimidated he felt before kick-off. He was subjected to a barrage of racist abuse from some Liverpool players in the tunnel before the match. This affected his performance on the pitch. 'Ordinarily, I would have risen above this behaviour, but it affected me. Billy (Bremner) and Jack Charlton retaliated in my defence, and had a go back at the players in question'.[8]

Johanneson's Cup final appearance at Wembley in 1965, despite a defeat for Leeds combined with his disappointing performance, was a symbolic step towards the increasing presence of black footballers in Britain in the decades to follow. In 1966, at Elland Road, Johanneson became the first Leeds player to score a hat-trick in a European club competition match v DWS Amsterdam in the Fairs Cup. Johanneson's career statistics at Leeds included 200 league and cup appearances and 67 goals.

Paul Eubanks, a broadcaster, teacher and writer, was born and raised in Leeds, and was encouraged to support Leeds United by his father who migrated to Britain from Jamaica in 1955. As a young schoolboy of Caribbean descent, Eubanks describes himself as being 'mesmerised' when he watched Albert Johanneson play at Leeds United's Elland Road stadium. Eubanks quickly adopted Johanneson as his number one football hero. "As a young boy growing up and playing football on the streets in Leeds with my friends, one of us would say, 'I want to be George Best'. Someone else would say, 'I want to be Bobby Charlton'. I would always say, 'I'm going to be Albert Johanneson'. I always wanted to be Albert".

Being Jamaican, my dad's number one sport was cricket. But within six or seven years he also fell in love with football and, especially, Leeds United. So he started to go and watch them play at Elland Road. Every time my dad took me to watch Leeds, my mum used to make us a pack-up and, often, it used to consist of Jamaican food including pieces of chicken. We were like two black peas in a sea of white as black fans at football matches were very rare back then. But I was only six or seven and, to be honest, I wasn't really that conscious of being with my dad in a place where we were the only black people in the stands. The Leeds fans absolutely adored Albert and, in all the games I saw Albert play at Elland Road, I never saw or heard him get any racist abuse from Leeds supporters. They admired Albert's skill and technique and as soon as Albert got the ball the crowd went mad! They all knew what he was capable of doing and would cheer him on by shouting, 'Albert! Albert! Albert!' There was no one else in the Leeds team at the time who could run with the ball from one length of the field to another in about three seconds. And you would hear hundreds of supporters shouting, 'Give it to Albert' if Leeds weren't doing anything with the ball.

Johanneson was warmly welcomed by the Caribbean community in Leeds. In 1963, he married Norma Comrie, a Jamaican in Leeds who worked as a pharmacist at the city's General Infirmary. Their wedding was also attended by some Leeds United players. Johanneson would often socialise in the West Indian clubs in Leeds and, occasionally, took a few Leeds players to these clubs. The players wouldn't be instantly recognised and could usually have a drink without being fussed over.

In 1970, after falling out of favour at Leeds, Johanneson joined York City in Division Four. Gerry Francis had also joined York towards the end of his career. Johanneson's transfer to York followed a period in which he suffered injuries, a loss of form, increasing self-doubt, intense competition from other players for his place in the Leeds team – including Mike O'Grady and Eddie Gray, a difficult relationship with Don Revie, and an increasing dependency on alcohol.

By 1973, Johanneson's professional football career in England had come to an end. He played his final game for York during the 1971/1972 season, was assessed by the club as being surplus to their requirements and not retained for the 1972/1973 season. Johanneson's drift into alcoholism intensified and life became extremely difficult for him as he sadly fell on hard times. During this period, Johanneson became permanently separated from Norma, his wife. Norma decided to go back to live in Jamaica with their two British-born daughters. From Jamaica, Norma and their two daughters relocated for a second time to settle in the US.

Years after Johanneson's career had ended; Paul Eubanks had an opportunity to meet him on a bus in Leeds. However, Eubanks felt unable to walk up to Johanneson and initiate a conversation. As Eubanks admits, 'All I kept thinking of was that he was my first ever hero. I was going to tap him on the shoulder and say hello, but I never did. Looking back now, I wish I had. Albert had fallen on hard times, but I was still completely in awe of him because of who he was'. In 1995, Johanneson died alone in his flat in Leeds at the age of 55. A police surgeon concluded that Johanneson's body had lain dead for up to a week in his flat before it was discovered.

In the summer of 1973, Clyde Best was preparing to start his fifth full season as a professional footballer in England. He had settled into his new flat in Ilford, Essex with Alfreida, his newly married wife. Best was also looking forward to watching the West Indies tour of England on television and eating Alfreida's fruit pies. The pies included peach, apple and plum ingredients collected from their new garden.

Clyde Best was born and raised in Bermuda and came to England to join West Ham United as a 17-year-old teenager. When Best arrived in England in 1968, it was his first time away from the Caribbean. By 1973, Best was one of the few black footballers I saw on British television. Dougie Brimson, an author, screenwriter and social commentator on football fan culture, suggests that being seen regularly on television was crucial to Best's exposure to young black audiences in Britain.

That Best played for West Ham is no accident. The club had always drawn talent from their local community and already had a number of black youths on their books, but the key to Best's success was TV. Programmes such as *The Big Match* took him into homes the length and breadth of the country and as one of only a handful of black players turning out regularly in the First Division at that time, he could not help but stand out. For the first time Britain's black youth had a player they could relate to and who provided proof that there was certainly room for them within the upper echelons of the national game.[9]

Best was a capable club cricketer in Bermuda as a schoolboy. He was encouraged to play cricket by his father, who was born and raised in Barbados. Best's father attended a junior school in Bridgetown which was later named after one of the island's greatest fast bowlers, Wes Hall. Best also had Guyanese roots through his paternal great-grandmother who migrated to Barbados from Guyana.

Best was an all-rounder for his school cricket team and for Somerset, his local club based in the west end of Bermuda. In one match, as a 15-year-old boy, Best played against a Middlesex Select team that toured Bermuda and included Ken Barrington and Garry Sobers, his cricket hero. In another match, Best played against a team in Bermuda which included Ray Illingworth and Fred Titmus.

As an enthusiastic and talented young cricketer, Best represented a club from the west end of Bermuda. In later years, he became an iconic figure playing for West Ham in the east end of London. 'In Bermuda, I was brought up with cricket', Best enthusiastically recalls.

We'd always hear about the three Ws because that's what my dad talked about and my dad was best of friends with Everton Weekes. They were buddies when they were young and went to the same school in Barbados. So I used to follow cricket at home because that is what we would always hear on the radio, the West Indies and cricket. Garfield Sobers was my number one guy. He was my favourite because he could bat, bowl and do everything. I even had a pair of Garfield Sobers cricket boots with his signature on them!

Best's father was keen for young Clyde to become a professional cricketer. He introduced Clyde to Everton Weekes during Clyde's first trip to Barbados in 1966. The same year the island celebrated its independence from British rule. Best's father was pleased to discover that Weekes had offered to coach Clyde if he came to live in Barbados. Despite having developed a passion for supporting West Indies cricket, which included the thrill of meeting Clive Lloyd and Lance Gibbs in Bermuda, Clyde decided to pursue a career as a professional footballer.

By the age of 15, Best was already a full international football star for Bermuda. During his first West Ham training session Best was introduced to West Ham's three 1966 England World Cup winners. Bobby Moore – England's World Cup winning captain, Geoff Hurst – England's World Cup final hat-trick goal-scoring hero, and Martin Peters – England's other goal scorer in the 1966 World Cup final. During an appearance for West Ham v Manchester City at City's Maine Road ground, Best was watched in the stands by one of Lancashire County Cricket Club's star players, Clive Lloyd.

At West Ham, Best continued to pursue his interest in cricket and played matches with some of his team colleagues. 'I played some cricket in England because at West Ham we had a team and we played village league cricket some Sundays. It wasn't that often but now and again against some local teams'.

It was nothing serious, just a bit of fun cricket which we played mainly in the off season when we weren't doing anything. Frank Lampard senior was a good player and, according to some people, he could have played cricket for Essex when he was younger. Mooro (Bobby Moore) wasn't bad, Ronnie Boyce was good, Geoff (Hurst) was good, Martin Peters wasn't bad and my friend, Clive Charles, was a very good player. In the summer time I played on Thursdays with a team of English guys. Albert Walker, who was the equipment man at West Ham, was a big cricket fan from Lancashire, and he would always tell me about Clive Lloyd, and if he had a good innings for Lancashire. And if England were struggling against the West Indies, I always reminded him of the result during the summer time. We'd always have fun with each other about that!

At West Ham, Best took another young black player under his wing, Ade Coker, who was also determined to make a career for himself as a footballer in England. Coker was born in Nigeria and arrived in England with his parents and elder brother at the age of 11. In October 1971, on an away trip with the West Ham first team at Crystal Palace, Coker was shocked to discover that he was going to make his debut 20 minutes before kick-off. Ron Greenwood, the West Ham manager, declared that Geoff Hurst was unfit to play and Coker would replace him.

The 17-year-old Coker made an immediate impact for West Ham by scoring after about seven minutes during a 3-0 victory. One of the other West Ham goals was scored by Clyde Best. Two black players had scored a goal each which, in the early 1970s, was extremely rare. Coker's goal and his overall contribution to West Ham's win at Crystal Palace was viewed by millions of viewers across the country. The match highlights were screened the following day on *The Big Match*.

I had an Ade Coker card in my football player trading card collection. Having an Ade Coker trading card in my collection, a black footballer who played for a First Division club in England, was something that I treasured for a long time. Coker also had a two-page self-authored feature in my *1972-1973 Topical Times Football* book. The article was dedicated to the story of his family's journey from Nigeria to Britain, his early career at West Ham, ambitions to achieve a regular place in the first-team, watching Geoff Hurst play in order to pick up tips, his close relationship with Clyde Best, and his hopes and dreams of playing international football for Nigeria.

Coker failed to achieve his dream to play international football for his country of birth. Following his dramatic debut, Coker only made 10 appearances in three seasons for West Ham before moving to the US, where he had a lengthy career playing domestic league football. Having lived in the US for a number of years, Coker was qualified to play international football for his country of residence and represented the US on a handful of occasions.

The occasions that Clyde Best, Ade Coker and Clive Charles appeared together for West Ham were further examples of ground-breaking achievements and progress against the odds in the 1970s for black footballers in England. Following on from Gerry Francis and Albert Johanneson, who played together for Leeds United in the early 1960s and followed by Trevor Lee and Phil Walker who played for Millwall during the mid-1970s. Best also remembers Brendan Batson as one of the few black players he played against in a reserve match for West Ham v Arsenal, which was Batson's first club. Batson was the first black footballer to play for Arsenal.

Cyrille Regis was born in French Guiana. His father had migrated to French Guiana from St. Lucia and worked as a gold prospector. His mother was born in French Guiana with ancestral roots in Guadeloupe. When Regis was four years old his father, a British passport holder as St. Lucia was still a British colony, migrated to Britain to seek a better future for his family. Regis spent a year in St. Lucia with his mother and siblings before they joined his father in 1963. By 1973, Cyrille Regis was a teenage schoolboy in London, and an enthusiastic cricketer and West Indies supporter.

Regis was, by his own admission, a much better cricketer than footballer during his years at primary school in West London. He was encouraged to develop his cricket skills by an Australian teacher who worked at his school. Regis played regularly for his school cricket team and played cricket at schoolboy level for his county. 'I was a bit of a bowler and really enjoyed the game', says Regis.

> I was an outdoor child. So I just wanted to play cricket outside, and I played much more cricket back then because football was just another sport I did without any real kind of passion.

In his mid-teenage years, Regis decided to devote more of his time playing football. This included playing for youth football teams with Mike Gatting, a future cricket captain of Middlesex and England. He joined Epsom and Ewell, one of the non-league clubs he played for, soon before Trevor Lee and Phil Walker left the club to play for Millwall. His talent as a non-league football star attracted the attention of West Bromwich Albion (West Brom) in the English First Division who signed him in 1977.

In the late 1970s, Regis, Laurie Cunningham – a British-born winger of Jamaican heritage, and Brendan Batson – born in Grenada and raised in Trinidad and London, who moved to West Brom from Cambridge United, emerged as black Caribbean football pioneers. Never before, had three black footballers played together regularly for a top-flight professional football club in England. Regis and Cunningham progressed to represent England at full international level and both were FA Cup final winners at Wembley. During the 1970s, admiring the talent, skill, courage and dignity of footballers with Caribbean heritage on television, continued to be a major pull factor in my passion for watching sport on television.

CHAPTER 5

Inspirational broadcasters, compulsive family viewing and the (shock of the new) colour television

A lthough football was a large part of my early 1970s television viewing experience, there were many other programmes which were added to my daily, weekly or annual 'must watch' list. I also enjoyed the shared experience of watching programmes with the rest of the family, sports or otherwise. Apart from the rare thrill of live football on television, there were the weekend football highlights, which provided a wide range of talking points for all the football fans in the school playground on Monday morning.

On Saturday night, there was *Match of the Day* on BBC which usually featured highlights from two matches in the First Division or the FA Cup. As *Match of the Day* was shown late on a Saturday night, and even though there was no school the following Sunday morning, some of us did not have permission by our families to watch it. Fortunately, by 1973, I was usually allowed to stay up and watch *Match of the Day* and offer my pearls of wisdom (!) about the highlights I watched with anyone and everyone at school the following Monday. The other option, if permitted by family, was to watch football and other sports, including showjumping, on the midweek late evening BBC *Sportsnight* programme presented by David Coleman.

For those of us who were unable to watch *Match of the Day*, you could catch up with the weekend's football action by watching the Sunday afternoon highlights on one of the regional independent television channels. I watched *The Big Match* in London presented by Brian Moore. Not just to watch the football highlights but to enjoy listening to the pitch, tone and delivery of my favourite match commentators.

Hugh Johns commentated on matches in the Midlands region, including games at Aston Villa, Derby County and Wolverhampton

Wanderers. Johns had a gorgeous, sugar-coated voice and would proclaim the score line as being 'one nothing' after a team scored the first goal in a game to take the lead. This contrasted with David Coleman's more commanding and precise delivery of 'one nil'. Another commentator I admired later in the 1970s was Gerald Sinstadt. He covered football matches in the North West, including games at Manchester United, Manchester City and Liverpool.

Sinstadt remains firmly embedded in my memory. He was the first football television commentator who I heard call out supporters who were racially abusing black players. During the Manchester United v West Brom match at Old Trafford in 1978, with Sinstadt as commentator, groups of Manchester United fans relentlessly booed the West Brom black Caribbean players – Brendan Batson, Laurie Cunningham and Cyrille Regis. I clearly heard this through the television speaker in our living room.

West Brom produced an exhilarating performance to win 5-3 with Cunningham and Regis scoring a goal each. For Batson, Cunningham and Regis, their individual and collective response to the constant racially motivated barracking from spectators was to channel their anger towards producing top quality performances. As Regis told me during an interview for an article for the *Caribbean Intelligence* website in 2015 about his life and career:

> When you went out there with 10,000 people abusing you. What do you do? It made you angry, but we learned very, very quickly it was what you did with the anger that mattered. So, we decided to use the anger as motivation. For me, it was all about showing them how good we were. It just inspired us to put the ball in the back of the net and run harder. [1]

The other sports I watched regularly on television included rugby union, horse racing and wrestling. Every year, I would pay close attention to the annual Five Nations international rugby union championship with England, France, Ireland, Scotland and Wales. Italy joined the competition in 2000 which led to the tournament being rebranded as the Six Nations Championship.

1973 was a unique year for the Five Nations Championship as, after all the matches were played, the final table had all five teams on equal points. The championship had finished in a five-way tie for the first time in its history. [2] For me, the annual highlight of the tournament was the England v Wales clash at Twickenham or the Cardiff Arms Park stadium. In 1973, Wales beat England 25-9 at Cardiff Arms Park. I always wanted Wales to win because their team during this period included Phil Bennett, Mervyn 'Merv the Swerve' Davies, Gareth Edwards and JPR Williams – players who completely captured my imagination. Since then, Wales have always been my favourite international rugby union team.

As for horse racing, the annual highlight was the Grand National at the Aintree racecourse in Liverpool. It was the only day in the year when everyone in our family, and our Jamaican neighbours who lived downstairs, placed a small bet and got excited about the outcome of a horse race. While the grown-ups went in the betting shop to place their annual bets, we would hang around outside. We were always curious about this mysterious smoke-filled shop with a dedicated clientele of mainly English, Irish and West Indian men, where children were not allowed to enter. My experience of watching the Grand National on television was enhanced by the captivating voices of the BBC commentary team. This included the authoritative and knowledgeable voice of Peter O'Sullevan, the BBC's chief horse racing commentator.

The finish to the 1973 Grand National was one of the most dramatic in British horse racing history. Crisp jumped the last fence way ahead of Red Rum, his nearest rival in second place. After being out in front for such a long period, over the punishing Aintree fences, Crisp was an exhausted horse. On the long run in to the finishing post, Crisp temporarily drifted from one side to another before moving forward again in a slow trot. As Crisp completely ran out of energy, Red Rum was quickly closing down on him. Red Rum then powered past Crisp with yards to spare to win the first of his three Grand National races.

My heart went out to the tired and defeated Crisp and I felt sorry him. Crisp was so brave to stay out in front for so long. Mrs Hines in the flat downstairs placed a small each way bet on Spanish Steps which finished fourth. She was able to claim a small profit on her bet.

By 1973 and throughout the 1970s, after the horse racing and before the start of the classified football results service, watching the wrestling on ITV's *World of Sport* presented by Dickie Davies was a

Saturday afternoon tradition. My great-grandmother was a huge fan of wrestling and we sometimes shared the pleasure of watching the wrestling with her. For some reason, like many other older women in Britain, my great-grandmother was thrilled by the violent confrontations, and the good guy versus bad guy theatrical macho performances delivered by the wrestlers in the ring.

Each week, before the bouts commenced on television, Kent Walton, the *World of Sport* wrestling commentator, introduced the action with 'Greetings, grapple fans'. Our favourite wrestlers included Mick McManus, the self-style south London tough guy. Kendo Nagasaki was the mysterious bad boy villain with a facemask who specialised in Samurai skills. Nagasaki's trademark move was the Kamikaze Crash, where he threw his opponent to the canvas and rolled over them with his shoulders.

Jim 'Cry Baby' Breaks usually became upset with his opponent or the referee and got involved in robust verbal exchanges with the audience. Gaylord Peacock was an extravagantly named wrestler who acted out an incredibly comic camp character. Gary 'Catweazle' Cooper's lucky mascot was a toad. Johnny Kwango's trademark manoeuvre was head-butting his opponents in the ring. Kwango was the only black wrestler I can recall watching on British television during the 1970s.

As mentioned earlier, at this stage in my young life, cricket was not a game I was eager to watch on television. However, there was one match I watched which enthralled me and helped to arouse my early interest in the game. It was the 1971 Gillette Cup semi-final between Lancashire and Gloucestershire at Old Trafford. The Gillette Cup, established in 1963, was one of the three major limited overs competitions which English county teams competed for during the annual domestic season.

The Gillette Cup was originally a 65 over per side competition before being reduced to 60 overs. The Benson and Hedges Cup, created in 1972, was a 55 over competition. Both competitions finished with a final at Lord's. The weekly Sunday John Player League, created in 1969, was a 40 over competition. Out of these three competitions, the Gillette Cup was the most prestigious and highly valued trophy. The Gillette Cup final was considered by some cricket supporters in England as the limited overs cricket version of the FA Cup final.

The 1971 Gillette Cup semi-final between Lancashire and Gloucestershire at Old Trafford started at 11 but during the lunchtime period an hour's play was lost because of rain. Gloucestershire batted first and scored 229 runs for the loss of six wickets. During the Lancashire innings, the player who came out to bat at number four was Clive Hubert Lloyd from Georgetown, Guyana. Lloyd hit an entertaining 34. Two years later in 1973, Lloyd would represent the West Indies for the first time in England.

The Lancashire v Gloucestershire game continued through the early evening as groups of spectators gathered around the boundary. Many of the Lancashire supporters had vacated their seats. They were now prepared for a celebratory crowd invasion of the playing area. David Hughes hit an incredible sequence of 24 runs, 4-6-2-2-4-6 off Jim Mortimer, Gloucestershire's off-spin bowler, to push Lancashire over the line for a memorable victory.

The match finished at ten minutes to nine in near darkness. Although, the darkness was not so obvious to me watching the match reach its conclusion on our black and white television. David Lloyd opened the Lancashire innings v Gloucestershire with Barry Wood. Lloyd humorously recalls that when concerns about the playing conditions were expressed by some of the players, umpire Arthur Jepson replied, 'I can see the moon – how much further do you want me to see?!'[3] The other umpire that day/evening at Old Trafford was Harold 'Dickie' Bird. There is much more from and about Dickie Bird later in this book.

In 1973, my routine of watching television experienced a dramatic change when my parents bought a new Phillips colour television set. Previously, we would have to pick up our small white television. Then move it from one position to another in the living room to improve the quality of reception. I was usually asked to carry out this task and act as the human television remote control and channel changer. Our new colour television was connected to a four-wheeled trolley and you could push and pull it around the living room. Amazing!

The BBC used the attraction of live sports coverage to introduce colour television to its audiences. Driven by the enthusiasm and determination of Sir David Attenborough, the Controller of BBC2, the BBC transmitted live colour coverage of the 1967 Wimbledon Tennis Championships. A few weeks before the official launch at

Wimbledon, Anthony Burgess, a novelist, was one of the guests on a trial broadcast for BBC TV executives of a BBC2 arts show called *Late Night Line-Up*. Burgess reported that other invited guests to *Late Night Line-Up*, as well as himself and the programme's host, Joan Bakewell, were unable to sit still in their seats. They kept moving up and down to peer at the monitors and catch a glimpse of themselves in living colour.

In July 1967, BBC2 switched from black and white images of the annual Henley Royal Regatta rowing event on the River Thames, to a colour camera which focused on Peter West, the presenter at Wimbledon who was 'artfully flanked by flowerpots and a green umbrella'.[4] The first match shown at Wimbledon 1967 in colour produced a British victory in a thrilling five-set contest. Britain's Roger Taylor beat Cliff Drysdale of South Africa on Wimbledon's prestigious Centre Court. A day before this historic broadcasting launch event, *The Times* newspaper suggested that it was:

> Impossible to assess how many 'colour parties' will be held round the few thousand sets installed. The Radio and Television Retailers' Association talks of 1,000-5,000 sets, 'probably nearer one'. The manufacturers body thinks it is in hundreds rather than thousands.[5]

Colour TV, partly driven by popular sports events transmitted in colour, helped to increase audiences and revenue for the BBC. The colour TV license was more expensive. Therefore, the more people who bought colour televisions and colour TV licences, which helped to fund the BBC as a public service broadcaster, the more money the organisation received. The growing demand in British households to watch television in colour also contributed to the increase in spending on new television sets. Between 1971 and 1993, households increased their expenditure on television at a faster rate than on other goods and services. Over that period average household expenditure rose by just over 40%, while spending on television and (much later during this time period) video, increased by over 80%.

Our new colour television was deliberately purchased to coincide with the 1973 England v West Indies Test series. After watching the first two Tests at The Oval and Edgbaston on our black and white TV, we were able to watch the third Test at Lord's in glorious colour. The first thing I noticed was how the green the grass was and, despite being a tiny visual image, how red the cricket ball was on a TV screen.

'It was just like that when Wimbledon was first shown on TV in colour in 1967 and many people commented on the how green the grass appeared', says Professor Joe Moran, a cultural historian and author of *Armchair Nation: An intimate history of Britain in front of the TV.*

With colour television and cricket, so much of cricket is about the atmosphere and the mood and some of that (in England) is to do with the weather. Cricket is a relatively slow-moving game, especially Test cricket, and so much of it is about the changing patterns of the day. If it's a sunny day or, for example, the shadows start to lengthen across the ground at the end of the day, and you can't really see that when you're watching it in black and white. I remember watching Test matches in the era when cricket was on television all day. With colour TV you got more of a sense of the weather, and the feel of the day and the atmosphere and ambiance, which you just don't get watching cricket on black and white TV. I remember when we changed from black and white TV to colour in the 1970s, and when you saw colour TV it was quite a shock. It was almost like being introduced to a new world.

So, back in 1973, were we behind the times, ahead of the times, or just around and about the right time to buy our first colour television? This was a question I felt compelled to ask Joe Moran. 'I think that 1973 was around and about the normal time', he replied.

Colour television really arrived in 1967 but hardly anyone had a colour TV then. So, it was really in the early 1970s that it really got going. 1976 was the year that there were suddenly more (BBC) colour TV licences in Britain than black and white ones, and it was a very gradual thing. So, it's the usual thing that happens with all innovations. People imagine that everything happens in one go but, actually, it's a gradual thing.

There were still black and white programmes being made during the early 1970s but by 1973 they were all in colour. So, 1973 was a very typical year for many people in Britain to get their first colour television.

Our new colour television also enhanced the viewing pleasure of the non-sports programmes we regularly watched, weekly or yearly. Every week on a Thursday evening, without fail, the whole family would gather around the television to watch the *Top of the Pops* music show on BBC. By 1973, most of the music I listened to was a combination of the records and cassettes we had at home, and what I enjoyed listening to on the radio. This was a mixture of pop, funk, soul, Motown, calypso, reggae and gospel music. On Sunday mornings leading up to lunchtime, we usually listened to a combination of Brooke Benton, Sam Cooke, Al Green, Mahalia Jackson, Johnny Nash and Percy Sledge. This was our regular Sunday blend of soul, light-touch reggae and reverential Christian music.

I also discovered Guyanese folk music records by chance, when my great-uncle Harry brought some of his vinyl records to our flat. Harry migrated from Guyana to Britain in the 1960s, before moving on to settle in the US. He brought over a collection of his vinyl records to Britain in the 1970s during a stay with our family in London. When Harry returned to the US, he left some of these records behind. I quickly assumed ownership of some of them including a *Songs of the Guiana Jungle* LP by Ramjohn Holda and The Potaro Porknockers, which introduced me to folk songs from Guyana. My favourite songs were *Lay Down Bessie, Mackenzie* and *Timberman*.

One of my mother's favourite television music shows in the 1960s was *Juke Box Jury,* presented by David Jacobs, who was also one of the original presenters of *Top of the Pops. Juke Box Jury* was a BBC music panel shown on Friday evenings. During each show, four guest reviewers discussed new records and predicted whether they would be hits or not. My mother enthusiastically remembers making sure she was home in time to watch *Juke Box Jury*. Especially when my mother's favourite *Juke Box Jury* panellist, Janice Nicholls, was one of the guest reviewers. Janice would typically end a review of a record by saying, 'Oi'll give it foive' (I'll give it five) in her distinctive accent from the Black Country, West Midlands region of England.

By 1973, *Juke Box Jury* had come to an end. So *Top of the Pops* was the only opportunity we had to experience the thrill of watching artistes perform the hits you heard on the radio. *Welcome Home* by Peters and Lee was a chart-topping hit in 1973 that I distinctly recall being performed on *Top of the Pops*. Peters and Lee were Lennie Peters and Di Lee, an unfashionable but quite charming and likeable easy-listening pop-folk duo. Peters, who lost his sight as a teenager, was the first blind performer I can remember watching on British television. *Welcome Home*, the duo's first single released in the summer of 1973, was an unashamedly sentimental number one hit pop ballad which I enjoyed singing along to.

Towards the end of 1973, Peters and Lee were invited to perform at the Royal Variety Show at The London Palladium in London – held in the presence of the Queen and the Duke of Edinburgh. This annual event was usually televised and watched by our family.

The two major live televised shows broadcast by the BBC, which we watched every year, were the Eurovision Song Contest and the Miss World beauty contest. The format of Eurovision was specifically designed and produced to show the simultaneity of television. It was, and still is, a live competitive music show featuring performers from across Europe and broadcast to audiences around the world. Both annual events became essential viewing in our household and in millions of homes across Britain. We watched these shows at home without any of us making wry comments, ironic remarks or exhibiting a sense of high-brow sneering.

During the Eurovision Song Contest, while my family were absorbed in the general sense of occasion of watching a live international event, and attempting to predict the winning song, I was usually focussed on hoping that the British song would win. This gave me someone and something to support and made the show much more interesting. Especially if it was a song I liked and heard regularly on the radio or watched on *Top of the Pops*. Britain's 1972 Eurovision entry, *Beg, Steal or Borrow* by the New Seekers, was a prime example.

One of our family's memorable Eurovision moments occurred in 1967. Sandi Shaw delivered a performance on stage in bare feet in Vienna, Austria to win the contest for Britain with *Puppet on a String*. The song gained over twice as many votes as the entry from Ireland which finished in second placed. My great-aunt Muriel called Sandi

Shaw 'Bare-foot Susie' after her 1967 performance in Austria. It was a Eurovision story that we enjoyed sharing during our annual family viewing of the contest.

In 1973 in Luxembourg, the British Eurovision Song Contest entry was *Power to All Our Friends* performed by Cliff Richard. Interestingly, Richard, who was born in India, arrived in September 1948 at Tilbury Docks at the age of seven with his parents and younger sisters. Following a five-week journey by sea from India and three months after the *Windrush* arrived at Tilbury from the Caribbean. Richard and his family were one of many families of British descent who left India after it won its independence in 1947.

Power to All Our Friends was a song which crept along before being interrupted by an uplifting and anthemic chorus. In my humble opinion, *Power to All Our Friends* was not on the same level of quality and likeability as Britain's previous entry, *Beg, Steal or Borrow* by the New Seekers. *Beg, Steal or Borrow* was an endearing pop-rock song with an admirable blend of poise and spirit. My enduring memory of the New Seekers was watching Peter Doyle sing and strum his acoustic guitar for all his worth to drive the band's 1972 Eurovision performance along to its end. *Beg, Steal or Borrow* came second in 1972. Could Cliff Richard do better a year later?

The 1973 contest was Cliff's second attempt at Eurovision glory after representing Britain in 1968 with *Congratulations*, which finished way behind the Spanish winner in seventh place. In 1973, as in 1969, Cliff was unsuccessful in claiming Eurovision glory as *Power to All Our Friends* finished in third place. *Power to All Our Friends* was two points behind Spain and six points behind the winning song from Luxembourg. Despite this, Cliff and his management could take plenty of comfort months later. The song rapidly became a hit record across Europe, including a peak of number four in the UK singles charts. Five years earlier, *Congratulations* may have failed to conquer Eurovision. However, the song still managed to shift over a million sales.

Britain would not win another Eurovision title until 1976 with *Save Your Kisses for Me* performed by Brotherhood of Man. *Save Your Kisses for Me* was a song that I didn't like, which won a song contest that, as I approached my teenage years, I became much less interested in. My interest in Eurovision dwindled as my interest diversified into admiration for other forms of music including The Stranglers, Jazz-funk, Mikey Dread, Big Youth and The Specials.

The Miss World beauty contest was broadcast each November from the Royal Albert Hall in London. The contest was created, owned and managed by the Morley family – Eric and Julia. Eric Morley also created the *Come Dancing* competition for BBC television. In 2008, *Come Dancing* was re-branded as *Strictly Come Dancing* complete with celebrity dancers performing as the star attractions.

There may have been quiet reservations amongst some of us watching a parade of women judged purely on their apparent beauty, body shape, and how they appeared in their national costumes, swimsuits and evening wear outfits. However, during the 1970s, the annual Miss World beauty contest was a glamorous, international and live popular event shown on one of the three available terrestrial television channels, BBC1, BBC2, and ITV.

In 1973, as in previous years, we all gathered as a family to watch a contest which, at its peak in 1968, drew an audience of 27.5 million people in Britain,[6] comparable to a British Royal family wedding. We always had our favourite contestants and, unsurprisingly, many of them were women from the Caribbean. Unlike the Eurovision Song contest, I expressed mild, bordering on disinterested, support for contestants representing the United Kingdom.

Andrea Levy, author of *The Long Song*, and *Small Island* – a tale of Caribbean migration, and personal and social relationships in wartime and post war Britain, was born and raised in London with parents from Jamaica. Her father arrived in Britain in 1948 on the *Windrush*. One of Andrea's vivid childhood television memories was watching Carole Joan Crawford from Jamaica win the 1963 Miss World contest. Carole Joan Crawford was the first woman from the Caribbean to win the crown. Sitting in her chair in the family's flat in North London, Andrea's mother was so excited that she kicked her legs in the air and clapped. Her face was full of pure happiness and excitement. One of the panel judges for the 1963 contest was the recently knighted Sir Learie Constantine.

In 1970, my mother jumped for joy when Jenifer Hosten from Grenada won the Miss World crown. Unfortunately for Hosten, her victory raised several questions when it was discovered that Eric Gairey, the Prime Minister of Grenada, was one of the judges. Eric

Gairey and the Mecca Organisation were adamant that there was no vote-rigging to enable Hosten to win the contest. The 1970 Miss World contest, with Bob Hope as the main compere, was also controversially memorable for variety of reasons. In quite bizarre circumstances, which reflected the country's apartheid system of racial segregation, South Africa was represented by two contestants. Pearl Jansen, a coloured woman who came second in the 1970 contest, was the Miss Africa South contestant. Jillian Jessup, a white woman who came fourth, was the Miss South Africa contestant. The 1970 contest was disrupted by a small group of feminist protesters who dressed-up to blend into the audience in the Royal Albert Hall. The protesters threw flour and smoke bombs, which they hid in their handbags, and shouted slogans, waved banners, shook football rattles and blew whistles. Some of the protestors attempted to rush on the stage. A militant left-wing group, unconnected with the feminist demonstrators in the Royal Albert Hall, had also placed a small explosive devise underneath a BBC van outside the venue.

There was further controversy following the 1973 Miss World contest, won by Marjorie Wallace from the US. Patsy Yuen, a Jamaican of Chinese descent who claimed third place, was the Caribbean success story of the 1973 contest. Months after winning the crown, Wallace was dethroned and stripped of her title by the Morley family. This decision was taken in response to her reported attachments with George Best – the Manchester United and Northern Ireland footballer, Tom Jones – the Welsh singer and Peter Revson – the American millionaire racing car driver.

For the Morley family and their Mecca organisation, which tightly controlled the Miss World contest, the clean-cut single woman public image of the title holder was paramount. In a carefully worded summary of how Marjorie Wallace's reign ended, *The Telegraph* newspaper reported that.

Mr Morley said yesterday that Miss Wallace 'felt it was fair. She agreed it was the right decision. We shook hands and parted friends'. Mrs Morley said later that the contest 'has become an international institution' likely to lead to world-wide publicity about the activities of Miss World. If that publicity were adverse, it would lead to a deterioration in the contest's status.[7]

After 1988, due to steadily decreasing viewing figures, the unfashionability of the Miss World contest for British television audiences, and increased criticism of beauty pageants as objectifying women, the Miss World contest was no longer shown on British terrestrial television.

CHAPTER 6

John Player League, John Arlott, the 1973 season in focus, and West Indian cricketers in England

B y 1973, I had still not developed a serious interest in watching cricket on television. There was a spark of interest generated by watching the dramatic climax of the 1971 Lancashire v Gloucestershire Gillette Cup semi-final. However, it was the Sunday John Player League competition, and the golden tones of one special cricket commentator, which helped cricket to penetrate my imagination and convert me to becoming follower of the game.

One Sunday afternoon in 1973, I settled into the living room at home and prepared to watch *The Big Match* football highlights. I had a lively exchange of views with my Barbadian father about whether we should watch *The Big Match* or live coverage of a John Player League cricket match on BBC2. After our chat, I conceded and considered watching the cricket instead.

The John Player League was created in 1969. As with the increasingly popular Gillette Cup and Benson and Hedges Cup competitions, Sunday league was part of English cricket's ambition to widen its appeal, attract more spectators to attend matches, and bring in an increase in sponsorship revenue.

The John Player League tobacco company, proud sponsors of Sunday limited overs cricket, produced advertisements, including one in the *1973 Cricketer Spring Annual* with an image of the John Player League trophy and the headline: 'All-action cricket-every Sunday in the John Player League!' The full-page advertisement confidently announced that:

Attendances have soared all over the country. And it's easy to see why! Attacking batting, tight bowling, keen fielding – all the elements of cricket at its most exciting are *guaranteed* by the 40-over formula. Last season saw the triumph of Kent. But the result was closely fought to the very end. And this season could be even closer. With every county taking up the challenge of all-action cricket, every county going all out to win, the result is anyone's guess. But the action guaranteed! Make a date with the John Player League.[1]

For the record, Kent won the 1972 John Player League title by just one point ahead of Leicestershire who finished as runners-up. As a reward for their success in 1972, the Kent players enjoyed a bonus prize trip to the Caribbean courtesy of John Player. The trip featured an 18-day limited overs representative tour with matches in Antigua, Barbados, Guyana, Jamaica, St. Lucia and Trinidad. Kent won four of these matches and lost seven. Kent were forced to acquire three replacements before the tour as Mike Denness, Alan Knott and Derek Underwood were unavailable as they were selected to play for England during the 1972/1973 tour of India, Pakistan and Sri Lanka. One of the replacements was Keith Boyce, the Essex, Barbados and West Indies all-rounder. In some of the fixtures on this tour, Boyce played against some of his West Indian team mates, who he would play with during the 1973 tour of England.

The John Player League introduced restricted run-ups for bowlers, and prize money and awards available for bowlers on each occasion they claimed four or more wickets in a match. In 1973, Dennis Marriott, the Jamaican-born Middlesex left arm medium pace bowler, was top of the John Player bowling rankings. Marriott produced a total of four wickets or more bowling performances in four matches for Middlesex. Prize money and awards were also available for batsmen for each six they hit during a John Player League season.

In 1973, as well as celebrating its fifth year of sponsoring Sunday league cricket, John Player produced an early edition of its annual cricket year book. The *1973 John Player Cricket Yearbook* featured full coverage of Test matches, the county championship, limited overs competitions, minor counties and schools' cricket. The book was edited by Trevor Bailey, who played with distinction for Essex and England, and featured contributions from Colin Cowdrey, Ted Dexter, Fred Trueman and Alan Knott, England's wicket-keeper for their 1973 home series of Tests v New Zealand and West Indies.

As might be expected, the arrival of a 40 overs a-side Sunday afternoon competition didn't appeal to all. Some cricketers were not impressed with the prospect of playing cricket on a Sunday. For many of them, this was an unnecessary intrusion on one of their free days. Yorkshire, Somerset and England's Brian Close insisted that the concept of John Player League cricket resembled a circus, 'Throw down some sawdust, everybody put on top hats and red noses and you've got the John Player League'.[2] An article in my *1973 Playfair Cricket Annual* recognised the entertainment value of the John Player League but was not convinced about the purity of the competition's format.

> The John Player League conjures up great enthusiasm with the television audiences on Sunday afternoons and on the grounds too, but only in the remotest sense is it cricket as it was originally designed. It is an entertainment which entertains a particular type of audience and does it well.[3]

Perhaps, I was part of what my *1973 Playfair Cricket Annual* described as a 'particular type of audience'. Within a few weeks of watching John Player League cricket, I looked forward to being entertained by each Sunday afternoon fixture. Watching the John Player League was one of my main visual cricket education aids. I found out more about cricket fielding positions with curious names such as the slips, third man, gulley and long-leg. I quickly understood when a bowler had delivered a wide, a no-ball, or had successfully completed a maiden over.

I clearly remember a batsman in one match, unintentionally, hitting an inside edge shot off his bat. The ball ran away past the diving wicket-keeper down to the long-leg boundary. The commentator described the batsman's shot as a 'Harrow cut'. Therefore, I could now add another term to my expanding cricket vocabulary. I also improved my knowledge of West Indian players, by watching them play for their counties in the John Player League every Sunday.

Steve Walcott was born and raised in Birmingham by parents who migrated from Barbados to Britain in the 1950s. He was a sports lecturer for 18 years at Solihull College in the West Midlands and also worked as a cricket coach. For Steve, watching cricket on television, including the John Player League, was part of his journey to becoming a cricket enthusiast and developing his knowledge about the game. 'I started following cricket on television as soon as I could remember', recalls Steve.

But I didn't just watch international cricket on television. I also watched county cricket, the Gillette Cup finals and the John Player League games every Sunday afternoon. I always pestered my dad to take me to Edgbaston to watch a Sunday league game, which he eventually did when I was nine years old. I'd either watch cricket with my dad or by myself. If my dad was at home and he wasn't getting ready for work, if cricket was on – cricket would go on the television. I would watch it with him and ask questions about things. Sometimes the commentators would say things which I didn't understand until I got much older. They would refer to the psychology of the game, which I just didn't get as an 8, 9, 10 and 11-year-old, and talk about things like scoreboard pressure, and each player having a certain type of mindset and so on. So, l learned about these things by watching cricket on television and my dad would sometimes explain things that I didn't understand.

Neil Sillett, an England cricket fan from Norwich, Norfolk, was named by his father after Neil Harvey, the great Australian batsman. Sillett's father also admired West Indian cricketers. 'My dad was a huge fan of Garry Sobers. According to dad, there was no one better than Sobers. That was it!' When Neil was a young boy growing up in Norwich in the 1960s and 1970s, one of his favourite players was Surrey and England's John Edrich, a local boy from Norfolk. Neil also remembers watching John Player League cricket on television as one of the main influences which introduced him to the game in the 1970s.

As a child, I'd sit on my little stool in our living room and watch a John Player League cricket match on the TV. We had one of those old fashioned 1960s coffee tables with four spindly little legs. I'd mark up a piece of paper with 40 squares, put the paper down on our coffee table, sit on my stool and, in my knowing way, try to score the match ball-by-ball. That was great entertainment for me at home on a Sunday afternoon! Sport was a lot easier to access at that time because you had cricket, rugby and football all on the BBC and Anglia TV. Now, unless you're prepared to pay ridiculous amounts of money each month, you just don't get to watch live cricket and some of the other sports on television.

Watching John Player League cricket had the bonus of listening to John Arlott's observant and humorous cricket commentary, delivered with his distinctive Hampshire accent and his natural gift for elegant, poetic and descriptive patterns of language. Arlott shared John Player League BBC television commentary duties with Jim Laker, the former Surrey, Essex and England off-spin bowler. Once again, my enthusiasm for a particular sport was partly driven by my admiration for a television and radio sports broadcaster. Edward Baugh, a Jamaican literary critic and one of the Caribbean's major poets, is one of many West Indians whose passion for cricket was enlivened by Arlott's commentary.

I believe that my own feeling for cricket was deeply enhanced by my first boyhood experiences of hearing that peerless poet among cricket commentators, John Arlott. My memory of the legendary 1950 England-West Indies series is inseparable from the rhythms of Arlott's voice, from his imagery, his always surprising choice of words, his timing and his elegance. Only a few days ago I happened to read a review of some recently published cricket books. The reviewer began with a definitive statement: 'Cricket needs its writers'. And in developing his point, he said, among other things, that anyone who had had the good fortune to watch the Oval Test in 1968 would have savoured that much more keenly if he had armed himself beforehand with Alan McGilvray's *ABC Cricket Book* and, having watched the game, had had the further good fortune of digesting Arlott's account of the last day's play.[4]

Andrew Carnegie was born in Jamaica and arrived in England as a 10-year-old schoolboy in 1967. Andrew's father arrived in England 10 years before him in 1957. A few months before the start of that year's West Indies tour of England, which ended in a 3-0 series defeat for the tourists. Andrew's father attended the second 1957 Test at

Lord's. Andrew played cricket as a 'batting all-rounder' for his primary and secondary schools in London, playing in teams, as he describes, 'with a mix of English and West Indian kids'. Andrew then progressed to playing club cricket for over 30 years, including a spell with a south London wandering club called South Lambeth, which had its origins in the South Lambeth British Rail depot.

During his time at the South Lambeth club, Andrew played with Reg Scarlett, who represented Jamaica and the West Indies. Andrew qualified as a 1A cricket umpire and umpired in league, junior and school cricket in England. He has precise memories of listening to John Arlott as a young cricket fan in 1960s Jamaica.

For me, John Arlott was the voice of cricket when I was growing up in Jamaica. His use of language over the radio set the theme, not just for what was happening during play, but also for the atmosphere, and it was beautiful to listen to. In the 1960s in Jamaica, before I came to England, there was a select time when you could get the cricket commentary from England on the radio. I lived with my grandparents at the time who were both keen on cricket and I remember we listened to (Basil) Butcher scoring a double century (209 not out in the West Indies second innings at Trent Bridge) against England in 1966. During the same match, I remember John Arlott describing Derek Underwood (who was making his Test debut for England) bowling a maiden ball to imply that his delivery wasn't hit for any runs. And Arlott also described in detail the direction of the breeze when another bowler came running in to bowl.

In 1973, Kent continued their success in the John Player League and retained the trophy they won in 1972. Their victory in 1973 was by six points with Yorkshire finishing as their nearest rivals in second place. Due to financial restraints employed by John Player, the Kent players were treated with a bonus prize weekend trip to Paris, instead of another extensive tour of the Caribbean! By 1973, after five years of the John Player League, three teams had won the competition. Kent in 1972 and 1973, Lancashire in 1969 and 1970, and Worcestershire in 1971.

In addition to their John Player League success, Kent were also victorious in the 1973 Benson and Hedges Cup final at Lord's after beating Worcestershire by 39 runs. Mike Denness was the Kent captain who led the club to a year of double success. During the following year, Denness became the first Scottish captain of the England cricket team. In 1973, another personal milestone was achieved by a Kent player. Colin Cowdrey, 10 years after strolling out from the Lord's pavilion with an arm in bandage to help save a Test match for England v West Indies, scored his 100th first-class century playing for Kent v Surrey at Maidstone.

The 1973 Benson and Hedges Cup final was one of the many significant moments of Brian Luckhurst's season as an opening batsman for Kent. Luckhurst top scored with 79 runs in the final at Lord's, made his highest first-class score, a double century for Kent at Derbyshire, and enjoyed a successful benefit year granted by Kent after years of loyal service. Luckhurst joined the Kent playing staff in 1954 as a professional at the age of 15. In 1973, he was selected for the last two Test matches for England v West Indies, replacing Surrey's Graham Roope and coming in at number three in the batting order.

Luckhurst also shared second place in the rankings and prize money available for batsmen for each six they hit during the 1973 John Player League season. Luckhurst hit eight sixes, as did two other batsmen, both West Indians, who shared second place. Roy Fredericks played for Glamorgan during the English domestic season and opened the batting for the West Indies in the 1973 Test series v England. The other West Indian six-hitting prize-winner was John Shepherd from Kent. Luckhurst described Shepherd, a combative all-rounder from Barbados, as one of the best all-rounders in the game. Shepherd made his Test debut at Old Trafford during the 1969 tour of England. This was the first of his five Tests for the West Indies. Shepherd was not selected for the 1973 tour of England.

The two other Kent players selected for England in the 1973 series v West Indies were Derek Underwood and Alan Knott. From 1969 to 1971, Underwood considered Luckhurst to be the premier batsman in England. None of the Worcestershire team defeated by Kent at Lord's in 1973 were selected to play for England v West Indies later that year.

Three Caribbean born cricketers played in the 1973 Kent v Worcestershire Benson and Hedges Cup final, John Shepherd, Ron Headley and Ivan Johnson. Shepherd was the only West Indian player for Kent during their 1973 two trophy winning season. Shepherd enjoyed a lengthy and successful career at Kent from 1967 to 1981. In 2011 he was appointed as the club's President.

One of the batsmen who opened the Worcestershire innings at Lord's was Ron Headley. He was Worcestershire's Jamaican born batting star and the son of George Headley. Ron would make his debut for the West Indies later that summer in the first Test at The Oval. Ivan Johnson, Worcestershire's Bahamian born all-rounder, who attended school in England, represented the England Under-19s team during their 1972 tour in the Caribbean. In the junior Test matches v West Indies, Johnson faced the bowling of Colin Croft, Joel Garner and Michael Holding, amongst others, and scored 438 runs. This included a century and three half centuries at an average of 62.57.[5] Unfortunately for Johnson, in the Benson and Hedges Cup final at Lord's, and a year on from his impressive performances in the Caribbean, he was cleaned bowled by John Shepherd for only two runs.

Vanburn Holder, a fast-medium pace bowler from Barbados, was the other Caribbean-born cricketer on the Worcestershire playing staff. Holder did not play in the final at Lord's but played in the last two Test matches for the West Indies during the 1973 tour. Holder established himself as a core member of the West Indies bowling attack v England.

Jim Cumbes and Ted Hemsley were two cricketers I always admired because they combined careers as professional cricketers with careers as professional footballers. In 1973, Jim Cumbes was a fast-medium pace bowler for Worcestershire and a goalkeeper for Aston Villa. In 1973, Hemsley, operated as a medium pace bowling all-rounder for Worcestershire and as a left-back for Sheffield United.

As well as being on the losing side in the 1973 Benson and Hedges Cup final, Cumbes failed to make an impact on the game by taking only one wicket and was run out for a single. Hemsley failed to take a wicket during his bowling spell but hit a score of 23 before suffering from the same fate as Cumbes, losing his wicket to a run out. Cumbes had a more successful season the following year as part of the 1974 Worcestershire team which won the county championship.

In 1972, Chris Balderstone, a cricketer-footballer who starred as a cricketer for Leicestershire and England, and as a footballer for Huddersfield Town and Carlisle United, produced a man of the match display at Lord's which helped Leicestershire beat Yorkshire to win the first Benson and Hedges Cup final. The Leicestershire captain that day at Lord's was Ray Illingworth, who led his team to their first domestic trophy v Yorkshire, Illingworth's former county. In 1973, Illingworth as England captain, would be a major contributor to the sequence of events which took place during the England v West Indies series.

In 1973, a year after enjoying cup-winning success at Lord's with Leicestershire, Balderstone endured a rocky period in his double sporting career. He was suspended by Carlisle United and stripped of the captaincy for choosing to play for Leicestershire until the end of the cricket season.

Peter Squires of Yorkshire was another cricketer who successfully pursued a career in two different sports. In 1973, Squires, a right-handed opening batsman for Yorkshire, made his first rugby union international appearance as a winger for England v France at Twickenham. Arthur Jepson was another sportsman who operated as a professional cricketer-footballer. Jepson was a handy fast-medium pace bowler for Nottinghamshire and a goalkeeper for Port Vale and Stoke City, near neighbours and rivals, from the late 1930s and in the years following the Second World War in the 1940s and 1950s. Jepson was one of the umpires during the 1971 Gillette Cup semi-final between Lancashire and Gloucestershire at Old Trafford. The first cricket match I can remember watching live on television, which famously ended in near darkness.

In 1973, Gloucestershire beat Sussex at Lord's by 40 runs to win The Gillette Cup final at Lord's. This was the first Gillette Cup final I can clearly remember watching on television. Alongside the FA Cup final and the Grand National, the Gillette Cup final became one of the other annual sports events that I eagerly anticipated watching live on television. Sussex batted second and were set a target by Gloucestershire of 249 runs to win. At one stage in their innings, Sussex were 120 for only one wicket, but behind the required run rate. Despite a solid enough start to their innings, their run chase crumbled as the light slowly faded with batsmen five to 11 all unable to reach a score of double figures.

Tony Greig, one of the two Sussex players selected for the 1973 series v West Indies, was run out for a duck. John Snow, the other Sussex player selected for the 1973 series, finished the match with his team's best bowling figures of three wickets for 31 runs. Arthur Fagg, one of the 1973 Gillette Cup final umpires, would be embroiled in controversy as an umpire during the second England v West Indies Test at Edgbaston.

Geoff Greenidge from Barbados was the only West Indian who played in the 1973 Gillette Cup final. Geoff's innings of 76 runs, as one of the Sussex opening batsmen, was his team's highest individual score in the final. He played his fifth and final Test for the West Indies during the 1973 home series in the Caribbean v Australia. Geoff was not selected for the 1973 tour of England.

There was another Barbadian born Greenidge who made a much more significant impact during the 1973 English cricket season. Gordon Greenidge grew up in the parish of St.Peter, where many of my relatives lived in Barbados. He also attended the same primary school as my father in Barbados, albeit some years after my father had migrated to Britain.

In 1973, Gordon Greenidge was the top English County Championship run scorer with 1,620 runs and his efforts helped to propel Hampshire towards their 1973 three-day County Championship victory. Hampshire won the County Championship by 31 points with Surrey in second place. This was Hampshire's second Championship win, their first in 13 years, and they were crowned champions as the County Championship celebrated its 100th anniversary.

Gordon arrived in England as a 14-year-old schoolboy from Barbados and joined his mother, who had been in England since he was eight. He lived with his family in Reading, a town in the English county of Berkshire, which would soon have a firmly established Barbadian community.

Although Gordon didn't envisage himself as wanting to pursue a career as a professional cricketer, a few years after migrating to England from Barbados, his talent as a schoolboy cricket player was identified. Gordon was selected for the Berkshire schools cricket team. He was genuinely surprised at being selected and thought he had been chosen because, 'I'm not being falsely modest when I say one of the main reasons was because I was West Indian. The selectors thought that since I was from Barbados I had to be good at cricket'.[6]

Gordon continued to learn his trade as a cricketer by playing in English conditions and on English wickets. He joined Hampshire at the age of 17 and made his debut for the county at 19. Gordon's first captain at Hampshire was Roy Marshall, a fellow Barbadian who played four Test matches for the West Indies. He continued to progress at Hampshire and became part of a powerful and destructive opening batting partnership with Barry Richards from South Africa.

Bitterness, controversy and exile often surrounded West Indian players who established cricket links with South Africa during its period of apartheid dominated rule, racial segregation, and state enforced discrimination. Despite this, there were examples on the English domestic cricket circuit, where West Indian players established professional working relationships with white South African colleagues. Gordon Greenidge and Barry Richards were an example of how this relationship could develop and flourish during the 1970s at Hampshire.

Eddie Barlow and Mike Procter were two examples of white South Africans who played against West Indians in England. Seven years after Hampshire's 1973 County Championship success, Wayne Daniel from Barbados who played 10 Tests for the West Indies, and Vintcent van der Bijl from South Africa, formed a formidable fast-bowling partnership during Middlesex's 1980 County Championship winning season.

According to Barry Richards, reflecting on Hampshire's 1973 County Championship victory, 'Our batting had always been a strength with Gordon Greenidge making a huge stride forward from a cavalier but careless cricketer into a world-class opening partner'.[7] Gordon was not selected for the 1973 West Indies tour of England, more of which will come later in this book. Despite his omission from the 1973 tour, in the years that followed, Gordon became the first post-*Windrush* Caribbean migrant in Britain to emerge as a high-profile and influential cricketer for the West Indies.

I briefly supported Sussex after feeling sorry for them when they were defeated by Gloucestershire in the 1973 Gillette Cup final. However, by 1973, and the immediate years that followed, Lancashire were the county team that I most admired. I was also drawn to Lancashire because I liked the noise their supporters made when I watched them play on television. More than 30 years before the birth of the barmy army faction of England cricket supporters, groups of boisterous Lancashire fans sang football fan-style songs in support of their team. My favourite was, 'Oh Lanky, Lanky…Lanky, Lanky, Lanky, Lanky Lancashire', which borrowed the rhythm and chorus lines from *Son of the Father,* an early 1970s chart-topping pop hit by Chicory Tip.

Another song belted out by Lancashire supporters with gusto at matches was *'Lancashire la, la, la'*. This was influenced by the *Banana Splits* opening and closing theme tune. The American produced *Banana Splits* was one of my must watch children's television shows during my early 1970s school summer holidays in England.

Before the start of the 1973 season, John Arlott made a strong case for Lancashire to win one of the three limited overs competitions and be contenders for the County Championship.

> Lancashire are admirably equipped for over-limit cricket and must always be a fair bet for each of those three competitions. They have, too, enough talent to exert a much stronger influence on the County Championship than they did in 1972.[8]

Arlott's case for Lancashire to have a successful season in limited overs cricket was made on solid ground and with an air of expectancy. Lancashire had won four limited overs trophies in the three years leading up to 1973. In 1970, Lancashire were the John Player League Champions. They were also Gillette Cup winners for three years in succession in 1970, 1971 and 1972.

In the 1972 Gillette Cup final v Warwickshire at Lord's, Clive Lloyd won the Man of the Match award, as adjudicated by Basil D'Oliveira, after scored a match-winning century to help steer Lancashire towards a six-wicket victory. The Warwickshire team v Lancashire at Lord's included four West Indians – Lance Gibbs, Alvin Kallicharan, Rohan Kanhai and Deryck Murray. Including Lloyd, five West Indians played in the 1972 Gillette Cup final and four of them were Guyanese, with Deryck Murray from Trinidad. All five would be selected for the 1973 tour of England.

Gibbs, who was 10 years older than Lloyd, was his first cousin. Lloyd's mother and Gibbs' mother were sisters who were both born in Barbados. Growing up as a young cricketer in Guyana, Gibbs was an influential figure and a role model for Lloyd. Gibbs and Lloyd also played for the Demerara Cricket Club in Georgetown.

An advertisement for the Gillette Cup competition in my *1973 Playfair Cricket Annual*, proudly declared that it was 'The Day Cricket's Favourite Competition' and asked a simple question at the bottom of the page. Will Lancashire win the Cup for the fourth time in succession? Unfortunately, for Lancashire and many of their expectant supporters, 1973 was not a successful season in terms of winning trophies. They were unable to add more silverware to their trophy cabinet at Old Trafford. Lancashire also had very little influence in the outcome of the County Championship and finished 12th out of the 17 teams in the league.

My initial attraction to Lancashire was also based on their one-day cricket achievements in the 1970s, and their entertaining and colourful cast of characters. For starters, there was the Indian Test wicket-keeper with a fascinating surname, Farokh Engineer. There were the two Lloyds. Clive Lloyd from Georgetown, Guyana, was Lancashire's vice-captain in 1973, and an integral part of Lancashire's exciting batting line-up.

Lloyd's route to playing county cricket with Lancashire was via Lancashire League cricket with Haslingden. After the 1966/1967 West Indies tour of India, where Lloyd made his Test debut, Wes Hall was offered a deal to play for Haslingden and replace Clairmonte Depeiaza, his fellow Barbadian. Hall was unable to play for Haslingden because he accepted a job offer from Banks Brewery in Barbados. With Hall now unable to take up the contract from Haslingden, the club approached Lloyd to join them. Lloyd accepted.

During Lloyd's time at Haslingden, a few of the English counties took an interest in him. Lloyd received approaches to play county cricket from Hampshire and Warwickshire. The offer from Warwickshire was an attractive one and better than the deal offered by Lancashire. Despite this, Lloyd felt compelled to stay in the Lancashire area and joined the county in 1969. Lloyd was replaced at Haslingden by Winston English, another cricketer from Guyana. English played for Guyana but was not able to break into the West Indies team. Much more of Lloyd will appear later in this book.

The other Lloyd was David 'Bumble' Lloyd. In 1973, David Lloyd took over the Lancashire captaincy from Jack Bond. David Lloyd would progress from here on an eventful career journey, which included becoming an England opening batsman, England team coach, journalist and broadcaster. In his autobiography, *Last in the Tin Bath,* David Lloyd paid tribute to Clive Lloyd and Farokh Engineer.

> If you want to assess the legacies of Clive Lloyd and Farokh Engineer at Old Trafford, then consider that they are still regulars at the ground and have remained residents in the area, adopted Mancunians the pair of them. It has been hard not to like these two champion blokes, who also happened to be two champion cricketers. Ask any long-term Lancashire member and they would tell you they are two of our own; forget the fact that they were imported from Guyana and Bombay respectively. They were certainly characters that endeared themselves to the people around Old Trafford. A sign of their popularity was that they both had successful benefit years with Lancashire despite their overseas status. [9]

John Abrahams, who joined Lancashire in 1973, and was a future team captain, was the first 'coloured' South African I'd seen on television. Abrahams' presence in the Lancashire team on television helped to broaden my understanding of the severe racial classification system which separated the population during the apartheid years in South Africa. Miss Abrahams, who was also a coloured South African, was one of my teachers at primary school. I once, excitedly, asked her if she was related to Lancashire's John Abrahams and was disappointed to discover that she wasn't.

Other Lancashire players, who made an impression on me during my increasing interest in cricket, included Frank Hayes. He was a young, richly talented batsman with flair, striking blonde hair, and another future Lancashire captain. Hayes would make a major impact on his Test debut for England during the 1973 series v West Indies. Peter 'Leapy' Lee was an all action fast-medium pace bowler. Lancashire may have finished the 1973 season without a trophy but Lee was the County Championship's highest wicket taker.

David Hughes' end of innings batting heroics for Lancashire v Gloucestershire at Old Trafford in the 1971 Gillette Cup semi-final was also one of the reasons for my early fascination with Lancashire. Some of the other compelling characters in the Lancashire team during the 1970s were 'Little Harry' Pilling and 'Flat Jack' Simmons. As a young boy, Jack and his family were close friends with Clyde Walcott. The Simmons family lived in Clayton-le-Moors, close to the Enfield Cricket Club ground. Walcott was a professional player for Enfield in the Lancashire League from 1951 to 1954.

By 1973, another Lancashire player who had pierced my imagination was Barry 'Sawdust' Wood, an opening batsman who played 12 Tests for England. Wood was not included in the England squad for the 1973 series v West Indies.

Len, my Guyanese friend who was a few years older than me, had already developed an affinity with Lancashire. Len would always pick Lancashire as his team when we played cricket against each other in one of the rooms in his family's house in Peckham, south London. I would represent Sussex. This room was reasonably spacious and, for some reason, had very little furniture in it. So, we could hit, bowl and throw a tennis ball around the room without risk of causing damage to any items of furniture or domestic appliances!

We used our imagination to invent match situations, and develop batting, bowling and fielding scenarios. Len would pretend to be Clive Lloyd or David Lloyd batting against me as John Spencer or John Snow. Len would then switch to become Peter Lee or Jack Simmons bowling at me pretending to be Peter Graves or Tony Greig.

I followed the progress of my favourite players, many of whom were West Indian cricketers at county teams in England. I mostly did this by reading cricket reports and score cards in the sports sections of newspapers I picked up at home, and watching Gillette Cup, Benson and Hedges Cup and John Player League matches on television.

In 1973, there were 21 West Indian cricketers registered and contracted to play for the 17 first-class counties in England and Wales. For Roy Fredericks, 1973 would be his final season for Glamorgan after joining the club in 1971. The start to his career at Glamorgan proved to be an eventful but painful experience. On a lively Sophia Gardens pitch, the home of Glamorgan cricket in Cardiff, Fredericks received a delivery from Vanburn Holder, a fellow West Indian playing for Worcestershire. The delivery from Holder rose sharply on Fredericks and broke his right forearm. Fredericks took six weeks to recover from his injury, and start batting again to develop his experience of playing in English conditions.

The West Indians playing for English counties in 1973 included Keith Boyce for Essex, Roy Fredericks for Glamorgan, Gordon Greenidge for Hampshire, Bernard Julien and John Shepherd for Kent, Clive Lloyd for Lancashire, Roland Butcher, Larry Gomes, Harry Latchman and Dennis Marriott for Middlesex, Garry Sobers for Nottinghamshire, Hallam Moseley for Somerset, Lonsdale Skinner for Surrey, Geoff Greenidge for Sussex, Lance Gibbs, Alvin Kallicharan, Rohan Kanhai and Deryck Murray for Warwickshire, and Ron Headley, Vanburn Holder and Ivan Johnson for Worcestershire.[10]

'In those days, there were a lot of scouts from England travelling around the Caribbean looking out for players. And if they spotted you, they would come up to you and say there was a club back in England who were interested in you', remembers Vanburn Holder.

I was approached in Barbados by Tom Graveney (Worcestershire) and Fred Titmus (Middlesex) during a MCC (Marylebone Cricket Club) tour in 1968. In those days Barbados had a colts team, which was a junior team that played matches over two days, and I played in a colts match v the MCC. Well, I must have played pretty well because after the match Tom Graveney and Fred Titmus came up to me and asked me if I'd like to play county cricket in England. They told me that I didn't have to make a commitment straight away, and I had a week or so to think about it, because they were off to play in Trinidad the next day and coming back to Barbados to play a four day game. When they returned to Barbados, they wanted to have another chat with me. I joined Worcestershire in 1968 and whenever you met another West Indian around the country playing for a county, you always had a chat with them. They were new to being in England, just like me, and playing for a county as well. By 1973, all the counties had one, or two, or even three West Indian players. Warwickshire had Gibbs, Kallicharan and Kanhai. When I was growing up in Barbados, as soon as you were able to walk you played cricket. I didn't have any formal coaching until I came to England and, until then, nobody was really telling me what to do and how to do it. When I came to Worcester in 1968 we had a coach, and had to be at the park ready at a certain time in the morning, come rain or shine! My game got better because of playing county cricket in England, because I was playing against players who were better and stronger than me. I think that if you do that, your game should improve, and playing in England made us (the West Indies) a better side. I'm not saying that my game wouldn't have developed back home (in Barbados). It would have happened, but it might have taken a longer time.

Eleven of the 21 West Indian cricketers contracted to play during the 1973 domestic season in England and Wales were selected to represent the West Indies during that year's tour of England. Warwickshire had four West Indian Test cricketers on their playing staff – Lance Gibbs, Alvin Kallicharan, Rohan Kanhai and Deryck Murray. In 1971, Warwickshire were so determined to sign Kallicharan that Alan Smith, the club captain and former England Test player, flew to Guyana to clinch the deal. Ahead of any potentially serious interest from other counties. Warwickshire's Dennis Amiss and Bob Willis were also selected for the England team v West Indies. So, Warwickshire suffered the most serious effect of losing important players to the England v West Indies series during the latter two-thirds of the 1973 season.

Gibbs, who recommended Kanhai, Murray and Kallicharan to Warwickshire, was one of the first high-profile West Indian Test cricketers in the post-war era to play county cricket. When Gibbs joined Warwickshire in 1967, he was one of the highest paid overseas players on the county circuit. Gibbs also played a key role in providing Colin Croft with his first taste of county cricket. In 1972, in conjunction with the *Guyana Chronicle* newspaper, he arranged for Croft to go to Warwickshire on a coaching scholarship.

1973 was Gibbs' final season as a Warwickshire player. During the season he seriously injured his bowling hand (right hand) fielding in the gulley for Warwickshire v Derbyshire. Brian Bolus played a square cut shot off David Brown, the Warwickshire and England fast-medium pace bowler. The ball flew to Gibbs. Trying to take a catch, he split his hand and required nine stitches between his fingers. The injury took about three months to heal in time for the England v West Indies series.

By 1973, while Vanburn Holder and other West Indians continued to raise their professional standards with county teams in England.

Some English players also recognised the impact that West Indian players had on their own development as cricketers. One of them was Dennis Amiss from Warwickshire, who opened the batting for England with Geoffrey Boycott in the 1973 series v West Indies.

At Warwickshire, we had Rohan (Kanhai), Alvin (Kallicharan), Lance (Gibbs) and Deryck (Murray). These four West Indian players were a big part of our 1972 championship winning side at Warwickshire, and all of them were star international players, were great to watch, and did some great things for our club. Rohan and Alvin played some brilliant innings for us, Lance took so many wickets, and Deryck was great behind the stumps, and he could also bat as well. We were very lucky at Warwickshire to play with such gifted players, and there is no doubt that you can learn from players like that, and this helped my game in many ways. They were always on hand to pass on help and advice. When Rohan was batting it really took the pressure off me when we were batting together. Rohan was such a great player and the opposition sometimes became frustrated because they just couldn't get him out, especially when he was smashing the ball over the place. It rubbed off on the chap at the other end and I was lucky enough to bat with Rohan on many occasions.

Two of the West Indian players who were not selected for the 1973 tour of England, Geoff Greenidge and John Shepherd, had recently finished their Test careers. Greenidge played his fifth and final Test for the West Indies during the 1973 series v Australia in the Caribbean. Shepherd played his fifth and final Test during the 1971 series v India in the Caribbean.

Harry Latchman was born in Jamaica and made his Middlesex debut in 1965. Latchman was released by Middlesex at the end of the 1973 season. The progress of Larry Gomes at Middlesex, one of the other West Indian players not selected for the 1973 tour of England, was noted in *Wisden*, who remarked that.

(In 1973) He (Gomes) made five first-innings fifties in his first eight matches at number one. Gomes passed fifty twice in his first two games, but later proved fallible outside the off stump. He did just enough, though, to convince most watchers that he is a potentially high-class batsman.[11]

Larry Gomes made his debut for the West Indies during the 1976 tour of England. After the West Indies had handed England a 5-0 Test series thrashing during the 1984 West Indies 'Blackwash' tour, Tony Cozier described Gomes' performances as the 'glue' which held the West Indies middle-order batting line-up together throughout the series. Clive Lloyd described Gomes as the rock in the West Indies batting order, and a player who operated in a similar style to Surrey and England's John Edrich. According to Lloyd, Gomes was a batsman who, before you knew it, had accumulated around 60 runs after taking guard at the crease.

Six of the West Indian players who were not selected for the 1973 tour of England, did not represent the West Indies during their careers. However, Hallam Moseley, a pace-bowler from Barbados, played representative cricket for his island, and Lonsdale Skinner, a wicket-keeper and middle-order batsman, represented Guyana. Ivan Johnson, who was born in the Bahamas and educated in England, represented the England Under-19s team. Johnson retired from first-class cricket a few years later to pursue a career in journalism in Britain and Australia, which included a spell with *The Sun* newspaper in Fleet Street, London. He later fulfilled his ambition to return home to The Bahamas and launch his own newspaper, *The Punch*.

As highlighted in an edition of *Backspin* cricket magazine, Johnson was just one of several young players who fell by the Worcestershire wayside in the 1960s and 1970s. This was a scenario that prompted John Arlott to tell Johnson that, 'Bring together all the talented and gifted players like you who left Worcestershire prematurely in the 1960s and 1970s and they would form a good County Championship side'.[12]

1973 was a very significant year for Roland Butcher's fledging cricket career. Butcher, who was born in Barbados and arrived in Britain as a 13-year-old schoolboy, had now spent a year at Middlesex and was listed as one of their playing staff. During this period, Butcher progressed from being just another hopeful young cricketer to a player full of potential. He was now on the verge of making his first-class debut. In 1972, Butcher made just one appearance for the Middlesex second eleven.

In 1973, Butcher's contribution to Middlesex's second eleven dramatically increased as he scored nearly 500 runs for the team. As Butcher vividly recalls, '1973 was an important year for me, because batting at three or four I was given an opportunity to establish myself and prove what I could do'.[13] Butcher sometimes travelled back to the Caribbean during the English domestic off-season to play club cricket. One of the clubs he played for in the Caribbean was the Young Men's Progressive Club in Barbados. He also played in a Shell Shield match for Barbados in Montego Bay, Jamaica. This provided the young Butcher with a platform to further develop his all-round cricket skills and secure a place in the Middlesex first-team.

In later years, Butcher became a key member of the 1980s Middlesex team. Alongside fellow Caribbean born players, Norman Cowans, Wayne Daniel, Wilf Slack and Neil Williams, they were known on the English county cricket circuit as The Jackson Five after the African-American family pop group. Norman Cowans, Wilf Slack and Neil Williams all played Test cricket for England. Other British-born players of Caribbean descent who played for Middlesex with Roland Butcher, or soon after his retirement, include Mark Ramprakash – whose father is from Guyana and Paul Weekes – whose father is from Montserrat.

Of the West Indian players contracted to play for clubs in England during the 1970s, I was always keen to check on the runs, wickets and catches accumulated by Clive Lloyd at Lancashire, Gordon Greenidge at Hampshire, Keith Boyce at Essex, and Lonsdale Skinner at Surrey. I was particularly interested in Lloyd for a number of reasons, one of which being that he attended the same high school as my mother in Georgetown, Guyana. I was further inspired to track the runs Greenidge scored after his vital contribution with the bat to Hampshire's 1973 County Championship success.

I kept a keen eye on Boyce's performances at Essex as he attended the same high school as my father in Barbados. My first trip to watch a cricket match was in 1974. I went with my father and Tony, his friend from St.Vincent who he served with in the British Army, and Mike – one of the lads who lived next door to us in our south London street. This trip to The Oval was arranged to watch

Boyce play for Essex v Surrey in a gloomy, rain-affected day of County Championship cricket.

My interest in Lonsdale Skinner was immediately alerted when I discovered in an edition of one of my Playfair Cricket Annuals that he was born in Plaisance, Guyana. Plaisance is a village on the east coast of the Demerara river and approximately six miles from the capital Georgetown. My continuing interest in Skinner was also fuelled by the fact he was a Guyanese cricketer playing for Surrey, our closest county cricket club. My maternal grandmother, who sadly passed away in Guyana many years before, and my great-grandmother, who lived with us in England, both came from Plaisance. I developed an early interest in Plaisance because of the stories my great-grandmother told me about her life there.

I once asked my great-grandmother if she could recall any families called Skinner from Plaisance. She thought long and hard but could not remember any. Despite this lack of certainty from her, I became increasingly curious about Lonsdale Skinner. During a chat with Skinner many years later, I discovered that in Plaisance he knew a cousin of mine, Beryl, also known as Bobby. The Grant family, including Eddy Grant, lived opposite Bobby's home in Plaisance. By 1973, Plaisance – born Eddy was a musician based in north London and had recorded a string of records with his band, The Equals, one of Britain's first multi-racial pop groups. The Equals biggest hit was *Baby, Come Back* which was a chart-topping record in 1968.

My 1973 Spring Annual edition of *The Cricketer* described Skinner as 'a reserve wicketkeeper and an aggressive opening batsman from Guyana, who has had a lot of success in the second XI'[14]. Skinner attended high school in south London, played for Surrey from the age of 14 at Colts level, joined the county as a professional in 1969, and made his first-class debut in 1971. In 1974, he was in the Surrey team which beat Leicestershire at Lord's to win the Benson and Hedges Cup.

For many West Indian cricketers who were unable to secure contracts to play for one of the 17 first-class county clubs in England and Wales, there were still opportunities to become a hired professional for a club in the competitive Lancashire Leagues. Learie Constantine's personality and impact as a player for Nelson, laid the foundations for other West Indian players in successive years to earn a living in the

Lancashire Leagues. Each team in the Lancashire League system consisted of 10 locally based amateur players and a paid professional who was the star attraction.

Some of the West Indians who played in the Lancashire and Central Lancashire Leagues – widely acknowledged as the two top club cricket leagues in the Lancashire area, included Clairmonte Depeiaza, George Headley, JK Holt and Clive Lloyd at Haslingden. Sonny Ramadhin, Garry Sobers and Frank Worrell for Radcliffe. Nyron Asgarali, Keith Barker, Conrad Hunte, Charlie Stayers and Clyde Walcott represented Enfield. Walcott described his time playing for Enfield as one of the happiest periods of his career.

Basil Butcher played for Lowerhouse and Bacup. Roy Gilchrist, George Headley and Everton Weekes also played for Bacup. Charlie Griffith, Manny Martindale, Bruce Pairaudeau and Collie Smith played for Burnley. Lance Gibbs also spent a season at Burnley following the West Indies 1960/1961 tour of Australia. Seymour Nurse played at Ramsbottom for three seasons following the 1960/1961 Australia tour.

Wes Hall played for Accrington and described his time in Lancashire as one of the defining periods of his life. According to Hall, he faced a collection of challenges, which included living with strangers far away from home in the Caribbean. For Hall and many other cricketers from the Caribbean playing in the Lancashire Leagues, it was their first experience of living for a considerable amount of time in a place with people who were not West Indian. Hall's experience coincided with the rigorous demands of being the star professional player for Accrington, and the person that people wanted to be around with.

In 1987, Viv Richards, after his controversial departure from Somerset with Joel Garner, spent a season playing Lancashire League cricket for Rishton. Richards, who was still the captain of the West Indies and, arguably, the best batsman in world cricket, arrived at Rishton in spectacular fashion. Following an overnight flight from the Caribbean, Richards landed on the playing area of Rishton's Blackburn Road ground in a helicopter! A group of reporters, television crews and photographers surged across the ground towards Richards. As Richards stepped down the helicopter's gangway, and on the outfield, he was quickly surrounded by a gaggle of excited school children.

In 1973, there were six West Indian players registered to play for clubs in the Lancashire League and the Central Lancashire League. Ken Arthur from Barbados joined the Church club as a replacement for Carlton Forbes, on the recommendation of Everton Weekes. Duncan Carter from Barbados continued his stay at Lowerhouse. Keith Barker, also from Barbados, confirmed his position at Rishton for the second season in a row as a player and a coach. Cecil 'Cec' Wright from Jamaica was contracted to play for Walsden. Two of the six players engaged by clubs in the Lancashire Leagues in 1973 played Test cricket for the West Indies. Roy Gilchrist at Crompton and Reg Scarlett at Stockport – both from Jamaica.

As a West Indian in Britain, playing cricket for a first-class county or for a side in a competitive club league as a professional, often under pressurised conditions as the club's star attraction, offered an additional way of earning a living. It also helped to develop an all-round professional approach to the game and improve the technique of many West Indian players, who had to quickly adapt to playing in English conditions.

Vasbert Drakes played league cricket in the Bolton League, county cricket for Sussex, Nottinghamshire, Warwickshire and Leicestershire, and for Barbados. He played 14 Test matches for the West Indies. Following his retirement from playing cricket, Drakes has worked as a coach for the West Indies A team and Test team, the Barbados Cricket Association (BCA), the Queen's Park Cricket Club in Trinidad, the West Indies Women's team, and the Barbados Tridents Caribbean Premier League (CPL) T20 team. As Drakes explains.

In Barbados you'd be playing on wickets where the ball would consistently go through to the wicket-keeper. Then all of a sudden, you go to England where the wickets are wet and damp. So it was a real challenge in England for West Indian players as the ball seams around a bit more and you had to constantly adjust to the conditions to achieve the results you wanted. And when bowling in England, your length had to change considerably because of the slowness of the wickets. You had to bowl a fuller length up to the bat and rely on subtle variation. This created a better awareness in you as a player because you have to adapt to the conditions and think about the most effective method that worked. A player's technique is all about the ability to be effective and to be able to adjust in any circumstances and in any conditions.[15]

Lance Gibbs once told me, during a telephone conversation (Gibbs was in the US and I was in the UK) about his experiences playing county and club cricket in England that, 'If, as a West Indian, you could master the conditions in England, you could play anywhere in the world'.

By 1973, West Indian players playing in the Lancashire Leagues became a rare sight, as regulations which prevented overseas cricketers playing for English counties became more relaxed. Clive Lloyd was an example of a player who left Haslingden and Lancashire League cricket to join Lancashire CCC. There were now alternative ways for West Indian cricketers to earn a living and play cricket as professionals. In turn, playing first-class county cricket provided an ideal training ground for them to play Test cricket in England. West Indian players on the county cricket circuit regularly played on the international grounds used for England v West Indies Tests. Also, there were more top West Indian players for me to watch on television playing domestic limited overs cricket in England, which inspired my developing passion for the game.

CHAPTER 7

Playing the game, Sure and Steadfast, trouble beyond the boundary, and at the crease at The Oval

A s my interest in cricket increased, I continued to be inspired by watching English county teams play each other and Test matches live on BBC television. With the 1973 West Indies tour being a memorable starting point. However, I rarely played cricket. I occasionally played some bat and ball with friends living on my street during the summer holidays. I always remembered our clear instructions to play on the pavement, and to avoid straying on to the road. On our trips to the local park, a 15-minute walk from our flat, we would head for the wooded area called 'the woods', play football or, whether there was any water in it or not, play in the paddling pool.

At my primary school we didn't have a cricket team but, in a year or two, we progressed to play cricket during some of our PE lessons. We had a football team which, in a couple of years, I would play for and score goals for as a centre forward. By 1973, I still thought of myself as my primary school's Allan Clarke. I attempted to emulate his Leeds United goal-scoring achievements for my school when we played against other schools in our area. Whenever I was selected for the school football team, I would immediately grab the number eight team shirt to wear. Allan Clarke wore the number eight shirt with pride and distinction for Leeds from 1969 to 1977. Clarke scored 151 goals in 364 appearances for the club and 10 goals in 19 appearances for England.

My primary school had a few informal after school cricket matches on our local park. They were quite straightforward arrangements and not seriously organised and competitive. Two teams were loosely formed from across the various year groups in the school. A few parents and teachers were recruited to join the teams and act as occasional umpires. I don't remember batting during these matches, but I clearly remember bowling medium-pace, left-arm around the wicket to both right and left-handed batsmen. During one match, Mr Burns, our school head teacher, suggested to me that, 'You've got a bit of swing there'.

At the age of nine or ten, I'm not sure I was able to swing a ball into or away from a batsman. But I did grip the ball between my fingers and across the seam – as discovered in 'how to play cricket' books borrowed from my local public library. It was probably a very welcome accident that I managed to bowl a few swinging deliveries, which troubled the batsmen in our local park. Despite this, Mr Burns' review of my bowling spell gave me a timely confidence boost, during my early attempts to play cricket at a vaguely competitive level.

During the summer of 1973, a casual enquiry made towards an acquaintance from school, would lead to me playing competitive junior cricket a few years later. One evening after school, I was walking back to our flat from somewhere. I don't remember where from or who I was with. But what I do remember is that David Johnstone was on the other side of the street.

David was a boy in the year above me at my primary school. I can't say we were close friends, but we knew each other well enough to greet each other on the street and say hello. David was dressed in a uniform which I'd not seen before. He wore a blue pullover and a hat which reminded me of the headgear worn by the puppet characters in the Thunderbirds show on television. I asked David where he was going. 'I'm going to Boys' Brigade' he replied. 'What's that?' I enquired. I'd never heard of the Boys' Brigade. 'Oh, you can play games and things and they check your nails to see if they're clean'.

The Boys' Brigade (BB) is an international youth organisation, founded in Glasgow, Scotland in 1883, with its roots in the Christian church. 'Sure and Steadfast' was the invigorating motto on the BB's anchor and cross badge. I was slightly baffled about the nail-checking. But the prospect of playing games and charging around with other boys sounded like a brilliant idea. As I quickly discovered, the junior section of the 92nd London, my local BB group, met once a week in a Methodist church hall. This nearly faced one end of our street. I just had to come out of our flat, turn right, and walk there in about five minutes.

Back at school the following morning, I discovered that a couple of boys in my class attended the BB, including my close friend Ian.

Maybe Ian had mentioned it to me but I can't recall him saying anything about it. Anyway, within a couple of weeks of making this discovery, I became a member of the BB.

By 1973, I had made strong connections with a variety of Christian denominations during my young life in England. I was a Roman Catholic from a family with a tradition of worship in the Roman Catholic Church, Anglicanism and Seventh Day Adventism in the Caribbean. I attended a Church of England primary school and was about to join a youth organisation connected to the Methodist Church. Within a couple of years, I also briefly joined a local Cub Scout group which was linked to a nearby United Reformed Church.

When I joined my local BB junior section, I also discovered more about what David described as nail-checking. Before all the fun and games started, some of us had our hands and nails inspected by the BB organiser in charge that evening. He wanted to see if they were clean. I guess it was one of the BB's methods of instilling some basic hygiene rules and routines, and aspects of self-discipline into our young lives. I didn't have a problem with it.

When I joined my local BB junior section, I looked straight ahead, and within a couple of years I was involved in all the games and sports we played. Either amongst ourselves in the Methodist church hall during the week, or against other local junior sections at weekends. These included athletics, cricket, football, gymnastics, tag races and table tennis.

The weekend BB day trips included funfairs, the zoo, and adventurous hiking and walking expeditions through rural areas and pristine suburban areas. These hiking and walking expeditions, which included the joy of tumbling up and down hills and grassy banks, were in areas in Surrey and Sussex. These were areas that most of us were unfamiliar with and beyond our immediate collective experiences.

As far as I recall, our junior section football team didn't win any trophies. Our football team was not as strong as our cricket team and our results were a mixed bag of wins, defeats and draws. I didn't care whether it was rain, drizzle, sunshine or hail. I just wanted to play every match for our football team on Saturday afternoons on various park pitches across south London. I was always upset when I was not selected to play for the team, or if I was named as a substitute.

When I started to play for the junior section football team, I operated in a central midfield role. This suited me fine because I wanted to be involved in as much action as possible during every match. For many of our games, my approach was quite straightforward. If in doubt, pass the ball to Gary Allen. Gary, who was a Chelsea supporter, was born in Britain to Jamaican parents. He was the best footballer I've ever played with in any form of organised football for BB, cubs, school, weekend league, work and other representative teams.

This was autumn/winter 1973, I was nine and Gary was a year or two older than me. Gary could pick a ball up from just outside our penalty area, move up the pitch by gliding past three or four opposition players, and then slide the ball past the opposition goalkeeper. He had immaculate balance, poise, skill and speed, and everything appeared to be easy for him. He often smiled quietly to himself when he easily swayed past opposition players on another slalom-style run towards goal. I was convinced that Gary had the potential to be a professional footballer. I haven't seen Gary Allen for nearly 40 years. If I ever met him, I would let him know how highly I rated him as a footballer and as an all-round nice guy.

As well as burning off serious levels of energy on football pitches, I played cricket more often with my friends in our local park, back gardens and, a few years later, against Len in the largely unoccupied living room in his family's flat in Peckham. I was reminded of playing house cricket as part of my growing enthusiasm for cricket in the 1970s, during a chat with Alex Tudor as part of my research for the revised and updated version of *They Gave the Crowd Plenty Fun*. Tudor, a British-born fast-bowler of Barbadian descent, who played 10 Test matches for England between 1998 and 2002, grew up in a cricket loving Caribbean family household in south London. During our chat, he fondly recalled playing cricket with his brother at home, sometimes damaging ornaments as they played for hours in their living room.

As soon as I became aware that the junior section of my local BB group had a cricket team, I urgently wanted to be part of the action. Another boy who joined the BB and the cricket team was my friend Dharmesh. He established himself in the side as the wicket-keeper. Dharmesh was the only boy from my class at primary school who played with me for the junior section team. He was also the only other player of Caribbean descent. Dharmesh's parents were from Berbice, Guyana.

A year or two after I joined the junior section cricket team, we won our local borough battalion league championship. I was the captain. I became captain because I wanted to involve myself in everything and anything on the field of play at all times. To be honest, I don't remember making any meaningful decisions during any of these games. Before each match one of our senior BB organisers selected the team and organised the batting and bowling order. During their stints as match umpires in each game, they usually made suggestions to me and the team about who would stand where in the field.

I opened the bowling (left-arm around the wicket to right-handed batsmen) and imagined that I was either Michael Holding or Dennis Lillee. Thundering in off a long run-up to cause mayhem and havoc to the opposition's batting attack. I attempted to bowl as fast as possible. If I bowled a few quick but wayward deliveries, I switched to bowling at a more medium pace and concentrated on accuracy. My memory recalls that in these BB junior section league fixtures, each team bowled a maximum of ten overs, with each bowler restricted to no more than two overs each.

I also opened the batting (left-handed). I was not a flamboyant batsman and was more concerned with adopting a patient approach, occupying the crease, applying my defensive technique and playing shots against poor deliveries. I was more of a Larry Gomes than a Roy Fredericks. My batting heroes were Roy Fredericks, Vivian Richards and Geoffrey Boycott. An ideal combination, I thought, of self-belief, determination, commanding stroke play, endurance, swagger and dedication to duty.

In the years that followed, I became more aware of the level of criticism aimed at Boycott's personality, the way he played the game, and the way he strongly divided dressing rooms and wider public opinion. From accusations of being a selfish cricketer with no regard for others, as an unattractive batsman to watch, and only concerned with his own accumulation of runs – to being intensely self-centred and a difficult person to work with.

Back in 1967, after his highest Test score of 246 not out v India at Headingley, scored off 555 balls and 573 minutes, Boycott was dropped for the next Test. This was as a disciplinary measure for slow scoring. Boycott described this decision by the England selectors as the deepest wound of his professional life. Despite all this, and observed from a far distance, I continued to admire Boycott's powers of concentration, dedication to self-improvement, defensive batting skills and overall technique.

I was also keen to run quick singles and twos. I was quick between the wickets, and I didn't hit a significant number of boundaries. I tried to impersonate the batting and running between the wickets displayed by Clive Radley of Middlesex and England. BBC television and radio cricket commentators described Radley as a very quick runner between the wickets. He was a player who worked hard to convert singles into twos. Martin Williamson, a cricket journalist and former Managing Editor of Cricinfo and ESPN UK, perfectly sums up Radley's qualities.

> Clive Radley was not the most gifted or graceful batsman, but he more than made up for that with determination, hard work, and the absence of anything approaching risk. He accumulated runs rather than stroked them, scurrying between the wickets quicker than almost any contemporary, with a characteristic slide in the final yards which enabled him to turn quickly. Watching him in partnership with the equally swift Graeme Barlow was a delight. His ability to eke out quick singles made him a valuable one-day player in a side which dominated the one-day knockouts from the mid-seventies. [1]

I was an enthusiastic fielder and didn't drop many catches. I did everything to restrict singles from near the wicket and cut off boundaries in the outfield. I couldn't field too far away from the wicket because I had a very weak throwing arm. Micky, one of the lads in our team, did not make a substantial contribution as a batsman or bowler. But Micky had, what I can only describe as, a bullet throw. He could pick up a cricket ball from any area in the outfield, and accurately throw it to the wicket-keeper or the bowler's end at high-speed. I often thought of Micky as a young south London version of Kent's Alan Ealham. Ealham was the first player I can remember admiring purely for his tremendous fielding skills and powerful throwing arm.

During a match in the 1975 BB local battalion league cricket season, I endured my most humiliating and frustrating moment on a cricket field. Opening the batting, as usual, I was scratching around against the bowling to add to my score of 3 or 4. I received a delivery, which was just a little short of a length and straight. I tried to pull the ball through mid-wicket to the boundary but completely played around it and missed. The ball rocketed into my groin area and I collapsed in a heap on the ground. For a moment, everything around me seemed to go quiet. I slowly got back on my feet to face the next delivery. I was still in pain and felt very uncomfortable down below.

As I gritted my teeth and nodded to the umpire that I wanted to continue, I saw his finger was raised and still. He had given me out LBW. I hadn't heard an appeal from the bowler or any of the opposition fielders. However, in the umpire's opinion, the ball would have continued to hit the stumps if my groin had not got in the way. As I hobbled off the field, I had a sharp exchange of words, including a few expletives, with a few of the giggling opposition fielders. There was also, let us say, a lively verbal exchange between the umpire and me.

I don't recall whether we won the match or not. But I do know that as result of the incident, several days later, I went to a sports shop and bought a pink protective box for my sensitive groin area. From that day on, I always wore my box whenever I went out to bat and for any cricket team I played for.

As the 1975 season came to an end, the painful experience of being struck down below and losing my cool was eradicated by the sweet joy of victory. Our junior section cricket team won the local battalion league and we each received a certificate. This was the first time in my young life I had been part of a winning sports team. It was the only time I can remember that we won this competition, but it was not my one and only cricket success story. This confirmed my increasing engagement with playing cricket, as well as being consumed by the game by watching it on television, with occasional trips to watch games played professionally at cricket grounds.

Towards the end of 1976, I had progressed from the junior section of my local BB group and joined the senior section. The senior section had a cricket team and I was determined to be part of it. Alongside the fact that a few friends of mine from primary school had joined the senior section, one of my key motivations to stay in the BB was that I wanted to play competitive cricket at a decent standard. Although, I felt slightly anxious about playing with and against boys who were four or five years older than me.

By the start of the 1977 season, I acquired two other essential pieces of cricket equipment to go with my shiny pink protective box. My first cricket bat was given to me by my father. It was a Stuart Surridge 'SS' cricket bat and I ensured it was well maintained and kept in good order. As instructed by the old English guy who owned the nearest sports shop to our flat, I wiped the bat down with linseed oil, as and when necessary, and waited for it to dry. I loved the arid smell of linseed oil as it slowly dried on my bat. I would briefly panic if I identified cracks on the bat's face or edges which ruined the look of my bat.

My other major cricket equipment purchase was a pair of St. Peter (SP) batting gloves. These were unique, stylish, all-in-one white padded gloves with no individual 'sausage fingers' or green thin rubber spike padding. The first player I can recall wearing these gloves was Tony Greig playing for Sussex and England. Dharmesh and I went on a shopping trip to a sports shop in Croydon so would could each buy a pair of SP gloves.

During the previous summer, Greig, a South African-born and raised England captain, was interviewed on a BBC television sports programme. The interview took place days before the first match of the 1976 England v West Indies series. During the interview Greig insisted, with his South African accent firmly intact that, 'You must remember that the West Indies, these guys, if they get on top they are magnificent cricketers. But if they are down, they grovel, and I intend, with the help of Closey (Brian Close) and a few others, to make them grovel'.

Greig insisted that England could seriously challenge the West Indies. He also wanted to get the media and public onside after recent England defeats. Following the interview, some people in the Caribbean community were now prepared for a politicised 'us v them' cricket confrontation. There were many in the Caribbean community, especially young people born in Britain, who were increasingly frustrated and angry about limited employment opportunities, social alienation, racial hostility, conflicts with extreme right-wing political organisations, and persistent harassment from inner-city police forces.

South African sports teams were still banned from international competition because of their government's apartheid system of racial segregation and state enforced discrimination. Since 1970, South Africa had been banned from the International Cricket Council (ICC) as widespread anger at the apartheid system steadily increased. The West Indies team and some of the Caribbean community responded to the racial battle lines that Greig's remarks appeared to promote. No further motivation was required. This helped to inspire the West Indies towards a convincing 3-0 series win.

To state the obvious, as a captain of any team in any competitive sport, making grand statements about what you intend to do to the opposition is always a risk. Unless you are 100% sure you can back it up with a convincing result. Although, as Greig genuinely appeared to claim, his point about using the word 'grovel' had been entirely unconnected with race.

During the summer of 1976, Greig rapidly evolved in the eyes of many West Indian supporters in Britain as a Pantomime-style boo-hiss villain. Greig was heckled, although much of this was in good humour, by groups of West Indian spectators at every ground during the series, but especially at The Oval.

Despite all this, I still wanted to wear my pair of SP batting gloves as worn by Tony Greig. It was certainly worth saving up my weekly pocket money to wear them. I wasn't concerned that at the shop we bought them, they only had right-handed pairs of SP gloves in stock. As a left-handed batsman, wearing right-handed gloves meant that my left thumb was unprotected. I eventually removed a rubber thimble protector from an old pair of batting gloves in the BB cricket kit bag. I inserted the thimble in the left-hand SP glove whenever I batted. This offered the thumb on my left-hand some much needed extra protection.

My new equipment was now ready to be used for the 1977 BB cricket season. In addition to one of my smart white short-sleeved school shirts, my canvass white (slightly-flared) jeans and a pair of blue and white trainers. In a few years, my trainers would be replaced by a pair of old white cricket boots which my father passed on to me. He wore them when he played cricket during his years serving with the British Army.

I didn't have all the 'proper' kit, but this didn't prevent me from being on the fringes of selection for my local BB senior team. I knew that, if selected, as one of the younger members of the team, I would be placed towards the end of the batting order and would probably not get an opportunity to bowl. But, at the age of 12, I just wanted to experience the thrill of stepping up in class and playing cricket for the seniors.

My opportunity arrived in one of the first matches of the 1977 BB cricket season. I was selected for a match at Worcester Park in Surrey. Once again, being a member of a travelling cricket team meant I could explore another suburban outpost on the fringes of south London. I was selected to play with Nick – my good friend from primary school who also joined the BB. Our team batted first in a contest which was usually limited to 12 to 16 overs per side. The full allocation of overs, restricted to each side, depended on when both teams assembled their players at the venue. As near to the evening starting time as possible.

As Nick and I were placed at 10 and 11 in the batting order respectively, we didn't expect to bat until the end of the innings if required. So, we took a walk to a nearby playground which was about 100 yards away from the ground's boundary ropes. Minutes later, I was involved in a brief verbal slanging match with a couple of white English lads. At the time, they were both messing about on the playground swings. One of the lads took a serious exception to me, as a black guy, appearing on his turf and casually wandering around the playground with a white friend. He then barked out a chant aimed at me that, 'The National Front is a white man's front. Join the National Front!'

Formed in the 1960s, the extreme right-wing nationalist National Front party enjoyed an increase in popularity and support in Britain during the 1970s. At the core of the National Front's ideology was a firm belief in white supremacy, hostility towards the presence of black and Asian people in Britain, anti-Semitism, the desire to prevent all non-white immigration to the UK, and the repatriation of non-white immigrants and their families back to their country of origin.

In 1973, the National Front represented by Martin Webster, who became one of the party's high-profile activists, received 16% of the vote in a by-election in West Bromwich. This was the first time the National Front had achieved a vote of more than 10% in any UK parliamentary constituency. By 1973, the National Front had firmly established itself as Britain's most important far-right party. One of the reasons for the party's temporary successes in the 1970s was its exploitation of the fears some voters had towards the arrival of thousands of Asians from Uganda. In 1972, the British government confirmed that Asians expelled from Uganda by Idi Amin's regime could settle in Britain.

Many black supporters, who attended football matches during the 1970s, faced the intimidating prospect of fending off racist abuse from a vocal minority of white supporters, and watching black players racially abused by sections of the crowd. The National Front, and other far-right organisations, openly attempted to recruit white football fans on the terraces or outside stadiums.

I was more than familiar with the threatening existence of the National Front but had not heard this chant aimed at me before. The two lads were smaller than Nick and me but were vaguely intimidating. They also viewed Nick as being part of their problem. Nick was a white boy with a black friend. Eventually, we walked away from the playground – back to our cricket match in progress to wait for our turn to field.

I was required to field near the boundary during the opposition team's innings. I was not very active in the outfield throughout their innings. There were no shots hit in my direction. However, I was unnerved to discover that about 50 yards behind me, there were three menacing skinheads and the two lads standing together in a group. The two lads had, obviously, decided to call up some reinforcements to try to give me hard time. They did their best to give me some serious hard stares and shouted a few threats. 'Come over here you black c**t' was one of them. I declined their invitation and didn't know whether to take their other threats seriously or not.

I just stood my ground, concentrated on the game, and looked back from time to time to see if they were getting closer to me. I also hoped that I didn't have to retrieve a ball hit past me and beyond the boundary. I might then have to face the challenge of confronting the group to get the ball back. Thankfully, after 15 minutes or so, the boys probably got fed up and bored with it all. They sauntered off into the distance without looking back. Our team won the match and I had an anxious laugh about the incident with Nick during the car journey home.

One of my most memorable cricket-playing experiences took place at the end of my first BB season in 1977. The confrontation with the

National Front sympathisers in Worcester Park became a distant memory after our team achieved 10 successive victories in the London District 11-a-side knockout competition. The final was scheduled to be played at The Oval.

I'd played in some matches leading up to the final. I usually came out to bat at the end of our innings, at the tail-end of the batting order, as and when required, and did my best in the field. I can't recall being asked to bowl during this stretch of victories. So, in truth, as one of the youngest players in the team, I didn't contribute a great deal to the team's success but was hopeful of being selected for the final. So I was delighted to receive the news that I was selected and listed to bat at number eight.

I packed my SS bat as used by Viv Richards and my Tony Greig-inspired SP gloves for The Oval final. I also took my great-grandmother's sky-blue floppy hat to wear as part of my kit. I discovered the hat at home and it, vaguely, resembled the white beanie-style hat I'd seen Clive Lloyd wear on television. When it was my turn to bat, I put the hat in my bag after some relentless teasing about it from a couple of my team mates in the dressing room. I conceded that my great-grandmother's sky-blue floppy hat wasn't masculine enough for me to wear at The Oval.

At The Oval, Dean Hall, our captain, won the toss and decided we should bat first. When my turn came to bat, I sauntered slowly and deliberately from the pavilion across The Oval turf to take my guard. I wanted to savour every moment of my walk to the crease. I took in a few deep breaths to settle my nerves. I also took a long time to reach the wicket. It was a long way from the pavilion fence!

Although I'd watched a few matches at The Oval in the years leading up to this moment. Walking across the ground made me realise how large the playing area was. It was so big, the area of the ground used for our final was just over half the area used for county and international matches.

My innings at The Oval was short and not very sweet. I faced about eight balls. Two of them, as I recall, were signalled by the umpire as wides. Oh well, I thought. At least I'd added a couple of runs to our innings score, despite not being able to hit a delivery. I then blocked one or two deliveries in immaculate fashion with my bat and pad close together. I then swung and missed a couple of deliveries and survived a confident LBW appeal. I was then cleaned bowled by a fast and straight delivery after hitting across the line to the onside. A failed attempt at a shot I had seen Viv Richards play in impressive style on television.

Unsurprisingly, my walk back to the pavilion seemed even longer than the walk I made coming out to bat. I had blown my big moment at The Oval by scoring a big fat duck. Our final total was 88 for 9 after our maximum allocation of 12 overs.

When the opposition batted, my fielding position was on the boundary. I only touched the ball once during their innings. I picked up a shot hit towards me. I then threw the ball as hard as I could towards one of our fielders. He was standing about 30 yards in front of me. He then threw the ball to our wicket-keeper after their batsmen had crossed for two or three runs. The bowler, wicket-keeper, batsmen, umpire and stumps appeared as dots on a far-flung horizon from my position patrolling the boundary.

As the opposition's innings progressed, Michael Aitken, one of our spin-bowlers, was hit for a six early in his allocation of two overs. The six landed on The Oval Test wicket which was being prepared by the ground staff. They were not impressed that a ball from such an insignificant match had landed on an important piece of turf. Aitken regained his form and poise and finished with impressive bowling figures of three for 13.

There was a dramatic finish to the match. The opposition required four runs to win off the last ball. Dean Hall bowled, their batsman swung and missed, and we cried for joy! Then, slowly, the umpire signalled that Hall's delivery was a wide. Three runs were now required off the last ball. Hall bowled, the batsman hit the ball high into The Oval sky. The ball came down and a catch was taken. My Oval cricket playing experience had ended in a victory for our team. Three cheers echoed from both teams as the trophies and cloth badges were presented at the bottom of the pavilion steps. Our team also received two pairs of batting gloves from Wisden Edwards as a special award. Another warmly welcomed addition to our team's cricket kit bag.

Trevor Bailey, who had a distinguished career with Essex and England, and who I enjoyed listening to as one of the cricket radio commentary voices on BBC's Test Match Special, was spotted watching the match with great interest from the pavilion. Some Surrey

CCC members were also watching the action with nods of approval from the pavilion. Tony Greig was also rumoured to have watched some of the match. Apparently, he was scheduled to be at The Oval that day to appear before a MCC Committee. I wonder whether Greig briefly caught a glimpse of a young, black schoolboy scratching around for runs at the wicket, wearing a pair of Greig-inspired SP gloves?!

After the presentation ceremony, both teams were delighted to be invited to the dining room where the 'real' players ate at The Oval. I also introduced myself to a new culinary experience by eating scones with jam and cream, which I washed down by drinking a cup of tea from a dainty tea cup.

Before we left The Oval, I grabbed a handful of turf from the outfield as a souvenir. I was inspired to do this after watching a recent home international football match between England and Scotland at Wembley. Scotland beat England 2-1. Some of the delighted hordes of Scottish supporters invaded the pitch after the final whistle. They celebrated victory against the old/auld English enemy by cavorting across the pitch, accidently smashing a crossbar and goalposts. Some of them dug up pieces of hallowed Wembley turf to take back over the border to Scotland as treasured souvenirs.

Without condoning the behaviour of the Scottish supporters that day, I must confess that the idea to remove some Oval grass came from their turf removal antics at Wembley. I took some of The Oval grass home and fastened it with sticky tape in a scrapbook. Alongside my Oval grass souvenir exhibit, I pasted in a press cutting of a match report written in one of our local newspapers. This was another one of my memorable playing experiences which cemented my engagement with cricket.

Within the next five years, our BB senior cricket team won a further two 11-a-side and three six-a-side London District knock out competitions. I played in the last two six-a-side victories and all three of the 11-a-side wins. The last of our 11-a-side wins was at the old Essex County Ground in Leytonstone. All of this and more would not have happened if I didn't casually enquire as to where David Johnstone, a primary school acquaintance of mine, was going – when I saw him walking down my street during a warm summer evening in 1973.

CHAPTER 8

Cricket and Caribbean diaspora, emerging idols, TV times and build-up to the first Test

B efore the start of the 1973 England v West Indies Test series, as my enthusiasm for cricket steadily increased, it never occurred to me to support any other international team than the West Indies. Part of this was a sense of inherited interest being brought up in a Caribbean home in Britain. Another notable influence was being part of a wider community, where the passion for cricket and the West Indies team arrived with some Caribbean migrants in Britain. 'Cricket was, by a long way, the primary form of recreation and social interest across the English-speaking Caribbean, and that's how I was introduced to the game in Jamaica', says Andrew Carnegie.

If you were able to play for the West Indies, you probably had much more recognition in the Caribbean than if you became a senior politician. Representing the West Indies team was the highest aspiration you could achieve at that time and we idolised all the players. For me, Garry Sobers was, at that time, the most celebrated cricketer in the Caribbean, even in Jamaica. I brought that feeling for cricket when I came to England, and the vast majority of West Indian people, especially the men, had that feeling for the game and the West Indies team when they came to live here (in England). I once randomly asked some friends, colleagues and associates, who all had parents born in the Caribbean who came to England, what they recalled as children growing up in their parent's household in England, and what their fathers did during the summer months in England. Did their fathers turn on the television to watch cricket on the television or listen to cricket on the radio? They all invariably said yes. So, this was a near religious experience, which was passed on and picked-up by kids who were born in Britain to West Indian families.

By 1973, there were a growing number of young British-born people of Caribbean descent who, whether they were avid cricket fans or not, wanted to see a vibrant West Indies team on tour in England. Many of them had forged a collective relationship with the first generation of Caribbean migrants based on a shared interest in, and identity with, West Indian cricket.

In 1958, my father saw one day of Hanif Mohammed's mammoth innings of 337, which saved the match for Pakistan v West Indies at the Kensington Oval, Barbados. Hanif's 337, made in 16 hours and 10 minutes, is still the longest innings in Test history. Four years later at the Kensington Oval, during a Barbados v India tour match, my father saw Nari Contractor suffer a serious injury after being hit on the head by a Charlie Griffith bouncer. As well as Keith Boyce, my father also attended school with Wycliffe Phillips, who played for Barbados and county cricket in England for Gloucestershire for three seasons from 1970.

During his time as member of the British Armed Forces, my father played as an all-rounder who bowled, batted and occasionally played as a wicket-keeper for his regiment's cricket team. He played in competitive and friendly matches in Warminster and across Yorkshire in England, and in Cyprus, Gibraltar and Ireland. He also completed an umpire's course and umpired matches between different regiments. There were a few West Indians in the same regiment as my father who played regularly for the cricket team. These included Tony from St.Vincent who was a lively fast-bowler and a very useful batsman. Another was Calvin Harvey, a wicket-keeper batsman who also played league cricket in Barbados.

During the 1970s in Birmingham, Steve Walcott's enthusiasm for cricket was passed on to him by his father from Barbados. Back home in Barbados, Steve's father knew Clairmonte Depeiaza, who represented Barbados and played five Tests for the West Indies in the 1950s. In 1955, Depeiaza, playing for the West Indies v Australia in front of his home crowd in Bridgetown, achieved the most memorable innings of his Test career. In the first innings of the fourth Test match of the series, with his fellow Barbadian Dennis Atkinson who hit a double century, Depeiaza scored his one and only Test century during a 347-run seventh wicket partnership. This is still a Test match record partnership for the seventh wicket.

Steve's father worked for British Rail throughout his working life in Britain and played club cricket for Birmingham Rail. He also played for various Barbadian and West Indian cricket clubs in the Birmingham Parks League. Steve's father stopped playing cricket in the early 1980s. Unfortunately, some of the venues used for the Birmingham Parks League, which was a flourishing league providing opportunities for people from all backgrounds in Birmingham to play competitive cricket, are no longer available or in use.

In 1973, Lainy Malkani, Director of the Social History Hub in UK, author and journalist, was a 10-year-old schoolgirl living in north London. Lainy's parents arrived in Britain from Guyana in 1962. Lainy was born in Britain. Her sisters, who were born in Guyana, arrived in Britain a couple of years later. In Lainy's household, her mother was the number one cricket enthusiast. However, her mother's passion for cricket and the West Indies team didn't always filter down to other members of the family, including Lainy.

Cricket in our household was massive because my mum was really fanatical about the game and absolutely loved it. Everything had to be done in the house before a cricket match started on TV. The dhal had to be done, the curry done, and the roti clapped and sorted! I always remember a spanking clean house and we had an armchair sofa which was positioned in front of the TV. And then, yes, mum would just sit there glued to the TV watching cricket. My sisters and I weren't into cricket to a massive extent, but my younger brother was really into it. He had a signed West Indies cricket bat and Rohan Kanhai and Alvin Kallicharan were his cricket heroes. It's only now, when I look back to how important West Indies cricket was to our culture and history, I remember the story that kept coming back to us that, 'Oh my God, there is someone on TV who really looks like us'. Kanhai and Kallicharan were from Berbice (in Guyana), and not very far from where our family lived. So, we all felt a connection with them. I liked the showbiz element of cricket, all the excitement, the strength of support for the West

Indies, and I do keep an eye out when the West Indies play here (in England). But, at the time, unless the West Indies were playing on TV, I thought cricket back then was boring. With all these people in a field, standing around for ages not doing very much, and then a ball is hit, and you can't see it clearly on the TV, and you've got to guess where the ball had gone.

1973 was a landmark year in the young lives of Dwight Stevens and Rod Westmaas. Dwight and Rod were from families who would experience cycles of migration and re-migration. This included returning to live in Britain in 1973 after spending significant periods of time back in the Caribbean.

Dwight was born in Britain to parents from Jamaica. Early in 1972, Dwight and his family went back to live in Jamaica. He attended school in Jamaica and his family followed the 1973 West Indies tour of England in the Caribbean. Life didn't quite work out as planned in Jamaica for Dwight and his family. So, they decided to return to live in Britain in late 1973. Dwight credits his father for influencing his early interest in West Indies cricket. Other influences and reasons soon followed.

I got into cricket through my father who watched a lot of cricket. He always enjoyed talking a lot about cricket and the songs about cricket my family and his friends sang. Another reason why we identified with cricket and supported the West Indies was because the English liked to talk about cricket and play the game in a much more structured and traditional way. But the West Indies were more flamboyant, and we were used to watching sixes being hit around the place and all this kind of thing. So, this is what first drew my interest in cricket, for me and some of my friends. And even though we grew up with football here in this country, and did other things like running, we played cricket as well. I also went to a grammar school with lots of English guys who were all into their cricket. So, when the West Indies beat England it was my chance to get back at them. So, the culture of West Indies cricket was very strong for me, and that was very important for me growing up here (in England).

The first member of Rod Westmaas' family to live in Britain was his father who arrived on a Bookers ship in 1959. Rod arrived in Britain a year later to join his father at the age of two years and 11 months with his mother and older sister. In 1969, Rod was sent back to Guyana to live with an uncle and attend Queen's College school in Georgetown. Rod quickly became, as he describes, 'the novel English boy in the school'. It took a while for Rod's English accent to be less obvious. So, he entertained the boys in his class by putting on an English accent when he spoke to them. Returning to live in Guyana also offered Rod an opportunity to engage with his family's connections with cricket in Guyana and the wider Caribbean.

My grandfather, George Hamilton Westmaas, was an umpire in British Guiana and my uncle, my dad's brother, was a wicket-keeper for British Guiana. His name was Leonard Adrian Westmaas. My father was an ardent cricketer and was a manager for a saw mill in Guyana in the Pomeroon, and with his colleagues he organised cricket matches for the workers who would play against each other in teams. In Georgetown, we lived in Crown Street and Clive Lloyd was a neighbour of ours. Lance Gibbs was a cousin of his and used to come around. So we had these connections with them and we were just down the street from the GCC (Georgetown Cricket Club) and my uncle Leonard played for the GCC.

Rod brought this experience and relationship with Guyanese and West Indies cricket on his re-migration journey back to Britain in August 1973, during the England v West Indies series.

When I came back to England in 1973, the secondary school that I had to go to do my O levels was a grammar school. When I was sitting down with the headmaster, because he had to interview me before allowing me to go to the school, he said, 'You know your team (the West Indies) is here and about to play us Brits right now?' I said, 'Oh, OK, that's very nice. I hope we win'. And that was during the interview to get into the school! Well, I eventually got in the school which was a school with very few people of colour, and I actually remember in

1973 bringing a newspaper into school one day and trying to show it to some of the guys in my class – as a way of trying to make friends. I said to them, 'Look at what we (the West Indies beating England at cricket) are doing'. And I recall some of the kids saying to me, 'Don't talk to Chalky', which was the nickname they gave me at school because I wasn't white. I really wound them all up!

My relationship with West Indies cricket continued to be rooted in a sense of my personal and cultural identity in Britain being intimately tied to the Caribbean. I seized the opportunity to support a group of players who came from the countries my family came from. In 1987, I was a few feet behind a dancing Wes Hall as part of the end of sugar-cane season Crop Over Festival procession in Barbados. Clive Lloyd attended the same high school, Chatham High, as my mother in Georgetown, Guyana. By the age of 14, Lloyd was captain of the Chatham High school cricket team in the prestigious Chin Cup inter-school competition. Basil Butcher, Roy Fredericks, Lance Gibbs, Alvin Kallicharan, Rohan Kanhai, Clive Lloyd and Joe Solomon were all Guyanese.

My mother fondly remembers going on school trips to watch cricket at the Bourda ground in Georgetown. My great-grandmother always reminded her to keep an eye on the 'bird ticket' spectators. These were spectators who watched the action inside Bourda for free, by getting a bird's eye view perched high up in one of the tall trees surrounding the ground. One of Clive Lloyd's childhood cricket memories in Georgetown is watching Garry Sobers score two centuries in a match for West Indies v Pakistan at Bourda in 1958. Lloyd watched the action from a tree overlooking the side screen. As a teenager, I was excited and honoured to be given a brief behind the scenes tour of Bourda, including the pavilion, by my cousin's husband.

As a representative symbol for success, cricket was an activity that 'we' (as West Indians living in Britain) had a strong tradition in and could beat England at. I/we used West Indian cricket victories on English soil to hit back at the elements within wider British society who seemed to be intent on keeping us down.

Of course, from a Guyanese perspective, the large contingent of Guyanese players in the 1973 West Indies team, including Rohan

Kanhai (captain), Lance Gibbs (vice-captain), and Clive Lloyd (the next captain), was something to admire and celebrate. However, during a Test match against any opposition, it didn't matter to me which West Indian batsman was scoring the runs, bowler claiming the wickets, or fielder taking the catches – Antiguan, Barbadian, Dominican, Guyanese, Jamaican, St Lucian, Vincentian, or Trinidadian.

By 1973, when the West Indies played matches in the Caribbean, the nationality of the majority of spectators was still determined by where the team played. This largely separated the units of support at West Indies matches in the Caribbean into Barbadians in Bridgetown, Guyanese in Georgetown, Jamaicans in Kingston, and Trinidadians in Port of Spain.

There was a difference in the West Indies cricket team/Caribbean spectator relationship when the West Indies toured or played in tournaments in England. The West Indies played in England to combined sets of supporters who had migrated from, or were descended from, a variety of British-ruled Caribbean territories. By the early 1970s many of these territories were independent nation states.

Therefore, in Britain, the West Indies cricket team were a Caribbean regional unit which represented a pan-Caribbean diaspora support base. Beyond the boundary – the regional, political, social, and ethnic tensions and rivalries between, and amongst, Barbadians, Guyanese, Jamaicans, Trinidadians and other West Indians in Britain, were usually reduced or temporarily put on hold. As the West Indies cricket team, a symbol of Caribbean regional unification, competed on the field of play, the relationship with the team produced a sense of unity in exile amongst the diaspora in Britain.

West Indies cricket provided some of the Caribbean diaspora in Britain, many of whom were facing serious challenges in establishing themselves against the barriers of racial prejudice, discrimination and indifference, with an additional common cause to focus on. The West Indies team continued to be, for me/us, a site of inspiration, self-belief and identity. For many in the diaspora, the players evolved into symbols of community and public representation. Cricket grounds in England during West Indian tours continued to exist as mass assembly points for some of the Caribbean community. They provided an open public arena for boisterous displays of West Indian camaraderie, collective expression, fun and an emotional release.

Many West Indians in Britain whether they were specifically interested in cricket or not, continued to respond positively to a team that played with a distinctive swagger, determination, panache and style. Watching the West Indies on tour in England provided me with a compelling source of satisfaction and entertainment. I was also energised by the atmosphere created by West Indies fans, when I watched matches on television and attended West Indies matches on tour in England.

Susan Price was born in Britain to parents from Barbados. Susan describes herself as more of a casual cricket follower than a serious cricket fan. But she fondly remembers the experience of watching the West Indies play on television during the 1970s with her Barbadian family.

Watching the West Indies was a huge family event for all of us, and we would all gather around the TV and watch it. Everyone in our house knew when the matches were coming on, and it was very exciting and fun at the same time. All my family and their friends were passionate about the West Indies team and just loved the game. I still can't remember all the names of the cricketers, but Gordon Greenidge was one of dad's favourite players. I wasn't really a huge cricket fan and had a limited appreciation of the game but everyone else in the house always watched it on TV. So, I was always caught up with the atmosphere and the noise in the house and everyone else's enthusiasm and excitement.

Watching the West Indies was not just about me wanting them to beat England. I wanted the West Indies to beat everyone. During the 1970s, when I started to watch Test cricket on television, the international opposition to the West Indies was provided by Australia, England, India, Pakistan and New Zealand. I indulged in regular banter with my classmates at primary school who supported teams the West Indies played against. With my friends Nick and Shakil, I felt I was holding up a sense of West Indian honour and pride when the West Indies beat England or Pakistan. Shakil's uncle was a passionate Pakistan and Manchester United supporter and we often exchanged forthright views about the teams we supported.

At the end of the 1973/1974 football season, it was with some satisfaction that I was able to remind Shakil's uncle that Leeds United won the First Division Championship and Manchester United were relegated to the Second Division. In the following year, during the inaugural cricket World Cup tournament in England, I eagerly reminded him about the nail-biting West Indies win in their final group fixture v Pakistan at Edgbaston. A last wicket partnership between Deryck Murray and Andy Roberts, in front of an equal number of passionate West Indian and Pakistani supporters, and neutral English observers, steered the West Indies to a one wicket victory with only two balls left. Take that!

As a teenager, soon after our family moved to outer London semi-suburban Thornton Heath, I asked for a Saturday job in a nearby grocery shop. That was a normal procedure back then as a teenager if you wanted a Saturday job. You just went from shop to shop and tried your luck. In response to my enquiry, the Indian guy behind the counter said that there were no jobs available as, 'We already have a black boy working here'. Willing the West Indies on to give India a hiding at cricket, was my way of hitting back at him for making those crude remarks. This was another example of 'weaponising' my support for the West Indies to strike back.

Although I was committed to the cause of West Indies cricket, I also admired and respected cricketers who played for English county sides and other international teams. As well as the dynamic fielding and the powerful and accurate throwing arm of Kent's Alan Ealham, and the athletic running between the wickets displayed by Middlesex and England's Clive Radley, I was always intrigued by the spin bowling guile of Kent and England's 'Deadly' Derek Underwood. I tried to mimic his trot to the wicket and final delivery stride when I attempted to bowl spin against my friends in the park.

In the school summer holidays in England that followed 1973, I enthusiastically waited for the start of any England home Test series. It didn't matter to me who England played. I just wanted to watch it. I would ensure that I was settled in position in front of the television before 11am. I always felt a mild tickle of satisfaction when I heard BBC's cricket coverage theme tune, *Soul Limbo* by Booker T and the MGs, playing through the TV speaker. With my mother at work, my father on British Armed Forces duty in a distant land, and my great-grandmother drifting in and out of the living room – with very little interest in watching cricket – this was often a solitary but pleasurable childhood experience.

In 1973, Zaheer Abbas was a member of the Gloucestershire team which won the Gillette Cup final v Sussex at Lord's. However, his contribution to Gloucestershire's triumph only included nine runs and one catch. A year later, I watched almost every run scored by Zaheer during his double hundred for Pakistan v England at The Oval on BBC television. Zaheer, who was one of the very few players, including Clive Lloyd and David Steele, I can recall batting while wearing glasses, scored 240 in a steady, unassuming but purposeful manner. This was an exhibition of batting by Zaheer which was easy on the eye and confirmed his status as one of my favourite batsmen.

During the 1977 Australia v England Centenary Test match at Melbourne, I was in bed struggling against sleep late at night and listening to the radio commentary on my little black radio with a withered white single earpiece. I was enthralled by the commentary, which vividly described the early stages of combat between Derek Randall, batting for England in Australia in the Melbourne heat, against an onslaught of fast-bowling from Dennis Lillee.

I willed Randall on, tucked under the covers in my bedroom in south London, to keep scoring, and then fell asleep. Randall's performance eventually provided me with a rewarding experience. I later discovered that he scored 174 and, during his innings in a characteristically eccentric manner, doffed his cap to Lillee after evading another bouncer.

During summer months spent with family in the Caribbean, I would often spend days playing cricket with assorted relatives, friends, and friends of friends. I was keen to prove that I was good enough to hold my own during any beach, street or yard cricket session. I refused to give up my wicket easily and, therefore, batted defensively. I admired the technique and dedication to accumulating runs and occupying the crease adopted by Yorkshire and England's Geoffrey Boycott. In Barbados, I was called a few names when I refused to give up my wicket. These included 'Englishman' and the more extended 'He batting like a real Englishman' which I was, strangely, pleased to hear!

In June 1973, the ninth West Indies Test tour of England began with a two-day match v Essex in Chelmsford. From 1968 to 1973,

West Indies did not win a Test series. After beating India 2-0 in a three Test series tour in 1968, they lost five series, drew two, and only won two out 31 Test matches. It was a period of very limited success. This period also included two defeats by England – home and away.

Following the home series defeat by England in 1968, there was a public outcry of disapproval across the Caribbean for captain Garry Sobers. The first three Tests were drawn and the series was deadlocked. After Sobers' generous declaration on the final day of the fourth Test in Port of Spain, Trinidad, leaving England with 215 runs to score in 165 minutes, the English seized their opportunity and claimed victory by seven wickets. England held on to win the series 1-0 after the final Test in Guyana was drawn.

Despite Sobers' catalogue of achievements and displays of individual brilliance, his declaration in Trinidad in 1968 was also not easily forgotten by some in the Caribbean diaspora in Britain. These included my father. For him, the Port of Spain declaration by Sobers produced a defeat which should have been avoided. Perhaps, this was another example of the West Indies not reaching their full potential towards the end of Sobers' captaincy.

'Sobers was a brilliant individual and you can't question that', insists Joseph 'Reds' Perreira, the veteran Guyanese cricket commentator, writer and sports administrator.

> But at the captaincy level he was a very attacking captain. Some might say he was an ultra-attacking captain. And, maybe, he wasn't patient enough to wait for things to happen. And, of course, he was so great that he, perhaps, expected others to be as good as him.

From 1968 to 1973, in addition to two series defeats by England, there was a series defeat by India at home in the Caribbean which was the first West Indies series loss to India, and two series defeats by Australia – both home and away. Both series v New Zealand were drawn – home and away. The home series v New Zealand was particularly disappointing from a West Indies perspective. All five Tests were drawn against a New Zealand team on their first tour of the Caribbean. New Zealand were widely considered to be the weakest team in international cricket. During all these Test series, bar the home series v Australia, the West Indies were captained by Garry Sobers.

The last series played by the West Indies before the 1973 tour of England was a 2-0 defeat by Australia in the Caribbean. This was Rohan Kanhai's first series as captain after he replaced Sobers. Sobers was unavailable for the start of the 1973 home series v Australia due to injury. As Sobers recovered from a knee operation, this was the first time since 1955 he was not a member of a West Indies team. His run of 39 Tests was the longest unbroken cycle of captaincy of any country in Test cricket.

Cecil Marley, the President of the West Indies Cricket Board, visited England to speak to Sobers who was still contracted to play for Nottinghamshire. There were two main reasons for the meeting between Marley and Sobers. To confirm Sobers' thoughts on who should replace him as captain and to discuss his availability for the remaining Test matches during the 1973 home series v Australia.

David Holford, his cousin, was Sobers' first choice as captain. Although Sobers was not selected for the Australia series, he considered Holford to be a better captain than himself. Holford also had considerable experience of captaining Barbados. Sobers' second choice as captain was Clive Lloyd. For Sobers, if the board were not prepared to select Lloyd for the start of the series, his third choice as captain was Rohan Kanhai. The West Indies Cricket Board decided to appoint Kanhai, the team's most senior and experienced player, as captain.

Following the 1972 five Test series in the Caribbean v New Zealand, when all the Tests finished in a draw, Lloyd was not invited to join the West Indies squad for the 1973 Australia tour of the Caribbean. Lloyd knew that his scores of 18 and five in the last Test v New Zealand in Trinidad had not reasserted his place in the minds of the West Indies selectors. However, this did not prevent him from being frustrated at not being selected.

Lloyd would now have to fund his trip from Britain to the Caribbean and fight for a place in the West Indies team with eye-catching performances in the regional first-class Shell Shield tournament. Under a cloud of disillusionment, Lloyd had accepted a contract to play grade cricket in Australia for the South Melbourne Club – as a replacement for Tony Greig.

A Lloyd century at Lord's, which powered Lancashire towards victory in the 1972 Gillette Cup final, caught the eye of the West Indies selectors. Lloyd was asked to be a standby, if Sobers was unavailable, for the home series v Australia. When Lloyd was in Australia playing for South Melbourne, it took the considerable influence of Forbes Burnham, the Prime Minister of Guyana, and Gough Whitlam, the Prime Minister of Australia, to release Lloyd from his contract. So, Lloyd could travel to the Caribbean via Britain to confirm his availability for the West Indies.

Lloyd's passage from Britain to the Caribbean was sponsored by the Guyanese government. He felt some unease about what could have been viewed as political interference, which supported his return to the Caribbean. Despite this, the journey for Lloyd was eventually worthwhile. After being disappointed to miss out on the first two Tests v Australia, he was selected for the last three. Lloyd scored a first innings century in the fourth Test at Bourda, his home ground in Georgetown. The Test ended in a 10-wicket defeat for the West Indies and was watched by Forbes Burnham and other Caribbean government representatives gathered for a summit in Guyana.

Sobers eventually declared himself fit to play in the second Test in Barbados. What then gradually developed was a temporary breakdown in the relationships between Sobers and Jeffrey Stollmeyer, a West Indies selector and Clyde Walcott, the West Indies team manager. Stollmeyer and Walcott were not entirely convinced that Sobers was fit and match ready. Sobers insisted that he was.

After deciding not to play for Barbados v Australia and in a two-day practice match in St.Vincent, Sobers was not selected for the rest of the series. The question on the minds of many cricket supporters in Britain, West Indian and English alike, was whether Sobers would make a re-appearance for the West Indies in England later in 1973.

Weeks before Kanhai's first Test as captain in Jamaica, the first in a five Test series v Australia, the island hosted one of 1973's major international boxing events. George Foreman and Joe Frazier fought out a world heavyweight boxing contest in the National Stadium in Kingston. The fight also became known as the 'Sunshine Showdown'. Both fighters were undefeated coming in to the fight, but the estimated 36,000 crowd in the National Stadium did not witness a lengthy and hard fought contest. Foreman knocked out Frazier in the second round.

A new undisputed world heavyweight champion was crowned in Kingston, Jamaica in January 1973.

Kanhai, despite leading the West Indies to a series home defeat v Australia, had made West Indies cricket history. He became the first Guyanese and first Indian-Caribbean to be appointed captain for a full Test series. Kanhai was also the first Guyanese player to be appointed captain since 1930, when Maurice Fernandes led the West Indies to their first Test victory v England in Georgetown.

The 1973 tour of England would be a serious examination for a West Indies team going through a very lean period. They had to reverse a substantial period of decline to register success in England for the first time in seven years. In 1973, as in their previous tour of England in 1969, the West Indies would share a summer of international cricket with New Zealand. In 1969, the West Indies played their Test matches in advance of that year's England v New Zealand Test series. In 1973, there was a role reversal in terms of the tour schedule in England. New Zealand arrived to play three Test matches v England in advance of the three Test England v West Indies series.

The West Indies squad for the 1973 tour was led by Rohan Kanhai (captain) with Lance Gibbs as vice-captain. Gibbs was also the West Indies vice-captain during their previous tour to England in 1969. Kanhai would become the first Guyanese to lead the West Indies on tour in England.

The rest of the squad included Stephen Camacho (Guyana), Roy Fredericks (Guyana), Alvin Kallicharan (Guyana), Clive Lloyd (Guyana) – who was also appointed as a tour selector and a member of the tour committee, Keith Boyce (Barbados), Vanburn Holder (Barbados), David Murray (Barbados), Grayson Shillingford (Dominica), Maurice Foster (Jamaica), Lawrence Rowe (Jamaica), Inshan Ali (Trinidad), Bernard Julien (Trinidad), Deryck Murray (Trinidad), and Elquemedo Willett (St. Kitts and Nevis). Esmond Kentish (Jamaica) was the team manager and Glendon Gibbs (Guyana) – who was related to Lance Gibbs – was the assistant-manager. Kentish and Glendon Gibbs were both former West Indian Test players.

Elquemedo Willett, a left-arm spin bowler from Nevis, was the first cricketer from the Leeward Islands to represent the West Indies. Willett made his debut for the West Indies in the second Test match of the 1973 series v Australia in Barbados. However, he was unable to break into the first team and play for the West Indies during the Test series in England. Garry Sobers was not selected for the tour matches due to his knee injury, but he declared himself available for the three Test matches.

During the 1973 tour, a group of the more senior and experienced members of the squad formed the West Indian Players Association (WIPA). The first WIPA committee members were Lance Gibbs, Rohan Kanhai, Deryck Murray and Garry Sobers. 'There was not a lot of consideration given to the thoughts of the players, and the terms and conditions of the players as professionals', insists Deryck Murray.

We felt that there was a need, particularly, in terms of the way our cricket was developing, for us as professional players to express our views and not be victimised. The Professional Cricketers' Association (PCA) had been formed in England and we felt that we should have a branch similar to that in the Caribbean. So, we discussed it, started it and formalised it to have regular contact with the board. So that if any of the players spoke to the Board secretary, for example, it wouldn't be taken as being out of line.

Throughout the 1970s, 1980s and beyond, WIPA continued to establish itself as the sole representative organisation for all players selected for the nation state and West Indies teams. In future years, Kanhai would also serve WIPA as the organisation's President.

In 1973, Andrew Carnegie was a schoolboy in south London preparing for school-leaving exams. He was also one of the many West Indians in Britain looking forward to the West Indies tour of England.

I remember the 1973 tour very well as it was Dickie Bird's introduction into international cricket umpiring. My father left England, temporarily, in late 1971 to go to America but came back in May '73 in order to follow the West Indies tour! He went to the matches in London, but I followed everything by watching on television and listening to the radio. I wanted to see Sobers play in his last tour of England and watch Lawrence

Rowe who, you could say, was the new kid on the block. I'd heard a lot about him as he scored a double hundred and a hundred on his debut.

In 1972, Lawrence Rowe scored 214 runs in his first innings and 100 in his second innings on debut v New Zealand to the delight of his home crowd in Jamaica. Without question, Rowe was an exciting prospect at the top of the West Indies batting order. Many cricket aficionados, both West Indian and English, wanted to see Rowe perform in England. Towards the end of the 1970s, Jah Thomas, a Jamaican reggae DJ and producer, was the lead vocalist on a record called *Cricket, Lovely Cricket.* The song was partly inspired by Lord Kitchener's 1950 *Victory Test Match* chorus line. Thomas' song paid homage to the Sabina Park cricket ground in Kingston, Jamaica and the cricketing prowess of two Jamaican players, Michael Holding and Lawrence 'Yagga' Rowe.

In 1973, there was disappointment for Andrew Carnegie and West Indian supporters looking forward to seeing how Rowe would perform in England. In the third West Indies v Australia Test in Trinidad in March 1973, Rowe twisted his ankle in the field after trying to stop an off-drive by Ian Chappell. He was carried off the field, injured and in pain, by Maurice Foster and Clive Lloyd. Rowe was now unable to play in the Test matches v England due to an ankle ligament injury. But he did make appearances in some of the tour matches. In the following year v England in Barbados, Rowe became only the second West Indies batsman, after Garry Sobers, to score a Test match triple century.

There would soon be opportunities for cricket followers in England to see Rowe play. Earlier in 1973, Rowe agreed to a three-year contact to play for Derbyshire. Although, during his first season in English domestic cricket due to qualification reasons, he was restricted to playing only for Derbyshire's second eleven team.

Stephen Camacho was in the frame to open with Roy Fredericks during the 1973 tour and, therefore, be part of an all-Guyanese opening partnership. Camacho's family history was strongly connected to the development of cricket in Guyana and the Caribbean in the late 19th and early 20th century. G.C Learmond, Camacho's maternal grandfather, captained Spartan Cricket Club in Barbados and played for Barbados, British Guiana, and Trinidad in inter-colonial cricket.

Learmond also represented the West Indies during the 1900 and 1906 tours of England.

Camacho and Fredericks were the opening pair for the last two Tests during the 1969 England tour. The pair arrived in 1973 after being top of the batting averages for Guyana during their first Shell Shield championship win. However, Camacho's 1973 tour came to a painful end during a three-day, pre-Test tour fixture v Hampshire at Southampton. A match which coincided with England's second 1973 Test v New Zealand at Lord's. The first four West Indies players in the batting order selected v Hampshire were Guyanese – Roy Fredericks, Stephen Camacho, Rohan Kanhai and Clive Lloyd.

Hampshire selected some of their younger cricketers versus the West Indies. For some of these young players, this was an ideal opportunity to impress the Hampshire hierarchy and, in turn, make a name for themselves against the tourists. One of these players was Andy Roberts from Antigua.

In 1973, Roberts was a young cricketer from Antigua attempting to carve out a professional cricket career playing for the Hampshire second team. A year earlier, Roberts and Viv Richards arrived in England from Antigua to attend coaching sessions at the Alf Gover cricket school in Wandsworth, south London. The trip to England was organised and paid for by a group called the Antigua Voluntary Coaching Committee. The group raised funds for Roberts and Richards to make the journey to England and improve their cricket skills by organising barbecues, second hand sales and dances in Antigua. Roberts made his Test debut for the West Indies v England in Barbados, within nine months on from his debut for Hampshire v West Indies at Southampton.

For Viv Richards, 1973 was a landmark year in his cricket learning curve and career development in England. Just over two months before Roberts' appearance for Hampshire v West Indies, Richards played his first competitive match on English soil for the Lansdown Cricket Club, Bath. The match was at a ground in the English Somerset seaside town of Weston-super-Mare. Richards announced his arrival in English cricket by scoring a half century. His innings also included a couple of sixes hit on, what he later described as, a pudding of a pitch!

For Richards, the presence of Roberts in the team was an inspirational force that propelled him towards being the next Antiguan to play for the West Indies. The regular selection of Roberts and Richards from Antigua for the West Indies helped to increase the pan-Caribbean representative spectrum of the team.

Nineteen months on from his first appearance in England for Lansdown, and months following the Test debut of Andy Roberts, Richards made his debut for the West Indies v India alongside Gordon Greenidge, another Test match debutant, in Bangalore. Richards and Greenidge experienced contrasting fortunes with the bat against the challenge set by India's high-class spin bowling attack of Bhagwath Chandrasekhar, Erapalli Prasanna and Srinivas Venkataraghavan (Venkat).

Richards scored four and three in each innings in Bangalore. Greenidge made an impressive start to his Test career, after the disappointment of not being selected for the 1973 West Indies tour of England, with scores of 93 and a debut century (107). In the next Test match in Delhi, Richards demonstrated his emerging talent and promise, which had prompted the West Indies selectors to pick him. Richards produced an outstanding 192 not out, and a memorable display of fielding, which included two excellent catches at short leg.

Back to Southampton, 1973. During the West Indies second innings v Hampshire, Andy Roberts bowled a delivery that struck Camacho in the face and inflicted a serious injury. Camacho was unable to continue batting and was forced to retire hurt on his score of 6. He was led from the field with broken glasses and blood pouring from his face. He was soon withdrawn from the West Indies squad for the rest of the 1973 tour. Following this injury, Camacho didn't play another Test match for the West Indies. A month away from the first Test at The Oval, the West Indies were now forced to search for a replacement to open the innings.

'The incident in Southampton really upset Stephen because he had a good domestic season (in the Caribbean), was on top form, and looking forward to scoring more runs with Freddo (Roy Fredericks). Stephen and Freddo were partners and close friends and were expected to give the West Indies strong starts in the tour', says Brian Camacho – a cousin of Stephen who is based in Trinidad. Alongside his career as an architect, Brian worked semi-professionally as a photographer and writer. He covered several West Indies series for a variety of outlets, including newspapers in India and St. Lucia.

Andy Roberts was fresh and new, and Stephen was a compulsive hooker. It was quite late in the evening and it was dark. I remember Jeffrey Stollmeyer (former West Indies Test cricketer, who was a team selector and future President of the WICB) telling me that number one – Stephen should not have been hooking and number two – they should not have been bowling fast bowlers when it was almost dark. The ball flew off the bat, fractured the bone just below Stephen's right eye socket, and a piece of the bone was sent a little bit inward. Surgeons in the hospital in Southampton operated on him, but it didn't heal, and he couldn't stop the eye from running. A year later, Stephen went to Jamaica and had more surgery, and the Jamaican surgeon was able to put the eye socket bone back in place, which had been sent inward. When this healed, Stephen's eye was perfect again.

Gordon Greenidge was the other West Indian playing for Hampshire that day, in a match the West Indies won comfortably by 174 runs. It was the first West Indies victory during the 1973 tour. Gordon was looking forward to this match after being ignored by the West Indies selectors. During the match v West Indies, Gordon produced two low scores of nine in Hampshire's first innings and 13 in the second innings.

Understandably, Greenidge still considered himself worthy of selection for the West Indies, especially with five scores of 50 or more during the English domestic season so far. This included an impressive innings of 196 not out v Yorkshire at Headingley. Geoff Greenidge, his namesake and fellow Barbadian, was also considered to be in the frame as a possible replacement for Camacho.

The West Indian selectors did not pick a Greenidge. Instead, they decided to select Ron Headley from Worcestershire to join the tour. Headley was now the main contender to open the batting with Roy Fredericks. Vanburn Holder, the fast-medium pace bowler from Barbados, was the other Worcestershire player in the West Indies squad.

For some, at the age of 34, the selection of Ron Headley was a surprise pick, but Ron was a seasoned professional with years of experience of playing in English conditions and on English pitches. Ron had represented Jamaica but had not played Test cricket. As Ron remembers, 'It was emotional for me to be finally selected to play my first Test match for my country. But why did I have to wait until 1973 when I was 34? It wasn't as if I was a youngster!'

And let's face it. If Steve Camacho had not been injured, I probably wouldn't have played. People still ask me the question, 'Why didn't I play for the West Indies earlier?' It's a great question but I just can't answer it. Especially during the period when the West Indies were always short of opening batsmen. In my opinion, I should have been playing for the West Indies in the '60s.

Clayton Goodwin, writer, journalist and author of *Caribbean cricketers: From the Pioneers to Packer,* and *West Indians at the Wicket,* interviewed Ron just before he was selected as a replacement for Camacho.

I saw Ron play for the first time in the early 1960s for Worcestershire v Essex at Leyton in August 1961 and I thought that his right shoulder was too far over to the offside when he batted. But he proved me wrong by hitting the top score of 67! That was just my opinion. But Ron was good enough to play for the West Indies, and he had the experience in English conditions, which was a definite advantage, and he did eventually come through. So, I was very pleased for Ron. But I was surprised when he got selected for the 1973 team because I thought that at 34 years old his chance had passed him by.

According to Reds Perreira, the selection of Ron Headley was, in the circumstances, a sensible one.

Ron was a good player, had a good career at Worcestershire, and he knew English conditions and a lot about the England players. The tour had already started, so instead of having to get someone selected from the Caribbean and up to England, it was a common-sense decision by the board to bring Ron into the team.

Ron Headley is the son of George Headley and was born in Jamaica in 1939. Ron arrived in England in 1953 with his father and Lindy, his brother. Lindy was another member of the Headley family who excelled at sport and represented Jamaica as a sprinter in the 1964 Olympics in Tokyo. Teddy Saunders, a cousin of the Headley family, represented Jamaica at football as a goalkeeper.

As a young man growing up in England, playing cricket and talking about cricket was a constant activity in the Headley household. West Indian cricketers were regular visitors to Headley's home and Ron decided at a young age that he wanted to be a professional cricketer. 'Growing up with my dad, many of the players would come to the house and so I knew these people. Sir Frank Worrell was my dad's cousin. But Frank didn't want the burden of being known as the cousin of George Headley, and very few people knew this because we all kept it quiet', Ron recalls.

So, Frank Worrell was simply Uncle Frank. Therefore, I was privileged at such a young age to meet them. But to me the so-called stars, and of course they were stars in their own right as cricketers, were just like my mum and dad. I was never stage struck but, of course, as a youngster I admired all of them because they were all great players for the West Indies. I don't know a time when I didn't want to play cricket for a living and I can't remember a day in my life, growing up as a youngster, when cricket was not the main focus of my life.

Ron persisted in his attempts to carve out a career as cricketer, despite his father's deep reservations and attempts to dissuade him. 'Dad didn't put any pressure on me to play cricket because he didn't want me to play cricket', Ron explains.

Dad always stressed the importance of education. He always told me to forget about cricket and thinking about playing cricket for a living. Dad was fortunate enough to have travelled to different countries through cricket and that was one of the best ways of being educated, because you mixed with different people at different levels in different countries. But for me, he stressed the importance of a formal education and wanted me to be an electrical or a mechanical engineer. When I was 15, my dad went back to Jamaica to be head coach. The rest of the family went back to Jamaica with him and I stayed here (in

England) to study and live with an adopted uncle. Before that, dad played his cricket in the Lancashire League with Haslingden and Bacup, and with Dudley in the Birmingham League for about four seasons. Midway through that period at Dudley, Dad also had an arrangement that he could also play league matches for a local team, the Ross-on-Wye cricket club. When I became 17, I played in the Dudley team my dad played for and won the Birmingham League with them. I also remember when I was about 14; I played in the Sunday team, Ross-on-Wye, that dad played in. So, I played with him on one or two occasions. On one occasion, I actually outscored him! So, you can imagine that I felt good because, thinking about it now, I played above my years.

In 1958, at the age of 15, Ron begged his father to let him sign for Worcestershire. George eventually agreed to let Ron accept the offer and become a professional cricketer for the county. Ron's prowess with the bat contributed to a golden period for Worcestershire cricket in the 1960s. Worcestershire won their first County Championship title in 1964. Worcestershire followed this ground-breaking success with another Championship win in 1965.

The Worcestershire team contained a group of cricketers described by Ron as 'serious players' including Basil D'Oliveira, Jack Flavell, Norman Gifford, Tom Graveney – who recommended Basil D'Oliveira to Worcestershire, and Don Kenyon, the club captain. All these cricketers were, or would be, England Test players. The South African born D'Oliveira made his Test debut during the 1966 England v West Indies series. According to Ron, 'We had a super team at Worcestershire then and we would have beaten a lot of Test sides'.

Throughout the 1960s and into the 1970s, the West Indies selectors ignored Ron as he steadily developed his career on the English county cricket circuit as a forceful left-handed batsman. In 1972, Worcestershire granted Ron Headley a benefit year and a 1973 edition of the *Cricketer* magazine reported that 'RGA Headley of Worcestershire will receive £10,014 from his benefit – £2,128 more than the previous highest for the county (TW Graveney in 1969)'. [1]

During the months leading up to the 1973 England v West Indies series, Ron Headley and Gordon Greenidge had a few things in common. Following Stephen Camacho's injury at Southampton, they were both opening batsmen playing for English county sides, and in contention to be selected for the West Indies. They were also both qualified to play cricket for England. According to Ron, during the 1960s, both West Indies and England selectors looked at him with a view to selecting him to play Test cricket.

Rothmans (a British tobacco company) had an arrangement with the England cricket set-up that every winter a team called the Cavaliers would tour Jamaica and Barbados made up of potential young England players and old England players. I went on two such trips because I was invited to go. On the trips that I went on, I was with players like Keith Fletcher and Alan Knott who, like me, were youngsters. Because someone like me was selected to play alongside a lot of English guys out in the Caribbean, and I was only 19 or 20 at the time, I knew England were looking at me. After Worcestershire won the championship in 1964, we went on a world tour. So, I couldn't play for the (Rothmans Cavaliers) team in Barbados, but I did play in the match in Jamaica. When I was in Jamaica, Gerry Alexander, who was then a West Indies selector, didn't leave my side. After the match, he said to me, 'Ron, I didn't know you could bat like that'. So I turned around to him and said, 'What do you think I've been doing in England all these years!' If England had selected me to play for them, I would have said yes, because I wouldn't have said no to playing Test cricket. But at the same token, England knew where my heart was, and it was with the West Indies. Therefore, at the end of the day, when they (the England selectors) assessed it, their bottom line was that I played too many shots. They felt that an English batsman had to play cricket in a certain way, and I played like a West Indian. Whilst that might have been admired in certain quarters, that didn't work in a conservative cricket English set-up, and that's something I always knew.

Camacho, who Ron Headley was selected to replace, was one of six Guyanese players in the original 1973 squad of 16 to tour England. Camacho's omission from the squad through injury reduced the

Guyanese contingent in the series to five players. However, this was still the largest contingent of players from Guyana to tour England as part of a West Indies squad with a Guyanese captain – Rohan Kanhai, vice-captain – Lance Gibbs and the next captain – Clive Lloyd. From a Guyanese perspective, this was a rare occurrence. One of the few times it happened was in the Caribbean in 1962 when five Guyanese – Lance Gibbs, Rohan Kanhai, Ivor Mendonca, Joe Solomon, and Charlie Stayers were all selected for the West Indies during the five Test series v India.

There were a few other significant reasons why 1973 was a landmark year for Guyanese cricket. In 1973, before the Australian tour in the Caribbean, Kanhai displayed his captaincy credentials by leading Guyana to their first regional Shell Shield, four-day title. This victory, ahead of Barbados, Jamaica, Trinidad and the Combined Islands, occurred during a period when the first-class season in the Caribbean was highly competitive and highly respected internationally.

Guyana ensured their first Shell Shield success after their final match v Trinidad in Berbice ended in a draw. Lance Gibbs was the leading wicket taker during the series and 1973 was a year of milestone achievements for him. At Sabina Park, Jamaica, Gibbs also passed Garry Sobers' record of 215 wickets for the West Indies during the Test v Australia. This was another personal achievement passed on his way to being the first spin bowler to take 300 Test wickets.

The steady rise in Guyana's contribution to the development of West Indies cricket from the mid-1950s onwards, which reached one of its major peaks in 1973, was a concrete example of the enduring legacy of Clyde Walcott's work in Guyana between 1954 and 1970. Walcott remembers his time living and working in Guyana as one of the most satisfying periods of his life.

Alongside most of the colonial territories in the Caribbean islands, Guyana's main export crop was sugar. Clyde Walcott, the West Indies team manager for the tours to England either side of 1973, the 1969 tour and the inaugural World Cup tournament in 1975, was employed by the Sugar Producers Association (SPA). The SPA was a group of British companies responsible for producing sugar for Guyana's export market. Walcott was invited to organise and develop cricket in Guyana's sugar plantations.

Jock Campbell, the head of Bookers, which owned the majority of the sugar plantations in Guyana, was instrumental in creating the opportunity for Walcott to carry out his work. The sugar plantations were in several areas across Guyana. This included the Berbice region, across the east and west Coast, and up and down the east and west bank of the Demerara river.

Another important part of Walcott's remit was to improve the quality and impact of Guyana's cricket in regional competitions. A positive by product of this project, if it resulted in progress and success, would be to guide and promote more cricketers towards the attention of the Guyanese and West Indies selectors. Towards the end of the 1950s, apart from Robert Christiani, Bruce Pairaudeau, John Trim and Clifford McWatt, there were very few Guyanese players who played a significant number of Tests for the West Indies.

In 1948 in Delhi, India, Christiani became the first Guyanese cricketer to score a Test century for the West Indies. Two years later in 1950, Christiani was the only Guyanese member of the victorious squad of 16 players which toured England. After his retirement, Christiani was also employed by Bookers and played a supporting role to Walcott during his work in the sugar plantations in the 1950s. Joe Solomon joined Walcott as a cricket organiser in the early 1960s.

By the 1950s, unless you played club cricket in Georgetown, it was still unlikely you would be selected to represent Guyana. This was a major obstacle for players outside Georgetown, including Berbice, with ambitions to play for Guyana and the West Indies. John Trim was the first cricketer from Berbice to play for the West Indies. Trim made his Test debut v England at Bourda, Georgetown in 1948. Years before the Berbicians who emerged and made an impact on Guyanese and West Indies cricket in the 1950s and 1960s.

In his autobiography, *Sixty Years on the Back Foot*, Walcott outlined his experience, with examples, of coming to terms with working in a new and challenging environment.

I had to organise the clubs and the competitions and advise on improving facilities, persuading the owners to put down concrete pitches in the outlying areas that would survive the harsh climate. New grounds were built, and such was the enthusiasm of the Indian population that immense strides were made in a very short time. There were several clubs on each estate and I decided to have them amalgamated into one club. If there were any disputes, I had to resolve them, and I remember one funny incident when a club protested that a game had finished too early. I invited the umpire who made the decision in to see me and asked him what time he called a halt. 'Five-thirty, sir,' he said. 'Did you have a watch?' I asked him. 'No, sir, but the train usually passes at five-thirty', he said. I was not sure how he knew it was on time![2]

In addition to his work as a cricket coach and organiser, Walcott also captained the Guyana national team in 13 first-class matches. His record as captain included six victories and five draws. In 1958, Walcott scored his last Test century for the West Indies v Pakistan at Bourda, Georgetown. In 1970, he was awarded the Golden Arrow of Achievement Award for his contribution to cricket in Guyana.

According to Walcott, despite the recognition for developing cricket in Guyana, there were some Guyanese who were uncomfortable that a Barbadian was appointed as Guyana's team cricket. Despite this, the majority of those concerned with the development of cricket in Guyana continued to support Walcott's work. Perhaps, being a Barbadian and not Guyanese was a positive attribute for Walcott to have in Guyana.

'Because Clyde Walcott was not Guyanese, in some ways, this made it easier for him to be accepted by the various groups in Guyana. Clyde Walcott was an outsider, he was a Barbadian, and he was much more diplomatic in the way he handled everything', suggests Professor Clem Seecharan. He wrote an award-winning book, *Sweetening Bitter Sugar: Jock Campbell – The Booker Reformer in British Guiana 1934-1966*, about Jock Campbell's role in shaping Guyana towards the end of its years under British colonial rule.

What Clyde Walcott did was to go on to these plantations and, at the same time, you had the creation of a lot of community centres. These centres were very important because you didn't just have cricket, but you had small libraries that were being created, sewing classes and cooking – so people could cook and eat nutritious food. Jock Campbell was a man with enormous foresight who realised that these things were very important for the people living in these communities. If it wasn't for the initiative of the SPA, and if it wasn't for Clyde Walcott, we probably would never have heard of Basil Butcher, Rohan Kanhai, Joe Solomon, Ivan Madray and later on – Roy Fredericks and Alvin Kallicharan. All these were guys from Guyana who played for the West Indies and came out of the sugar plantations. Every time you raise this issue with people who come from the Corentyne area in Guyana, they can name about 10 or 15 other people who preceded these cricketers, and who they thought were worthy enough to represent Guyana at some point. But they came from the backwoods and nobody went with any torchlight looking for them at all. So, it took somebody like Clyde Walcott with a torchlight. Who went out there and said, look we have got people here who are just as good, if not better, than the guys you have playing for the clubs in Georgetown. And that was the context of how these cricketers emerged in Guyana after the Second World War.

In 1973, Basil Butcher and Joe Solomon were both offered honorary life membership of the MCC. Of the six Guyanese players selected to tour England with the West Indies in 1973, three of the players selected were from Berbice – Roy Fredericks, Alvin Kallicharan and Rohan Kanhai. Three of the players were from Georgetown – Stephen Camacho, Lance Gibbs and Clive Lloyd. This represented an ethnic, regional and social cross section of Guyanese people with African, Indian and Portuguese heritage.

If Kanhai's suitability for captaincy on the 1973 tour was principally based on knowledge and experience of playing in English conditions, he was an ideal choice. From the late 1950s and throughout the 1960s, Kanhai played for Aberdeenshire in the Scottish League, Milnrow and Blackpool in the Lancashire League, and Ashington Cricket Club in the Northumberland County League. Newcastle is the nearest major city to Ashington.

Kanhai's impact at Ashington was significant enough for a pub to be named after him. The Rohan Kanhai Pub is a popular drinking establishment in Ashington and no more than a 10-minute walk from the cricket ground. There are a few pictures of Kanhai on the walls of the pub, with information about his cricket career printed on the pub's food menus.

In 1973, Tim Cooke and his brother were looking forward to travelling to Lord's and buying tickets for the England v West Indies Test. This was the last Test of the series and Rohan Kanhai's last Test in England. In the 1950s, Tim was a young schoolboy whose introduction to cricket was watching matches at Ashington Cricket Club. When Tim got a bit older, he sometimes helped work the scoreboard at Ashington, pulling the big canvass rollers around, and watching Kanhai play for the club in the Northumberland County League. 'I think Rohan Kanhai was probably the first person who I saw, in the flesh, who wasn't white, and I remember him playing for Ashington', Tim thoughtfully recalls.

This was in the 1950s and seeing someone like Rohan Kanhai in Ashington was quite a rare sight. I was about six or seven years old and, looking back, I think it was probably quite brave of him to venture into darkest Northumberland in those days. And to think that he is so warmly remembered there now, including a pub in Ashington which is named after him.

The edition of the BBC *Radio Times* magazine, available for viewers and listeners just before the start of the Test series, promoted its coverage of 1973 tour with a front cover picture of Kanhai backed by seven West Indies players. The fact that this edition of the *Radio Times* magazine was dominated by a group of sportsmen from the Caribbean of African, Indian and Portuguese descent made it a unique cover image in 1970s Britain.

Captain Kanhai is pictured in front of his players kneeling on one bended knee. He has a bat in his right hand and a ball gripped in his left hand. Kanhai is smiling, in good spirits, and ready to lead from the front to claim victory on English soil. The other members of the West Indies team pictured from left to right are Inshan Ali, Maurice Foster, Elquemedo Willett, Grayson Shillingford, Lawrence Rowe, Stephen Camacho and David Murray.

It's probably safe to assume that this picture was taken before the start of the tour. Stephen Camacho withdrew from the squad after the tour match v Hampshire through injury. Rowe, due to injury, only played in some of the tour matches. Willett, Shillingford and David Murray were also not selected for the Test series. So only three of the West Indian players pictured – Kanhai, Inshan and Foster – played in the Tests.

The promotional text across the centre of the picture attempted to excite BBC viewers and listeners with the prospect of the 'carnival atmosphere of Test cricket in Barbados – now at the Oval, where England face the West Indies in the first Test.' Available to view on BBC1 and BBC2 and to listen on BBC Radio 3. The BBC television commentary team was Richie Benaud, Denis Compton and Jim Laker. A strong line-up of distinguished ex-Australian and English Test cricketers, introduced by the dapper, debonair and slightly upper-crust, Peter West.

Benaud's first stint as a BBC television commentator, working with Brian Johnston and Peter West, was the 1963 England v West Indies series. I particularly liked the contrast of listening to Benaud's sharp and occasionally whimsical Australian accent. Combined with Laker's engaging, and almost fatherly, Yorkshire accented vocal delivery.

Late on Saturday night, as scheduled in the *Radio Times*, after the third day's play at The Oval, BBC1 viewers could tune in to *The Spinners – go International* show. Singers from around the world were organised to welcome The Spinners back home to Liverpool, where the group were formed, at the end of their 1973 British tour.

The Spinners were a four-man, family entertainment folk group. My great-grandmother enjoyed humming or singing along to The Spinners whenever they appeared on television. The Spinners also had their own show on BBC1. In 1973, their series of television shows celebrated its fourth anniversary. One of The Spinners was a bespectacled Cuban born Jamaican singer called Cliff Hall. During the early to mid-1970s, Hall was one of the most regularly watched West Indian entertainers on British television.

On Monday night, after the fourth day's play at The Oval, following the traditional Test match rest day on a Sunday, BBC1 viewers could also relish the prospect of watching the *Charlie Williams Show*. Williams was a Yorkshire born comedian with a Barbadian father and an English mother. His father was a merchant seaman who also served with the Royal Engineers in the First World War.

At school, Williams played for the cricket team and was captain of the athletics squad. But it was his ability as a footballer that captured the attention of a collection of clubs who offered him trials. Williams spent four months on trial at Leeds United before signing for Doncaster Rovers. During the years following the Second World War, he made a career for himself as one of the very few non-white players in English professional football. From 1948 to 1959, Williams made 171 appearances as a centre-half for Doncaster Rovers.

Williams became more of a nationwide household name in Britain after his football career ended. He pursued a career as an entertainer and developed a comedy act which earned him a reasonable living in the working men's clubs, theatres and cabaret across the north of England. By 1973, Williams became one of the first non-white comedians on British television to achieve mainstream success.

I can clearly recall watching Williams perform on *The Comedians*, a show on Sundays on ITV. *The Comedians* featured performances by a collection of stand-up comedians. Williams had a unique act based on being a mixed-race man with a broad Yorkshire accent telling 1970s style comedy club jokes. As a family, we may have been uncomfortable with some of the racist humour Williams turned against himself, which helped to increase his popularity. Despite this, what also made Williams compulsive viewing for us was that his father was Barbadian. There was nothing like a clearly identifiable Caribbean connection to someone on television to immediately capture our attention.

On this Monday night special edition of the *Charlie Williams Show* in 1973, one of the special guests was Sacha Distel. I was mildly fascinated by Distel as he was the only identifiably French person who appeared on British light entertainment television. Distel was a suave and handsome crooner with an obvious, and somewhat cartoon, Gallic charm and sense of romance.

My mother would sometimes insist, when we watched Distel's performances on television, that he possessed a rather high opinion of himself. 'He thinks he's God's gift to women' my mother would occasionally remark. Distel was also a notable guest on some of the *Seaside Special* shows on BBC1. *Seaside Special* was a popular variety entertainment show filmed at various British seaside resorts during the 1970s. As a family, we often sat in our living room and enjoyed watching *Seaside Special* on Saturday evenings.

Cy Grant arrived in Britain from Guyana during the Second World War to join the RAF, and later become a barrister. Grant also experienced a degree of success as an actor and entertainer on television, film and stage. During the late 1950s, he became the first black person to appear regularly on British television on the BBC's *Tonight* programme. *Tonight* discovered that calypso was an ideal vehicle for humorous commentary on the daily cycle of news and current affairs. So, Grant was often invited to perform witty and observant calypsos on a particular item of news. This made Grant a well-known television personality in Britain for Caribbean and non-Caribbean people alike.

By 1973, Clyde Best, Cliff Hall, Johnny Kwango and Charlie Williams, people who I've referred to in previous pages. Alongside the singer, Shirley Bassey (who was one of my mother's favourite performers), born and raised in Wales to a Nigerian father and a British mother, Don Mitchell, Nichelle Nichols – who played Lieutenant Uhura in *Star Trek*, and the Trinidadian actor, Rudolph Walker, were some of the personalities in the 1970s who I derived a sense of inspiration from. They were part of a small crop of black and mixed-race performers I could watch on British television.

On Saturday nights we usually huddled around the television to watch *A Man Called Ironside*, an American detective series. Raymond Burr was the lead actor who played the show's central figure, Robert T Ironside, a paraplegic detective. Ironside was the first character who was a wheelchair user that I saw on British television. Each week, Ironside faced the challenge of solving a grisly crime. We were always thrilled to see Mark Sanger, Ironside's black afro-haired colleague played by Don Mitchell, appear on screen. Mark was a member of Ironside's team who, as well as being his assistant and bodyguard, often had the responsibility of pushing Ironside around in his wheelchair.

Rudolph Walker starred in a 1970s television comedy series called *Love Thy Neighbour*, which featured a pair of married couples, one white British and one black Caribbean. The couples lived next door to each other in an outer London suburb. The men worked together in the same factory. Most of the comedy in *Love Thy Neighbour* was based on the racial hostility between the two men, featuring a flurry of racist insults, fist-shaking, relentless conflict and one-upmanship.

Eddie Booth, the white male neighbour from Manchester, was played by Jack Smethurst. Bill Reynolds, the black neighbour from Trinidad, was played by Rudolph Walker. One of the other major causes of antagonism between the two men was their political differences. Eddie was a trade union leader at their factory, and a supporter of the main opposition Labour party led by Harold Wilson. Bill was a supporter of the ruling Conservative party led by Edward Heath who, in 1973, was the British Prime Minister. Meanwhile, the two wives, with Trinidadian actress Nina Baden-Semper playing Barbie, Bill's wife, comfortably developed a friendship with each other. As well as being friends, the two wives were usually weary of their husbands' tiresome behaviour.

In 1973, a *Love Thy Neighbour* film was released for cinema audiences. In one scene during the film, Eddie and Bill use cricket as a vehicle to assume their superiority over each other. An England v West Indies, white v black, cricket confrontation is set up in a side street alongside the factory. Eddie is prepared to bat and, with a crate positioned as the stumps, waits for Bill to bowl. One of the Indian workers is in position as the wicket-keeper, with two West Indians in the slips. Eddie insists, as Bill prepares for a long run-up to bowl, that he is not intimidated by Bill's theatrical warming-up antics. A group of factory workers watch the action and are entertained by the thrill of confrontation.

Bill adopts a Wes Hall-style run-up and bowling action. He is intent on bowling the fastest delivery he can. Bill's first delivery thumps into a very delicate area of Eddie's body just below the waist. Eddie is not wearing a protective box and hops around in pain. Bill joyfully appeals for an LBW decision to an imaginary umpire. A few of Eddie's friends enjoy a laugh at his painful predicament.

Bill, clearly enjoying Eddie's discomfort, asks him if he wants to retire hurt. However, Eddie wants to repair his wounded pride. He takes a tin sandwich box cover from the Indian wicket-keeper's work bag. He uses this as a protective box and insists on facing another delivery. Brimming with confidence, Eddie hits Bill's next delivery in the air. The ball crashes through the windscreen of Mr Granger's car.

Mr Granger, played by Bill Fraser the popular comedy character actor, is the boss of the factory. His car was just slowing down to park behind the start of Bill's bowling run-up. Eddie is petrified of Mr Granger's reaction. Bill quickly accepts responsibility for the damage caused to the car. He delivers this favour of saving Eddie from Mr Granger's retribution for a purpose. Bill tells some of the factory workers gathered together, both black and white, that he will gain maximum satisfaction when Eddie is forced to apologise to him for taking the blame.

During the 1970s, I also experienced the emergence of Norman Beaton, a Guyanese actor, in *The Fosters*. This was a family situation comedy featuring a black Caribbean family based in London. *The Fosters* helped to introduce Lenny Henry to a wider television audience. Beaton's wife and Henry's mother was played by Isabelle Lucas, a Canadian born actress of Barbadian descent who migrated to Britain in the 1950s.

The Fosters was soon followed by the production of *Empire Road*, a soap opera/drama series written by Michael Abbensetts, a Guyanese playwright, about West Indian community life in the Birmingham/ West Midlands area of Britain. Two of the main characters in *Empire Road* were played by Norman Beaton and Rudolph Walker.

Apart from these regular sightings, when a black person appeared on television it caused a flurry of excitement in our flat. Someone would shout, 'There's a black man (or woman) on the TV!' Whoever was at home would scamper to get to the living room in time. But after a few scenes, the black actor would, inevitably, quickly disappear from the screen. Following this, there would be a short period of speculation as to whether he/she was from the Caribbean. This was based on a surname spotted during the end of programme credits.

For example, if he/she had Shillingford as a surname, you could safely bet next week's rent that he/she was from Dominica. Phone calls were then made to family and friends to share the excitement of seeing a black person on television. Therefore, by 1973, for me and many other Caribbean people in Britain, the West Indies team playing England on television, the majority of whom were players with African or Indian heritage, was a highly anticipated live event.

'Around 1973, I was living with my family in Luton on a huge council estate called Farley Hill', says Colin Grant, historian, author and broadcaster. Grant was born in Hitchin and raised in Luton with parents from Jamaica. 'There were around 2,000 families on the estate and most of the families living there were Irish with a scattering of English and half a dozen families from the Caribbean'.

As children we were more interested in football and basketball and my father was much more interested in gambling than watching cricket. But any time a black person was on the television was a cause for celebration at home. So, anytime we were watching television and the West Indies cricket team were playing, we'd watch and root for the West Indies without a shadow of doubt. We recognised the importance of cricket and that West Indian cricketers played with a certain kind of flair and ambition, compared to their English counterparts, and with a sense of Caribbean individuality. And, ordinarily, it didn't seem as if the West Indian players were always playing safe which we also admired.

Back to the edition of the *Radio Times* magazine, available for its readers just before the start of the 1973 series. Peter Gillman, a British writer and journalist, shared his experiences of watching cricket in Barbados. This was based on his visit to the West Indies v Australia Test match at the Kensington Oval, Bridgetown, in March 1973. This was the second of a five Test series in the Caribbean. Peter Gillman observed during day one of the Test.

In the players' pavilion, Kammy (Cammie) Smith, the former Barbadian opening bat, surveys the crowded stands and the open ground on the far side, rapidly filling. The crowd could go over 10,000 he guesses. There are more screams as a fielder makes an acrobatic stop. 'In England a Test Match is like a funeral', he says. 'Here, it's a carnival'.[3]

After his Test cricket experiences in Barbados, Gillman was convinced that the 'carnival atmosphere' which West Indian supporters had brought to England since the historic 1950 tour, would continue from the first 1973 Test at The Oval. Gillman's *Radio Times* article was titled, *Cricket, lovely, cricket*. By 1973, the enduring legacy of the *Victory Test Match* song by Lord Kitchener and Lord Beginner after the historic 1950 Test victory at Lord's was still evident.

During the 1970s, the significance of West Indies cricket tours for the Caribbean diaspora in Britain, whether you were a serious cricket fan or not, steadily increased in importance. The cricket ground continued to serve its purpose as an outdoor public meeting space, as well as a venue to watch cricket. Thousands of people from across the Caribbean diaspora in Britain prepared to attend the Tests in 1973 or follow the series on BBC television and/or radio.

With two Test matches in London at The Oval and Lord's, and one in Birmingham at Edgbaston, the three Tests were scheduled to be played in two cities with substantial Caribbean communities. In the areas of each ground dominated by West Indian supporters, the interaction with events on the field and with each other was guaranteed to be raucous, fun, loud, and create a boisterous atmosphere. There was plenty of fun to be had.

By 1973, as more Caribbean people had settled in Britain, there were also more opportunities for West Indian cricketers to meet family and friends during their tours of England. Some family, friends and supporters of the West Indies team organised leave from their jobs to coincide with a cricket tour. For example, back in the 1960s, Basil Butcher would often visit his sister and her husband who migrated from Guyana to Britain and settled in Crystal Palace, south London.

In 1973, for the first time, Maurice Foster met his grandfather who managed a barbershop in London. Lance Gibbs had two sisters in England who both worked as nurses. 'I had family in England', says Vanburn Holder. 'I had a brother and an uncle in London, but the Guyanese in the team seemed to have family everywhere!' Clive Lloyd had a cousin in London and was married to Waveney, a Guyanese woman from Berbice who he met in London. Some of the West Indian players contracted to play county or/and club cricket including Lloyd, Alvin Kallicharan and Deryck Murray had, or would soon have, children born in England.

On the following West Indies tour in 1976, Michael Holding was one of the few players who had not visited England. However, he still had a connection to England through the experiences of his mother. She studied in England to become a teacher and enjoyed her time in what she still called 'the mother country'.

The West Indies team to face England at The Oval in 1973 was Roy Fredericks, Ron Headley, Rohan Kanhai (captain), Clive Lloyd, Alvin Kallicharan, Deryck Murray, Garry Sobers, Bernard Julien, Keith Boyce, Inshan Ali and Lance Gibbs. It's interesting to note that five out of the top seven players in the West Indies batting order were left-handed. Kanhai and Murray were the two exceptions. Inshan Ali was the only West Indian selected for The Oval with no experience of playing county or club cricket in England.

Maurice Foster was another member of the 1973 West Indies squad who had no county or club cricket experience in England. However, during the tour, Foster received an offer to play for Kent which was supported by Colin Cowdrey.

I remember we played Kent during the 1973 tour and I scored a century, and after the game I went into the office with Colin Cowdrey. He asked me to sign a contract and said, 'Sign here!' He wanted me to play for Kent but I turned it down because at the time I was fortunate to have a good job in Jamaica. My family was there and I would have had to relocate for about three months a year in England. So, after I finally worked it all out, thinking about the stress of having my kids in England and everything else, for me it wasn't worth it. Years later, I met Colin Cowdrey in Barbados and he recognised me and said, 'You know Foster, you should have taken up that contract at Kent. Then you would have played a lot more for the West Indies!'

The England team selected for The Oval was Geoffrey Boycott, Dennis Amiss, Graham Roope, Frank Hayes, Keith Fletcher, Tony Greig, Ray Illingworth (captain), Alan Knott, John Snow, Geoff Arnold and Derek Underwood. Snow was one of the five cricketers named by *Wisden* as a cricketer of the year in 1973. Snow was the only non-Australian in the list alongside Greg Chappell, Dennis Lillee, Bob Massie and Keith Stackpole. Snow was the only player selected for the England v West Indies series to receive this annual accolade from *Wisden* in 1973.

Ray Illingworth captained England when the West Indies last toured in 1969. This was his first series as Test captain. Illingworth described England's victory v West Indies in the third and last Test of the 1969 series at Headingley, his home ground, as one of the most memorable moments of his cricket career.

In 1973, Illingworth was unable to repeat his county captaincy success during the previous year by lifting a trophy for Leicestershire. In 1972, he captained Leicestershire to victory in the Benson and

Hedges Cup final at Lord's. This was Leicestershire's first major domestic title. However, Illingworth did have one award to reflect on months before the start of the 1973 series v West Indies. Earlier in the year, Illingworth attended a ceremony at Buckingham Palace with his wife and two daughters to receive a CBE award from the Queen. This was followed by a photo session at Lord's, where he was accompanied by his family and Rachael Heyhoe-Flint, England women's cricket captain.

The only change for England from their last Test versus New Zealand at Headingley was Frank Hayes who replaced Chris Old. Therefore, the selectors were convinced that a middle-order batsman was more suited to The Oval than a fast-medium pace bowler. At The Oval, Frank Hayes prepared to make his Test debut with Ron Headley and Bernard Julien, the two debutants selected to play for the West Indies.

For Rohan Kanhai and Ray Illingworth, the success and/or failures of their teams, and the result of the series, would play a major part in deciding their immediate futures as Test captains. Would Kanhai and Illingworth, who were both approaching the end of their international careers, lead their teams against each other in the series scheduled from February to April 1974 in the Caribbean? The Test at The Oval was the first of eight consecutive England v West Indies Tests. Scheduled from July 1973 and finishing in April 1974 at The Queen's Park Oval in Trinidad.

1973 was also a breakthrough year in Harold 'Dickie' Bird's distinguished and eventful career as an international cricket umpire. During the 1970s and 1980, many cricket supporters, both English and West Indian, appreciated Bird's personality and mild eccentricities. Whenever England played the West Indies in a televised match, and there was an appeal from the West Indies to Bird to give an English batsman out, 'Come on Dickie!' would be my father's cry from the sofa. As he pleaded to Bird through the television screen to uphold the appeal. Whenever Bird umpired a match I attended or watched on TV, his presence would add considerable value to the events taking place on the field.

After leaving school, Bird joined Barnsley Football Club, his hometown club in South Yorkshire. Bird signed as an amateur player for Barnsley at the age of 15 because he wasn't old enough to sign professional forms. He played for Barnsley in the Northern Intermediate League against some of the top football clubs in the north of England including Leeds United, Newcastle United and Sheffield Wednesday. One of the footballers Bird played against was John Charles, who attained legendary status for Leeds United, Juventus and Wales.

One of the footballers Bird played with at Barnsley was Tommy Taylor, who Bird also played football with at school. Taylor went on to play for the Barnsley first team, Manchester United and England, before his tragic death in the Manchester United air crash in Munich in 1958. The accident claimed the lives of 23 people including Taylor and seven other Manchester United players.

During his time as a youngster at Barnsley Football Club, Bird also played for Barnsley Cricket Club in the Yorkshire League. The cricket club is about 30-minutes' walk away across Barnsley from the football club. After suffering a knee injury playing football, Bird weighed up his options and decided to focus his time and effort in playing cricket. 'I thought that football could be a short career, but cricket would give me longer career, and I was proved right,' Bird told me as he reminisced about his career choices as a young sportsman.

Bird played cricket for Barnsley as the team's professional. During his time playing for Barnsley, Bird often opened the batting with Michael Parkinson, who would become a popular and well-known journalist, author and television chat show host. On one occasion playing for Barnsley, Bird shared a batting partnership with a young schoolboy who was determined to succeed as a professional cricketer. Their partnership abruptly ended when Bird's batting partner hesitated to run a single. This resulted in Bird being run out. The batsman's name was Geoffrey Boycott. In Bird's debut Test as an umpire at Headingley in 1973, he witnessed Boycott at close quarters score a century for England v New Zealand during their first innings.

Bird played for his home county of Yorkshire before ending his playing career at Leicestershire. His conversion to umpiring began after a quiet drink with a fellow ex-professional cricketer who was also an MCC committee member.

One night, I was talking to John Warr, who was a fast bowler for Middlesex, and who played for England, and he said to me during a drink we were having together, 'Have you ever thought of becoming an umpire Dickie?' And I said to him, 'You must be joking. I've never given it a thought'. He said, 'No, I'm not. I think you'd make a success of it'. After we spoke, I then thought to myself, there might be something in that. So, I went home and wrote a letter to Lord's to become an umpire. The captains met, then the Test and County Cricket Board (TCCB) met just after that, and I was taken on to the first-class umpires list.

Bird umpired on the domestic county circuit for two years before his rapid rise to Test cricket. Bird's first outing as an international umpire was the 1973 England v New Zealand Test on his home ground at Headingley. This was the third and final Test of the series, which England won by an innings and one run. Bird was so excited to umpire his first Test that he arrived at Headingley well before the gates opened. 'I got to the ground very early in the morning', says Bird as he remembers his excitement.

I think I got there about six o'clock on the first day and I could not get into the ground! I didn't want to be late, so I got there early by three hours because I've always been a stickler for time. I was there before the ground staff and the people who attended the turnstiles, so I had to wait for the ground staff to open the main gates. I just sat in the football stand end in the ground, right at the back, with nobody about. I was just thinking about what might happen during the day, and that kept going in and out of my mind. But I remember my first Test in '73 went very well and I enjoyed it.

Ronald Griffiths was a popular West Indian spectator at international cricket matches in England who regularly declared that he was Geoffrey Boycott's biggest supporter. Griffiths interacted with events on and off the field by walking around the boundary edge and, whether they wanted to hear it or not, shouted out advice and commentary to players, umpires and spectators.

During the 1973 England v New Zealand Test at Headingley, Griffiths was especially critical of Bird's decision to signal a wide after a delivery by England's Chris Old. In response, Bird took off his umpire's jacket and walked over to where Griffiths was sitting. Bird then invited Griffiths to put his jacket on and replace him as umpire. This produced howls of laughter from some of the Headingley spectators.

David Constant and Tom Spencer were scheduled to stand as umpires for the first 1973 England v West Indies Test at The Oval. Bird's next Test match as an umpire would be alongside Arthur Fagg, a former England Test cricketer. Fagg's major contribution to cricket folklore was his record setting achievement playing for Kent in 1938. He became the first and last batsman to score a double-century in each innings of a first-class match. As Bird and Fagg prepared for the second England v West Indies Test in 1973, they would not have expected the drama and controversy, on and off the field, which presented them with a set of serious umpiring challenges.

Right: Rupert Hunte, a great-uncle, proudly wearing his Militia Band uniform in Georgetown, Guyana. In 1951, Rupert was the first member of my family to migrate to Britain

Below: Queen Elizabeth II and British Prime Minister, Edward Heath, attend the 'Fanfare for Europe' gala concert to celebrate Britain's entry into the EEC, 3 January 1973 (Photo by Hulton Archive/Getty Images)

CARICOM Secretariat headquarters building in Turkeyen, Guyana. CARICOM was established in 1973 (*Photo by author, 2009*)

Ian Porterfield scores the only goal in the 1973 FA Cup final for Sunderland against Leeds United (*Mandatory Credit: Allsport Hulton/Archive*)

Right: Leeds United rosette worn by a friend's brother at the 1973 FA Cup final. The rosette was given to me a few years after the final at Wembley

Below: England, take cover. Cover of Radio Times magazine (28 July to August 1973 edition). West Indies players from left to right – Inshan Ali, Maurice Foster, Elquemedo Willett, Grayson Shillingford, Lawrence Rowe, Stephen Camacho and David Murray. In front, Rohan Kanhai

Above: England v West Indies 1973 tour souvenir programme with photos of captains – Rohan Kanhai (left) and Ray Illingworth (right) – on the cover

Right: West Indies 1973 tour to England magazine cover. West Indies players from top left (clockwise) – Bernard Julien, Keith Boyce, Lance Gibbs, Rohan Kanhai, Garry Sobers, Inshan Ali. Origin unknown (*Photo kindly supplied by Shafeeza Ali-Motilal*)

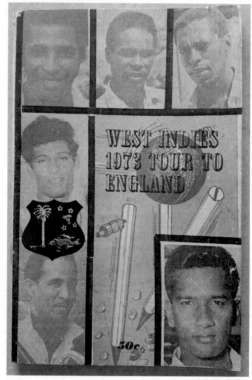

CHAPTER 9

The Women's World cup ends and build-up to the first Test continues

During the weeks leading up to the first Test at The Oval, England were considered by some to be slight favourites to win the 1973 series v West Indies. Months after their narrow 2-1 series defeat in India, England's 1973 home international summer started with a 2-0 series win v New Zealand. The New Zealanders provided England with a stiffer examination than was widely expected. According to my *1974 Playfair Cricket Annual*, England played cricket which survived in the end to win the series but, at times, they inspired little confidence.

After being widely acknowledged as the world's best team in the mid-1960s, the West Indies had not won a Test match in England since beating England at Headingley in 1966. The West Indies had not won a series since their 1966/1967 tour of India, or a single Test match since beating New Zealand in Auckland in 1969. They played 20 consecutive Tests without a victory. In addition, they suffered a 2-0 home series defeat by Australia months before the start of their 1973 England tour.

The 1973 England tour was another opportunity for the West Indies to erase the threat of long-term decay. Unlike the West Indies team which toured England in 1969, many of the 1973 team had considerable experience of playing cricket as professionals against English players in English conditions.

In 1973, 10 years on from attempting to impersonate Wes Hall in his back garden in north London, Mark Cripps was playing cricket for his school team and with school friends for Arkley Cricket Club. Mark followed cricket as closely as he could through the newspapers, the *Playfair Cricket Monthly* (which had just merged with *The Cricketer*), and BBC television and radio coverage of Test matches, Gillette Cup, Benson and Hedges Cup and the John Player League.

Like many young cricket enthusiasts in England, Mark knew just about every county side by its batting order. But he was also aware there was a crop of new faces arriving with the West Indies team in England.

It was now a time when the careers of many in that West Indies team from the 1960s – Worrell, Griffith, Hall, Sobers and others were coming to an end, or had come to an end. So, the big question was, how were they going to do and who was going to take up the mantle from those great names? This was counter-balanced by England who had all these super names, but during the 1970s they didn't always play well together as a team. So, I felt the series was in the balance but there were probably more question marks about the West Indies team than the England team, because the England team hadn't really changed. There were plenty of familiar names in the England team, give or take a few changes here and there.

EW Swanton, the cricket journalist and broadcaster, suggested on the morning of the first Test that the lower West Indies batting order would not score as many runs as the English lower order. The selection of Frank Hayes would make for a more balanced England side and improve their batting line-up. Swanton expressed concern about the West Indies ability to cope with English bowlers using the conditions to move the ball late in the air or off the pitch. However, Swanton also recognised that many West Indian players had developed a significant amount of experience of playing in England on the English county cricket circuit.

In addition, despite the West Indies series loss to Australia in the Caribbean, Swanton observed that the West Indies had been a difficult team to beat. Therefore, England would face a much more serious challenge from the West Indies compared to the New Zealanders earlier on in the summer of 1973. Swanton summarised his article in *The Daily Telegraph* newspaper by writing.

All in all, though, one can conclude that England's second opponents of the summer have a much greater wealth and variety of talent than the first, and that, supposing the luck runs evenly,

Illingworth will have done extremely well if in this, his 11th series as captain, he emerges on top.[1]

Clayton Goodwin recalls his thoughts before the start of the series.

The West Indies had played themselves into good situations in some of the Tests leading up to England in 1973, but they weren't able to develop or land a killer punch. Just like a boxer who hustles and bustles and looks quite good but runs out of energy. I think some people felt the West Indies would do that again in England and lose 2-0 or 2-1. England, on the other hand, had lost in India and beat New Zealand, but New Zealand had put up a good fight despite losing 2-0. So, England weren't that powerful either, but I thought most people expected England to win, partly, because of home advantage.

'We thought we could win the series because many of us had played for a couple of years in county cricket, which had opened up to overseas players around 1968 to 1969', says Deryck Murray. As he remembers the mood in the West Indies team ahead of the 1973 series.

So, it hadn't been long that many West Indians had been playing county cricket in England. But by then we were very familiar with the English players and we were, I think, quietly confident that we could win, but we were also aware that the West Indies team was coming off a period where we hadn't won a Test series for about five or six years. We were all looking forward to the tour with great expectation and, in some ways, we felt that not having won on tour for quite some time was not a true reflection of the ability of the individuals that we had. So, for us, it was really a question of taking on the task and pulling together as a team.

The first 1973 England v West Indies Test at The Oval coincided with the end of a historic global cricket tournament, which was also played in England. The first Women's World Cup. On the day of the first Test at The Oval, the International Cricket Council (ICC) agreed a plan at its annual meeting for a men's international cricket tournament to be staged in England in 1975. Each match in the tournament would have a maximum of 60 overs per team. All the current Test playing countries would be invited to participate.

In 1973, two years before the first men's cricket World Cup tournament in England, the final match of the inaugural Women's World Cup, England v Australia, took place at Edgbaston. The patron of the tournament was Jack Hayward, a millionaire business man, philanthropist, and a future chairman of Wolverhampton Wanderers Football Club, who spent £40,000 to sponsor the tournament.

England beat Australia by 92 runs and confirmed victory in a tournament that featured seven teams playing matches over a period of seven weeks. Australia, England, a Young England team, Jamaica, New Zealand, Trinidad and an international team which included four Australians, two English, and four players from the Caribbean – two Jamaicans and two Trinidadians. Five cricketers from South Africa received invitations to play for the international team, but the Jamaican and Trinidadian governments refused to permit their players to play with or against the South Africans.

The tournament was played using a round robin league table system with no knock-out matches. The players attended a reception at 10 Downing Street, complete with an informal speech of welcome given to the teams by Edward Heath, the British Prime Minister. At Edgbaston, after England beat Australia in the final, Princess Anne awarded the World Cup trophy to Rachael Heyhoe-Flint, the England captain and a close friend of Jack Hayward.

From the 1970s onwards, Rachael Heyhoe-Flint's name was synonymous in my mind with women's cricket. For many years, she was the only female international cricketer I could call to memory. This was hardly surprising as Heyhoe-Flint was a major pioneering figure who overcame many barriers to help develop women's cricket in Britain and beyond.

By 1973, women's cricket in the Caribbean had not progressed to a stage where an adequately resourced, organised and talented pan-Caribbean team was able to play in competitive international tournaments. Earlier in the year, there was some encouragement for progress in the development of women's cricket in the region. This included Barbados becoming the latest Caribbean country to join the International Women's Cricket Council. The Caribbean now had three members of the International Women's Cricket Council with Barbados joining Jamaica and Trinidad. Three years later, the West Indies women's team played their first competitive fixtures v Australia in the Caribbean.

CHAPTER 10

The first Test at The Oval, London, July 26 to July 31, 1973

On the morning of Thursday 26 July, two days before the final match of the inaugural women's World Cup, the players representing the England and West Indies men's teams began the first Test of the 1973 series at The Oval. Captain Kanhai won the toss for the West Indies and decided to bat first. I was ready and waiting to follow the series with ball by ball coverage available on BBC television and radio. The stage was set.

The first morning session was a difficult one for the West Indian batsmen. The English bowling attack, led by Geoff Arnold and John Snow, made the ball seam and move in both directions off the pitch. Roy Fredericks survived a couple of confident LBW appeals.

The first wicket to go down in the 1973 series was Ron Headley. Playing his first Test and opening the batting with Roy Fredericks. After about 70 minutes at the crease, Ron padded up to a delivery from Tony Greig and was trapped LBW for eight runs. Umpire Tom Spencer immediately responded to Greig's appeal. Ron was given out. This was a shot Ron couldn't recall playing at any time during his career.

'It was a very lively morning session at The Oval. In those days, The Oval was always green and lively during the first half of the day, and it was green and lively that morning with plenty of movement. I was used to these conditions having grown up playing in England, but Tony Greig did me LBW', Ron remembers.

Before lunch, the ball began to swing, and it was the only time in my whole career that I let a ball go. It swung big, it swung late and I was absolutely plum LBW. It was an easy decision for the umpire to make as it was knocking middle stump out of the ground. But Ray Illingworth paid me a compliment as I walked in to go for lunch. He gave me a glare, and I glared back at him, and he said, 'OK Ron. Well played. We really should have had four or five of you guys out by lunchtime'.

During the lunch break, a BBC reporter spoke to a group of West Indian spectators. He wanted to get their reaction to the slow start made by the West Indian batsmen. 47 for one after the morning session. One confident spectator insisted that the West Indian batsmen still had five days to make the England players 'suffer in the field'. He was not worried about the slow start. According to him, the West Indies just needed time to get going and 'get their eye in'. 'After lunch we will be giving them races out there. Plenty of races'. He also confidently predicted that the West Indian batsmen would score heavily off John Snow's bowling. As a result, by the end of their innings, Snow would 'have his shirt torn off his back'.

Illingworth had to be content with just one West Indian wicket at lunch. After lunch, Fredericks and Kanhai were soon dismissed and the West Indies were 64 for three. Kanhai had only scored 10 when he was cleaned bowled by Tony Greig. However, Illingworth's satisfaction with the state of play slowly evaporated. As the afternoon progressed, the shift in control of the match swung towards the West Indies after a partnership of 208 for the fourth wicket delivered by Clive Lloyd and Alvin Kallicharan. Both were left-handers from Guyana who the English bowlers struggled to control. After two other Guyanese batsmen, Fredericks and Kanhai, had been dismissed.

Back in 1963 at The Oval, the West Indies won the fifth and final Test. A win by eight wickets clinched the series 3-1. The rapidly developing and seemingly unbreakable bond between the West Indies team and the Caribbean diaspora was illustrated at the end of the Test. Basil Butcher and Conrad Hunte, the West Indies vice-captain who scored a not out century, were out in the middle together in the West Indies second innings. The West Indies were on the brink of victory. Thousands of West Indian spectators lined up just beyond the boundary. They were determined to celebrate across The Oval turf.

Butcher hit the winning runs with a drive off Brian Statham into The Oval outfield. The inevitable crowd invasion soon followed. Butcher recalls that some of the English press described the invasion as 'The Charge of the Dark Brigade'. In 1963, many of these spectators were Caribbean migrants who had been in Britain for only a few years. They were ecstatic to see West Indian victory on England soil.

Hunte was knocked over and partially submerged by the invading spectators. After the match, Hunte described the invasion and the jubilation experienced by his fellow West Indians at The Oval.

When Butcher hit that winning stroke, Statham was bowling from the Pavilion end. Butcher made the single that gave us the victory and kept on running towards the pavilion. He was safe. Most of the English players were able to beat the crowd in the race for the pavilion, but I ran the single towards the wicket at the far end and, as I raced back towards the pavilion trying to avoid my countrymen, I was brought down by a perfect rugby tackle. I lost my bat in the process. I lay there on the ground terrified at being trampled upon as I looked up into the jubilant and excited faces of my compatriots. I need not have feared for my life or for my bat. Some West Indians got hold of my feet as I kicked and struggled to be free, others got hold of my arms and shoulders, some supported my waist and back, and carried me shoulder-high through a clear path in the crowd to the pavilion steps. There they carefully put me down and said: 'Now go in!' I was safe indeed.[1]

From the safety of the player's balcony at The Oval, Hunte became more concerned about his bat which had disappeared. It was the bat which he scored most of his runs with on the 1963 tour. Hunte appealed to the crowd below for his bat from the player's balcony. Perhaps it had been taken by a spectator as a precious souvenir. There was a positive end to the Conrad Hunte 1963 Oval bat mystery. A West Indian supporter had picked up the bat and handed it to a policeman at The Oval's pavilion entrance. The bat was then returned to Hunte.

Ten years later at The Oval, Clive Lloyd's first century in England was the first in the 1973 series which thousands of West Indian supporters at The Oval, and watching on television at home, were able to celebrate. The difference from 1963 was the West Indian crowd at The Oval and watching on television also consisted of an emerging second generation. The 1973 series in England was the first where a generation of young Caribbean people, who had migrated to Britain as children or were born in Britain in the 1950s/1960s, like me, were able to share this intense cricket experience with their older Caribbean family and friends.

The other difference was that, increasingly, many of the British-born West Indian supporters had a combined Caribbean family heritage. Like me, they were born to parents from different countries in the Caribbean who developed relationships with each other in Britain. For example, some of these young people had Dominican fathers and Jamaican mothers, Guyanese fathers and Trinidadian mothers, or St. Lucian fathers and Barbadian mothers. There were also the growing number of mixed-race young people who had a Caribbean parent and a British or Irish parent.

The sheer delight at Lloyd's achievement at The Oval resulted in the first major pitch invasion of the 1973 series. Lloyd swept a delivery from Illingworth off leg stump over square leg for a boundary to reach 99. A section of the crowd responded by invading the playing area. They had incorrectly judged that Lloyd had scored his century.

Alan Gibson, one of the BBC radio match commentary team, described the disruptive invaders, many of whom were young schoolboys, as both black and white in appearance. Many of them, both West Indies and England supporters, some of whom were friends with each other, ran on the field from behind the boundary ropes. The playing area at The Oval was finally cleared after about five minutes.

The premature crowd invasion did not upset Lloyd's concentration. Lloyd hit Illingworth's next delivery for a single through the offside to reach his century. Despite a plea from The Oval PA announcer that spectators should remain in the stands, there was a repeat invasion. 'Here they come' announced an exasperated Alan Gibson to listeners following the match on BBC radio.

Lloyd holds up his hand. He is being surrounded by youngsters. They form a good considerable part all over that end of the wicket. There must be about 50 people treading on the pitch at this moment. It really is, I trust I shall not be thought to be stuffy for saying so. It is a fairly deplorable sight, and it could have done the pitch no good at all.

'Well, this really is absolutely stupid', an irritated Jim Laker told viewers, like me, watching and listening to his commentary on BBC television. One ecstatic West Indian supporter ran up to Lloyd and insisted on pouring him a drink of rum and orange juice. Lloyd swiftly drank some of it and handed the drink back to the spectator. He then raced back to his seat in the crowd.

Alvin Kallicharan was caught behind the wicket by Alan Knott off Geoff Arnold for 80. Reza Abasali, a Trinidadian cricket historian and broadcaster, told me that Kallicharan in action at The Oval in 1973 is one of the photographs on the walls of The Extension Bar near his home in El Socorro, Trinidad. This photograph, which has pride of place as the largest on display in the bar, shows Kallicharan confidently hooking a delivery from John Snow during his first innings score of 80. Kallicharan told me that Snow was the best England fast-bowler he faced during his Test career.

After Lloyd scored his fifth Test century, which was his first in England, he finished day one on 132 not out. The West Indies finished day one on 275 for four. Lloyd was out LBW first ball the following morning on day two. Lloyd unconvincingly played across the line and missed a straight delivery from Arnold. He failed to add to his overnight score. The West Indies were all out for 415. Boyce, coming in at number nine in the batting order, backed up the efforts of Lloyd and Kallicharan with an exhilarating 72. This included a mighty blow off Greig which landed in the seats just in front of The Oval pavilion.

At the end of the second day England were 117 for two. Dennis Amiss and Graham Roope were back in the dressing room after being removed by Boyce. Boycott survived two confident LBW appeals and an appeal for a run out before achieving a half-century. On Test debut, Hayes quickly demonstrated his youthful zeal. His first runs in Test cricket was a boundary confidently hit through the covers. He struck the final two deliveries of the day, bowled by Inshan Ali, for a six followed by a four. Hayes masked his pre-match debut nerves and tension in front of the Oval crowd. Before his debut Hayes remembers that, 'I felt terrible and didn't want to play'. Boycott and Hayes would return the following morning.

On day three, England were bowled out for 257 in their first innings. Boycott was the only English batsman to post a score of over 50 runs. Boycott was out for 97, caught by wicket-keeper Deryck

Murray down the leg side off Julien. This was Julien's first Test wicket. The dismissal of England's premier batsman.

Keith Boyce's performance with the ball produced exaltations of noise and unrestrained delight amongst sections of the West Indian crowd. Boyce dismissed Greig for 38 caught at second slip by Sobers. With Greig back in the dressing room, Boyce immediately clean bowled Snow. One West Indian spectator in a grey suit couldn't contain his joy at Boyce being on a hat-trick delivery. He walked up to Boyce in the middle of the pitch and gave him a quick kiss on the cheek. There would be more congratulatory kisses offered to players from both teams by West Indian supporters as the series continued.

Geoff Arnold was the next batsman in. Arnold tentatively prodded at Boyce's potential hat-trick delivery. The ball nipped back off the pitch, beat Arnold, and just cleared the top of the bails. The ball flew in the air at a furious speed before it smacked into Murray's wicket-keeper gloves. At the end of this intense period of suspense, Boyce's potential hat-trick delivery was judged by the umpire, Charlie Elliott, to be a no-ball.

Boyce was denied a Test hat-trick but he produced an impressive first innings return of five wickets for 70 runs. This was Boyce's first stint of bowling in a Test in England. Combined with his score of 72 in the first innings, which helped the West Indies to establish a 158 first innings lead, his contribution to the Test so far was keenly observed by my father.

'I wasn't expecting the most exciting of series and, as I recall, I didn't notice any real excitement during the build-up', says Clayton Goodwin. 'But that all changed for me when I remember the sensation of watching Keith Boyce break through the England batting in the first Test on television at The Oval'.

Boycott's first innings dismissal on 97 meant that he was just three runs short of a consecutive Test century. His last century was scored in the third and final 1973 Test v New Zealand at Headingley. Boycott, a few days before the first Test at The Oval, as the captain of Yorkshire, warmed-up for his role as England's premier batsman by scoring a century in a county game v Nottinghamshire at Bradford. As Ron Headley confirms, Boycott, who Dickie Bird described as the best self-made player in the history of the game, was the number one target for the West Indies bowling attack.

Boycott was the wicket we all wanted because he was the best and we had to dig him out. Boycott could bat all day and all night if you let him. So, once we got Boycott out, we felt we had a chance at both ends.

'Boycott was a fighter like Trueman and Illingworth. A typical Yorkshireman and they never gave up easily', remembers Lance Gibbs.

There were some England cricketers who you could get on top of and stay on top of them. But Boycott would fight. He played within his limitations, he knew his strengths and he knew his weakness, and this was something he used. He wasn't the type of player who could destroy an attack, but he would stay there, and if you're playing a Test match over five days, and a man like Boycott bats all day in the first day and gets over 100 runs, he could go on and make a double or a triple century against you the next day.

'Boycott was the man we always wanted to get out. But in some ways, we wanted Boycott to stay in because he might score a hundred, but he might also take a whole day doing it,' says Vanburn Holder.

Boycott wouldn't try to take the bowling apart like, say, Viv Richards or someone like that. If we couldn't get him out, some of the guys would say let him stay out there because he's not doing any harm, and he's scoring slowly. Clive Lloyd used to say to me about batsmen that, if you can't get them out, don't let them knock you all over the park, and I think that's a good philosophy. Sometimes, it's just best to keep a batsman quiet.

The West Indies batting performance in the second innings at The Oval, 255 all out, was less commanding than their first innings. However, with a lead now increased to 413, and setting England an unlikely second innings target of 414, the West Indies were still in a very strong position to win the Test. Kallicharan scored 80 as he did in the first innings. This was a considerable achievement as he batted in both innings with a broken finger. Garry Sobers was the other player to pass 50 with a score of 51.

Headley outscored Fredericks in the second innings. Fredericks was trapped LBW by Arnold for three. Headley was also dismissed by Arnold, bowled for 42. Despite being out for only eight runs after 70 minutes in the first innings, Headley regarded this score as more valuable to the West Indian cause than his second innings score of 42. According to Headley, his long stay at the crease in the first innings prevented England from taking more wickets before lunch on day one. Lloyd followed his first innings century with a less impressive score of 14.

The early development of England's second innings on day four was hampered by the control and artistry displayed by the spin bowling of Gibbs. He captured three England wickets for 36 runs by the end of day four. The prize wicket was, once again, Boycott, caught and bowled by Gibbs for 30. Graham Roope, batting at number three, was out in the same manner as Boycott. Caught and bowled by Gibbs. England's end of day four total was 126 for five. England were now staring down the barrel of a first Test defeat.

In 1971 at the age of 17, Steve Stephenson arrived in Luton, Bedfordshire with his brother from Jamaica. The principal reason for Steve's journey from Jamaica to live in Britain was to further his studies. By 1976, Steve had joined the Luton United Cricket Club, which was formed in 1972. Most of the players in the Luton United team were from the Caribbean, or of Caribbean descent, with a few players from India. Steve was also part of a group which started the Luton Carnival. 'With just one truck and one generator', he told me with pride.

Steve would also soon organise reception events for visiting West Indian teams on tour in England. He organised these events for over 25 years. Before the 2019 Cricket World Cup in England and Wales, the West Indies team paid their respects to Steve as a long-standing supporter, at a ceremony and dinner event at the Bristol West Indian Phoenix Cricket Club.

As with some West Indians who migrated to Britain in the 1950s, 60s and 70s, Steve had not met many people from Guyana and other islands in the Caribbean at home. 'In Jamaica, we used to go to the stadiums to watch cricket and football and sometimes you would see people from other islands, but I never really had a chance to speak with a lot of them', remembers Steve.

One of my Guyanese mother's early migration experiences was meeting large numbers of West Indians, for the first time, from other Caribbean islands after arriving in Britain in the early 1960s. As she would occasionally remark, 'I didn't meet a Jamaican until I came to England'.

By 1973, for Steve, and many other Caribbean people in Britain, cricket grounds in England continued to become public assembly points for boisterous camaraderie and collective expression during West Indies tours. The event was not just the cricket match. The cricket was part of a whole day of social activity. During the five days of a Test, in the cricket ground or watching at home on television, island loyalties, and ethnic and social differences between West Indians in Britain were usually blurred or temporarily erased.

Steve and two of his Jamaican friends were three West Indian supporters from Luton excited at the prospect of travelling to watch the final day of The Oval Test. For Steve, this was the first cricket match he attended in England.

I left Luton at five in the morning with two other Jamaican guys, the Hunter brothers, and one of them had a little Ford Anglia car. We drove to The Oval and in those days you could park at the ground, queue up, and buy your tickets for the match. The first thing I noticed when I got into the ground was all these Caribbean men sitting together making noise. They all had bags of food and drink, and we sat next to the 'bell man' who took his shirt off! During the day a dumpling would pass by, then a fritter would pass by, and the different rums were coming out from people sitting around us from different islands, and we noticed that everyone was sharing. So, we opened our bags and started sharing too. We had some mangoes with us and all sorts, and cans of Skol lager, those little cans of beer they used to have then. There was constant shouting, bantering and joking with the policemen around the boundary, and one of the guys took off a policeman's hat and the police cheered back. I remember that Clive Lloyd came to field near us on the boundary and everyone got really excited and called out his name. And every now and then some people started to burst out tunes and sing songs like Harry Belafonte's, *Daylight Come and We Want Go Home* (the *Banana Boat Song*) and that sort of thing. It was a brilliant atmosphere and a really good experience for me. It was my first real experience of meeting people from all the other Caribbean islands, and everyone was really positive with each other. In the 70s, there was a little bit of tension between different groups of Caribbean people in Luton, but most of it was because of ignorance and separation – as people from different islands in the Caribbean are separated by water. We used cricket and carnival to break that down, and when I went to The Oval in '73 it showed me that there could be unity between us in England.

Just after lunch on day five, England were bowled out for 225 in their second innings. This was the same second innings total as the West Indies. Boyce continued his all-round display of brilliance with the ball taking six wickets for 77 runs, and 11 wickets in total for the Test. For England, the stand out batting performance in their second innings was produced by Frank Hayes, one of my favourite players in county cricket. I still have an image of Hayes imprinted in my mind, after I watched him play for Lancashire during the 1970s on television – as an exciting, youthful and talented batsman with striking blonde hair.

After scoring a modest 16 runs in his first innings on debut, Hayes top scored in England's second innings with an undefeated century. His seventh wicket partnership of 93 runs with Illingworth temporarily held up the West Indian pursuit of victory. On 97, Boyce bowled a generous full toss to Hayes which was dispatched down to the fine leg boundary. Small groups of spectators dashed on to the field to congratulate Hayes on his century, including some West Indian supporters. Hayes also received generous congratulations from most of the West Indian players. Tony Cozier, reporting on his fourth West Indies tour as a journalist and broadcaster for the BBC radio cricket commentary team, proclaimed, 'This has been a fine innings indeed by Hayes'.

101 not out. England 248 for 8. Frank Hayes in his first Test match for England getting a century and a kiss from a West Indian, male spectator I might add. And he wiped his cheek after receiving it. But it really has been a splendid innings

indeed. 101 not out in his first Test match, and it's not very often that we have a player who marks his first Test match with a century.

'Frank got a hundred on his debut and I remember it very well. I was really pleased for him', recalls Ron Headley, who also made his Test debut at The Oval in 1973.

Frank was a very good player and he didn't necessarily bat like an Englishman, and I'm not being unkind when I say that. He had a bit of flair about him and he played very well off the back foot, and most of the English players didn't. We were winning the Test match. So, therefore, we weren't looking to save runs and were on the attack the whole time. So, really, more credit to Frank for getting his century.

Over 45 years later, Hayes gave me a philosophical response when I asked about his debut century memories at The Oval.

To be honest, when you're in good nick, and I frequently wasn't, you can be batting for Lancashire, you can be batting for the Lancashire second team, you can be playing for your local club side, you feel as if it's your day and everything is going for you. At The Oval in 1973 I was at the top of my game. I played well, got a ton and that was that. You sort of take it in your stride. You don't really realise at the time what you've done, and it's only when you look back that you realise and think about what you've achieved.

Hayes was more animated when I asked him about the West Indian crowd response to his century, which included a kiss on the cheek from one of the invading spectators.

The reaction by the West Indian crowd to my ton in 1973 was fantastic! They really loved their cricket, and obviously they wanted to see their team play well, but it wasn't just about their own side. They were quite delighted to see me score a ton and I got a great ovation from them, and I think some of them were a bit disappointed that I didn't quite make it a few years later (during the England v West Indies 1976 series).

Graham Dransfield, who in 1973 was a 17-year-old Yorkshire and England supporter, watched Hayes reach his century on television at his aunt's house in Southport.

In the summer of 1973, I was a sixth former and had just finished my A levels at school in Lancaster. I remembered watching Hayes score his hundred at my aunt's house in Southport by the seaside in her light and sunny 'telly' room. I applauded when Hayes got his century while sitting on my auntie's sofa. I was really pleased for him because, even though I was a diehard Yorkshire fan, I didn't mind Lancashire players scoring hundreds for England! Perhaps because my family lived in Runcorn and I sometimes went to watch Lancashire play at Old Trafford. But mostly because he was not a Southerner, and us northern cricket fans have a bit of a bond when it comes to England cricket team selection.

The two centuries at The Oval in 1973 were both scored by Lancashire players, Frank Hayes and Clive Lloyd. Alongside his more experienced and seasoned colleagues, Hayes finished on 106 not out at the end of the Test. He was the only English batsman in the second innings to pass 50 runs. *Wisden* later confirmed that Hayes was now only the fifth English batsman to score a century on debut since the Second World War.

Before Hayes, the last English player to score a century on debut was John Hampshire v West Indies at Lord's in 1969. After Hampshire reached his century, two West Indian spectators dashed on to the field to congratulate him with hugs and handshakes. After the Oval Test, Kanhai remarked that Hayes was a wonderful young player. According to Kanhai, Hayes was not afraid to play his shots and had a bright future for England.

West Indies beat England at The Oval by 158 runs. It was their first Test win since 1969, and their first win in England since 1966 at Headingley. At the end of the match, groups of spectators, including some delighted West Indies supporters, ran on the field to secure a spot in front of the pavilion. Three of these West Indian supporters were Steve Stephenson and his two friends.

We all ran on the pitch at the end of the match, ran up to the front of the pavilion and cheered and waved at some of the West Indies players, and I remember feeling really excited when Deryck Murray, Keith Boyce and Bernard Julien waved back at us.

A buoyant West Indies now had a 1-0 lead to take to the second Test at Edgbaston. A crucial foundation block was in place for the West Indies to win the 1973 series in England.

CHAPTER 11

The second Test at Edgbaston, Birmingham, August 9 to August 14, 1973

The West Indies made one change for the second Test at Edgbaston. Vanburn Holder's right-hand fast medium pace was preferred to Inshan Ali's left-arm wrist spin. Inshan was excited about the prospect of playing cricket in England for the first time. He sprung a surprise for groups of excited pupils at Preysal Government School, his former school in Trinidad, when he attended a farewell function there before his departure to England.

Inshan was also thrilled to be part of Garry Sobers' last tour of England. Sobers was Inshan's hero when he was a young aspiring cricketer in Trinidad. A year later, Sobers, alongside Inshan, were the special guests at the opening of a new set of cricket nets at Preysal Government School. Inshan was satisfied with his performances in the first-class tour matches and proud to play for a team which won its first Test since 1969. So, he was disappointed to be dropped for the Edgbaston Test.

Perhaps, Inshan's bowling figures of 0 for 52 and one for 49 at The Oval influenced the West Indies selectors to make their decision. Or, maybe, Holder's fast medium pace was a more reliable selection for Edgbaston than Inshan's mercurial spin-bowling talent. This was a Test the West Indies did not want to lose. The Oval Test would be Inshan's first and last Test appearance in the series, and his one and only Test in England during his career.

With Holder from Worcestershire now back in the West Indies starting line-up at Edgbaston, this was the first time a team on tour in England had selected 11 county cricketers for a Test. For England, Brian Luckhurst replaced Graham Roope and Chris Old came in for John Snow. This was Dickie Bird's first appearance as a Test umpire during the England v West Indies series. Bird would share his umpiring duties at Edgbaston with Arthur Fagg.

As in the previous Test at The Oval, Kanhai won the toss and decided to bat first. Caution was the watchword for the West Indies batsmen in conditions which, for much of the first day, were cold and bleak with a lush outfield. The English bowling attack, led by Arnold and Old, made full use of the conditions which offered some movement in the air and off the seam. A restrained approach by the West Indies was also a reaction to the early dismissals of Headley, Kanhai and Lloyd, which left the West Indies first innings in a perilous state at 39 for three.

At the end of day one at Edgbaston, the West Indies were 190 for five with Roy Fredericks on 98 not out. His day long occupation of the crease was an exercise in restraint and composed defiance. Fredericks applied his cautious approach to the playing conditions and the match situation. He reached his total score of 150 on day two after a marathon session of eight and a half hours. It was an innings completely without his usual collection of dashing strokes.

The Daily Mirror's assessment of the first day at Edgbaston featured some unflattering headlines, including *Kill Joy Roy* and *Go Slow Calypso*, to describe the innings by Fredericks and the general slow progress of play. Illingworth's exhibition of tight bowling on day one contributed to his first innings bowling figures of one for 37 from 32 overs. Nineteen of Illingworth's overs were maidens. John Woodcock, writing in *The Times* under a headline which declared, *Illingworth turns screw and silences calypsos*, summarised Fredericks' innings on day one as a 'vigil'.

> Throughout his vigil, Fredericks played no more than half a dozen attacking strokes. There were a couple of drives, a hook or two, and a punch wide of mid-on off Illingworth. For most of the time, he pushed defensively and inscrutably forward. Lloyd had managed two flamboyant drives, and Kallicharan found some gaps in the covers with lovely timing.[1]

The West Indies were bowled out on day two for 327. For the third Test innings in succession, the top West Indies run scorer was Guyanese, Roy Fredericks. Another notable feature of the West Indies first innings was Bernard Julien scoring his first half century in Test cricket.

During the second afternoon at Edgbaston, a sequence of events took place which this Test has often been remembered by. England were 23 for no wicket with the two openers, Geoffrey Boycott and Dennis Amiss, unbeaten and at the crease. Boyce bowled a delivery to Boycott. Some of the West Indies players, who confidently appealed to umpire Arthur Fagg, felt that Boycott had edged the ball through to Deryck Murray, the West Indies wicketkeeper. Fagg turned down the appeal for a catch behind the wicket. A few West Indies players, led by Kanhai standing at first slip, visibly expressed their displeasure at the decision.

'I remember that there was no question in our minds that Boycott hit it', says Murray.

I caught it and we were all in utter disbelief that it wasn't given out. I remember Rohan was at first slip and, in an effort to try and restrain himself, he walked around in a little circle in his first slip position, but Arthur Fagg thought that was showing dissent and disrespect to him as the umpire. It was just one of those incidents! We all knew it was very difficult to get Boycott out as he was difficult to dislodge, because he always put a very high price on his wicket. So, when you thought you got him out, the last thing you wanted was a 'technicality', which meant that he was not walking back to the pavilion.

Dennis Amiss, Boycott's opening batting partner, was standing next to Arthur Fagg. 'I honestly can't picture it now whether Geoffrey hit or not, but obviously there was an element of doubt as far as he was concerned. And if there is an element of doubt, you don't go', insists Amiss.

I do remember the remonstrations by the West Indies players. But sometimes decisions don't go your way in cricket, and it can be difficult to take, especially when you've got a player of that class batting. Geoffrey was probably our best batter and for the West Indies it was frustrating because they thought he was out. I know that some of the West Indies players took it to heart and were disappointed and poor Arthur Fagg was at the end of it.

Ron Headley was standing at square leg. In Headley's opinion, the West Indian team's response, to what they believed was an umpiring error, was not especially demonstrative.

> I was standing by Dickie (Bird) at square leg and thought that Boycott nicked it, and we all appealed, but Arthur Fagg said not out. I thought Fagg made a mistake but, listen, we all make mistakes. After that, I looked round and thought that Keith Boyce, who was a bit of a fiery character, was going to burst a blood vessel! But he just took the ball, picked it up, and didn't really say a word. Rohan was at first slip and all he did was to put his hands up in the air, then on his hips, look up at the heavens, turn around to look at the pavilion, turn back round, clap his hands and say, 'Come on boys' to get us going again and we just got back into our stride.

Boycott was involved in another incident at Edgbaston which, for him, was a painful experience. To keep the scoreboard ticking over, Boycott and Amiss pursued some quick singles. Towards the end of play, Boycott hit Boyce to mid-wicket and charged up the pitch for a single. Amiss refused the run and sent Boycott back. After colliding into Deryck Murray, and stubbing his bat into his chest, Boycott managed to run back and regain his ground.

Two months earlier in England's second innings v New Zealand at Trent Bridge, Nottingham, another misunderstanding between Amiss and Boycott resulted in Boycott being run out for a single. Amiss went on to score a century. 'I ran Geoffrey out at Nottingham in 1973, which has been well documented over the years, and he never lets me forget it!' says Amiss.

> Geoffrey always says that, if it wasn't for me, he would have gone on to get a hundred or a 150. We have a laugh about it now and he has a bit of fun about it at my expense. I went on to score a century at Nottingham and Geoffrey wasn't happy about it. Raymond (Illingworth) called us for a meeting at the top of the stairs at Lord's and he backed me against Geoffrey, which gave me a lot of confidence that he backed me against our number one batter. In the following match at Lord's v New

Zealand, we were very careful and only ran twos when they could have been three or four. We also only ran singles when there should have been twos.

At Edgbaston v West Indies, Boycott required attention to his injury on the field from the England team's physiotherapist. His ribs were badly bruised. Despite still being at the crease after not being given out by Arthur Fagg, Boycott received sympathy for his injury from some of the West Indian fielders.

The atmosphere on the field at Edgbaston was tense for the rest of day two. Boycott finished day two on 32 not out and England were 96 with no wickets down. Boycott and Amiss prepared to bat on the following morning. Boycott had to receive pain-killing injections before he could bat on day three.

Fagg was unimpressed by, what he viewed as, sustained and visible dissent shown to him by some West Indian players. He considered leaving Edgbaston and refusing to stand as umpire for day three. Fagg insisted that Kanhai should apologise to him.

'There was an appeal for a caught behind off Boycott and some of the West Indian players thought he hit it', recalls Dickie Bird who was standing next to Ron Headley at square leg.

Sometimes you hear all sorts of noises, don't you? It could have been anything, but the West Indies were adamant that Boycott had hit it. So, they weren't very happy with Arthur Fagg. So, of course, Arthur wanted an apology from Kanhai and after he didn't apologise, Arthur said he was going home, and I had to do both ends. There weren't any third umpires in those days, so that's how it was. If one umpire was ill during a match you just had to do both ends. Arthur packed all his bags and said he was going home. So, I said to him, 'I can't advise you because I've only just started on the Test match panel, but I think you should go back on the cricket field, because you could lose your job if you don't come back'. But, anyway, Arthur stormed out and Alan Oakman did square leg umpiring for me the next morning, while I took both ends. Alan was a former umpire, a coach at Warwickshire, and the match was at Edgbaston (the home of Warwickshire).

There was also time for a brief comedy moment at the start of day three. Bird and Oakman, who was also a former England Test cricketer, arrived at the middle together to umpire. Oakman turned to Bird and confessed that he'd forgotten to bring the bails out to re-start the Test. The bails were still back in the dressing room. Oakman trotted off the field to retrieve the bails to the bemusement and amusement of the crowd at Edgbaston. After the first over, and to Oakman's obvious relief, Fagg returned to the field to continue umpiring. Bird takes up the story again.

> Well, Arthur came back on to the field eventually, and then there was some intimidatory bowling by the West Indians. Well, that's what me and Arthur Fagg thought. So, we got the two captains and the two managers into the umpires' room at the lunchtime interval (on day three). We got Kanhai and Illingworth with (Esmond) Kentish, the West Indies manager and Alec Bedser of England. We said that we wanted to piece over the cracks between the players and the umpires and cut out the short pitch bowling from the West Indies. From that moment on, the Test match was played in a tremendous spirit, and it was a very enjoyable match. After the match, Rohan Kanhai went up to Arthur Fagg and shook him by the hand. Kanhai apologised to Arthur and that was it.

Boycott was 56 not out on day three when he felt unable to continue. He retired hurt, still in pain after his collision with Murray on day two. Amiss, also on 56, was dismissed after being caught at the wicket by Murray off Julien. Keith Fletcher, after experiencing a stroke of fortune when he was dropped by Sobers at first-slip off Julien, was the other English batsman to pass 50. Tony Greig initiated one of the most exceptional moments of the day. During his innings of 22, Greig hit Gibbs for a straight six on top of the Edgbaston pavilion roof.

Boycott attempted to resume his innings with England on 249 for six but soon returned to the dressing room. After being struck on the arm by a delivery from Holder, and unable to add to his score of 56, he retired hurt for the second time in England's first innings. Boycott's major contribution for the rest of the Test was carrying out liquid refreshments for England fielders during the intervals for drinks.

Holder and Sobers claimed three wickets each. The ever-reliable Holder performed well on his return to the West Indies team and justified the faith shown in him by the selectors. He completed the bulk of the bowling work for the West Indies in England's first innings at Edgbaston – 44 overs for his three wickets.

England posted a first innings total of 305 all out on the morning of day four – 22 runs behind the West Indies first innings score of 327. The West Indies completed their first innings run scoring rate at just over two runs per over. England completed their first innings scoring at just under two runs per over. Therefore, the run scoring at Edgbaston was deliberate, slow and low on entertainment value.

The West Indies second innings produced another score of just over 300 runs. They finished on 302 with Lloyd top scoring with 94. A Guyanese batsman had now top scored for the West Indies in the series for the fourth innings in a row. Sobers made his first substantial contribution with the bat during the series with a half-century. Captain Kanhai also discovered some form with a half-century. Arnold was, again, one of the England bowlers to impress with final bowling figures of four for 43.

Lloyd and Sobers, the first and second highest run scorers for West Indies during their second innings, both escaped with catches dropped off Illingworth's bowling. Sobers played forward to Illingworth and edged the delivery to Hayes, who dropped a catch fielding in the slips. Soon afterwards, Lloyd attempted a sweep shot off Illingworth. Lloyd top edged the delivery. The ball flew to Arnold at deep square leg but he couldn't hold the catch. Illingworth later suggested that England would have won the Test if they had held their catches.

England's second innings finished on 182 for two at the end of the final day. The West Indies bowling attack in the second innings was depleted due to Boyce suffering from a heel injury. As the Test progressed towards a certain draw, Fredericks and Kanhai also shared some of the bowling duties. Boycott's persistent injury problems meant that Luckhurst opened the batting with Amiss.

Stranded on 86 not out at the end of play, Amiss was 14 runs short of being the first Warwickshire player to score a Test century for England at Edgbaston, the county's home ground. After the Test, the five England and West Indies Warwickshire team mates – Amiss, Gibbs,

Kallicharan, Kanhai and Murray, enjoyed a drink together in the West Indies' team dressing room. Gerry Cotter, cricket writer and author, summarised the final sessions of the Test with a sense of frustration.

> The West Indies' second innings was a bit more interesting as Lloyd made 94 and Sobers 74, but Kanhai, reasonably enough, saw no need for a declaration and they were finally all out for 302, leaving 227 minutes for England to reach 325. They simply had some batting practice and strolled to 182 for two. It was one of those games which are best forgotten. [2]

Steve Walcott was five years old during the 1973 England v West Indies Test series. Steve's Barbadian father took him to the Test at Edgbaston. This was Steve's first visit to a cricket ground, and he has vague memories of what happened that day. However, in years to come, his father would remind him that, for some reason, he got very excited when Frank Hayes lost his wicket in England's first innings. For the record, making his second Test appearance, Hayes was caught by Alvin Kallicharan off the bowling of Vanburn Holder for 29 runs.

Eric McClymont was one of the West Indian supporters at home watching the Test at Edgbaston on BBC television. Eric's father migrated to Britain from Jamaica in the late 1950s. Eric mother arrived from Jamaica in 1960. Eric, from his home in South London, was 13 years old in the summer of 1973 and his family's cricket correspondent.

> 1973 was the summer that I really got into cricket. I was a big football fan at the time, but I wasn't really into cricket. But I had to watch the cricket on television, because when my dad came home from work, he wanted me to tell him about it. Also, my dad worked for London Underground and did a lot of shift work. So, sometimes he would call home and expect me to report to him about who was in, who was out, and how many runs had been scored. So, I thought the best way to do this was to write the information down and read a report to him on the phone! My dad didn't play cricket, but he loved the game, knew how to set a field, and taught me about fielding positions. So, when I watched the Tests on the television, I could tell him on the phone who was fielding where. During the 1973 tour I got

into watching and finding out more about great West Indian players like Kanhai and Sobers who were coming to the end of their careers and Clive Lloyd, who was establishing himself. I was also a big fan of Roy Fredericks because of the way he rolled his shirt sleeves down and he always wore his West Indies maroon cap. Fredericks had a good series in 1973 and I'll always remember telling my dad about his century at Edgbaston.

With the second Test drawn after a reasonably even contest, the teams travelled back down to London for the third Test with the West Indies still in a strong position. The West Indies could win or draw the series. England were now unable to win the series. However, England were still able to win the third test, draw the series 1-1, avoid defeat, and retain the Wisden trophy.

In response to the crowd invasions at The Oval, the authorities and ground staff at Edgbaston prepared the boundary with fences around the ground between the spectators and the outfield. During the Test all spectators remained behind the boundary fences. There were no interruptions to play as there had been at The Oval. Meanwhile, our new Phillips colour television had arrived in our flat. Just in time for the third and final Test at Lord's.

CHAPTER 12

The third Test at Lord's, London, August 23 to August 27, 1973

A t Lord's, for the third consecutive Test match, Kanhai won the toss and decided to bat first. In complete contrast to the previous Test at Edgbaston, the bright and sunny weather at Lord's made conditions much more favourable for the team batting first. Ron Headley, who scored one and 11 at Edgbaston, after being dismissed by Chris Old in each innings, was dropped for the Lord's Test.

Headley was replaced by Maurice Foster who was top of the Shell Shield batting averages when he represented Jamaica during the 1973 first-class regional tournament. Foster was Headley's captain when they played together for Jamaica. Headley did not play another Test match for the West Indies. Headley and Foster represented the West Indies together on one occasion only at the second England v West Indies 1973 ODI at The Oval.

With Headley not selected for Lord's, Roy Fredericks had a new opening batting partner. Deryck Murray, who described himself as not the most enthusiastic opening batsman, was moved up the order to open with Fredericks. This was not the first time that Murray had opened the batting for the West Indies. Murray was asked to open on a few occasions, including with Stephen Camacho v England in Jamaica in 1968. Foster was scheduled to bat at number seven, which was Murray's usual batting position.

By 1973, Kanhai and Sobers were two legendary figures in West Indian cricket history, who were coming to the end of their Test careers. They had both pierced my young imagination. Not just as cricketers but as revered Caribbean folk heroes. Kanhai and Sobers now prepared to make their final Test appearances in England at Lord's. For England, Chris Old's appearance at Edgbaston was his only Test outing in the series. The England selectors replaced an unfit Old with Bob Willis, who was a young fast bowler making his return to international cricket after an absence of 24 Tests.

Dickie Bird was appointed for his second consecutive Test as an umpire alongside Charlie Elliott. Bird was not the original choice to stand at Lord's. He received a telegram from Lord's informing him that he was selected to replace Dusty Rhodes, the original choice. A press statement was released which confirmed that Rhodes had an eye infection. This prevented him for umpiring. According to Bird, the real reason for the change was because the West Indies wanted him to umpire at Lord's. Perhaps, during the previous Test at Edgbaston, Bird had earned the respect of Kanhai and the rest of the West Indies team.

This was a major disappointment for Rhodes. England v New Zealand at Trent Bridge, earlier in the summer of 1973, would be his eighth and final Test as an umpire. However, Bird had to seize this unexpected opportunity to umpire his first Test at Lord's. Unbeknown to Bird and Elliott, this Test would provide some extraordinary challenges for them to overcome as umpires.

David Thorpe, now an actor and comedian, was born in Sheffield and grew up on the Isle of Wight before moving to London as an 18-year-old. 'By 1973, there were three cricket teams I was fond of – Yorkshire because I was born in Yorkshire and it was my childhood dream to play for the county. Hampshire because I lived there and Essex because that was my dad's team', says David. As a schoolboy from the Isle of Wight, David attended the second day of the 1973 Test at Lord's. It was the first cricket match he attended.

My dad took me to my first ever cricket match at Lord's in 1973 and it made a huge impression on me, and so that '73 England v West Indies series was my starting point. Garry Sobers was a hero of mine and the other player in the West Indies team I adored was Keith Boyce. I watched him play for Essex, which was my dad's team, on the John Player League on television on Sundays. We got to Lord's early and my dad, bless him, made some people move out of the way so I could get a clear view of some of the players practising before the match in the nets. One of the players I clearly remember watching hitting some balls around was Dennis Amiss. It was great, because you could just watch the players up close and there was no security around to get in the way.

At the end of day one at Lord's, the West Indies were 335 for four. The West Indies had amassed more runs in the first day at Lord's than their first innings total at Edgbaston, which finished on day two. Murray's innings as an opener came to a premature end when he was bowled by Willis, who claimed a creditable three wickets at the end of day one. Fredericks was at his exhilarating best and scored a half century. Lloyd was dismissed for 63 and Sobers was not out on 31. However, the first day was undoubtedly dominated by Kanhai, who displayed an overdue return to dominant form by scoring 156 including 21 boundaries. This was his one and only Test century at Lord's.

After disappointing scores of 10, 0 and one in his first three innings in the series, Kanhai completed his century after striking Willis through mid-wicket. A misfield by Luckhurst at mid-wicket allowed Kanhai to quickly return for a second run to reach 100. A West Indian spectator in a green shirt managed to reach Kanhai on the field. He shook the West Indian captain by the hand. A couple of policemen patrolling the boundary prepared to intercept the spectator as he made his way back to the stands. On day one, three Guyanese batsmen, Fredericks, Lloyd and Kanhai, had made a major impact on the outcome of this Test and the series.

Kanhai was the first West Indian batsman to be dismissed the following morning on day two. He was caught by Greig at second slip off Willis. Kanhai's innings of 157 was his highest Test score in England. It was also the highest individual score during the 1973 series. Kanhai's 157 confirmed that a Guyanese batsman had been the top run scorer for the fifth consecutive West Indies Test innings. The legacy of Clyde Walcott's work in Guyana had, once again, borne fruit years later, in front of a full house at Lord's with a substantial presence of delighted West Indies supporters. As the third Test progressed, and the West Indies consolidated their winning position, I continued to feed off the joyous energy from the West Indian supporters clearly audible via our new colour television's speaker. It was an uplifting experience.

It was this combination of Caribbean camaraderie, atmosphere, collective cries of joy, bells, horns and whistles, which compelled me to watch the West Indies on television and, in the following years, watch them play on tour in England. As Vanburn Holder remembers with a chuckle, 'It seemed like everyone in the crowd at Lord's was West Indian and it felt and looked like the English in the crowd were sometimes outnumbered!'

They really gave us all a lift, man, and they really spurred us on, and we weren't allowed to feel down during that tour. Because they would always get behind you and they genuinely wanted us to do well. In the evenings, we would usually get invited somewhere, at an embassy, or invited to a party or something like that, but you still had to adhere to the committee and the management and not overdo things or abuse your body, if you know what I mean! The other thing was that you were never able to be by yourself, because somebody would want to be with you all the time, wanting to talk about cricket, and wanting to ask questions. We wanted to come out and enjoy ourselves, but we couldn't always do that because our fans were always around and wanted to talk about the matches. After playing, we didn't want to talk about cricket all the time, but I always preferred it that way than the other way. Where the West Indians we knew and met in England didn't want to talk to you because they weren't interested.

'Cricket gave West Indians something to cheer about and shout about because racism was still huge in England in the 1970s', says Maurice Foster.

It really gave West Indians in England something to brag about and feel good about and, you know, some of them lost their jobs during that tour. Because some of them wanted to watch the West Indies play and would just take off from work and come and watch us. So, when they went back to work the following day, they found out that they didn't have a job. Many West Indians told me stories like that during that series. For us it was great to be away from the Caribbean and still have that huge support. And, I feel, that is something that is missing from our cricket now – the willingness to achieve, and the commitment and focus to play for the people in the Caribbean and West Indians in England.

Sobers began day two at Lord's after an eventful Thursday night which, for him, continued until the following morning. Unbeknown to the thousands of expectant spectators at Lord's, and all of us watching on television at home. Sobers began Thursday night with a meal with Clive Lloyd and some Guyanese friends in London. He then met up with Reg Scarlett, an old friend and a former West Indies cricketer living in London. Sobers and Scarlett then enjoyed the rest of the night in a club, drinking, dancing and reminiscing, before returning to the West Indies team's hotel bar for more drinks.

Sobers took a cold morning shower without having had any sleep. He then joined the rest of the team on the journey to Lord's. Resuming his innings and watched by an expectant Lord's crowd, Sobers hit his 26th and final Test century, which was his fifth in England. It left him two centuries behind Don Bradman, Test cricket's master centurion. Eighteen runs short of his 150, Sobers explained to umpire Charlie Elliott that he had to leave the field. His stomach pains were becoming unbearable. Back in the West Indies dressing room, Sobers requested a drink of port and brandy mixed which Kanhai delivered. Two port and brandy drinks were consumed by Sobers (for medicinal purposes) to combat his stomach pains. Sobers then returned to the field to continue his innings.

Maurice Foster, playing in his only Test during the tour, was caught by Bob Willis off Tony Greig for nine. Foster, who made his debut for the West Indies during the 1969 tour in England, recalls his short innings in 1973.

On my first tour in England in 1969 I really struggled, and I didn't get any runs until we played Somerset in one of the county matches. I was never familiar with the conditions in England back then and I had to make some adjustments during the tour. So, when I came back in 1973, I was a much better player and, if you look at that tour, I topped the averages in the county matches. So, I was more than disappointed to get just one innings in the last Test against England at Lord's, which I remember very well. I was batting with Garry Sobers and the first ball I received from Geoff Arnold I hit for four. I was then out hitting a long hop straight into the hands of long on.

Sobers finished with a score of 150 not out and enjoyed a free-scoring partnership with Bernard Julien. Dickie Bird described Sobers' 150 at Lord's as one of the best innings he had seen as an umpire. Trevor Bailey, from his position in the BBC radio commentary box, reported that it was 'a superb innings in every possible way'.

West Indian runs continued to flow at Lord's when Bernard Julien joined Sobers in the middle. *Wisden* reported that, 'Thereafter Julien gave the English bowlers little encouragement, striking the ball cleanly, powerfully and in a mainly orthodox fashion to all parts of the ground in a thrilling display'.[1] Julien previously produced an example of his hard-hitting stroke play with a quick-fire performance of 23 runs in the West Indies second innings at The Oval. This included four boundaries and one six. He scored his maiden Test half century in the second Test at Edgbaston. Julien describes his partnership with Sobers at Lord's, alongside the jubilation of the West Indian supporters, as one of the outstanding moments of his career.

At Lord's, Julien became the third West Indian player in the Test to hit a century. This was his first century in any form of first-class cricket. Julien reached his century after striking a full toss delivery from Greig for four. As the ball reached the boundary ropes, there was a further release of unbridled joy from some West Indian supporters. Once again, this was immediately followed by an invasion of the field and an interruption to the tempo of the Test. One female West Indian supporter managed to reach Julien on the field. She gave him a kiss on the cheek as a reward for his efforts.

A scattered number of policemen also came on to the field. They proceeded across the turf in a gentle military slow march, from all corners of the ground, to establish a semblance of control and authority. Jim Fairbrother, the head groundsman at Lord's, also made his way across the field to the middle. Understandably, Fairbrother was deeply concerned about any potential damage to the pitch caused by the invading spectators.

The West Indies declared their first innings at 652 for eight immediately after Sobers reached his 150. A slightly confused young David Thorpe watched the declaration made by captain Kanhai. David was sitting next to his father in the stands with a close view of the Lord's pavilion.

I saw Garry Sobers score his century and what I next remember vividly is seeing Rohan Kanhai waving from the pavilion after Sobers had moved on to score 150. I wasn't really sure what was going on. All the players immediately stopped and started to troop off the field. My dad helped to explain to me what had happened. Kanhai had just declared the West Indies first innings and it was now England's turn to bat.

652 was the second highest innings total scored by a team in a Lord's Test match. It was an imposing total, and the West Indies would not be required to bat again for the rest of Test. England were 88 for three at the end of day two. Boycott, still the West Indies bowling attack's number one target, lost his wicket cheaply for only four runs after being caught by Kanhai at first slip off Holder.

By lunch on day three, the England first innings reply began to crumble with Tony Greig out for 44. Greig played and missed at more than a few delivers. However, he survived and led a brief but courageous resistance with Keith Fletcher who scored 68. Boyce, Gibbs and Holder shared the wickets and Sobers took a collection of exceptional catches. Alongside the memorable moments in the previous Test matches, and the dramatic events towards the end of the third day at Lord's, the catches taken by Sobers at Lord's are among some of the distinct memories I have of the 1973 series.

I had not seen fielding like this so close to a batsman on the leg side. I stared at our new colour television in awe. Sobers, standing close to the wicket, and only a few yards away from the bat, in a backward short leg (or leg slip) position, brilliantly caught Fletcher – the top scorer, and captain Illingworth, off Gibbs in successive balls. One catch was taken with his right hand and the other taken with his left.

In 1955, during Australia's first tour of the Caribbean, Gibbs was influenced as a young man by watching Ian Johnson bowl for Australia v West Indies at Bourda, Georgetown. Johnson, an off-spinner and Australian captain, bowled at an end at Bourda where the breeze took the ball out. The ball turned back in after it dropped on the pitch. This was a special Johnson delivery which Gibbs described as 'a two-way family favourite'. I shared my unforgettable memory with Gibbs about his wicket taking combination with Sobers at Lord's in 1973. Gibbs explained, on the telephone from his home in Florida, his right-arm spin bowling and field placement strategy behind these wicket taking deliveries.

Leg slip is where Sobers fielded for me and he took a lot of catches for me in that position. Sobers was left-handed. So, as a left-hander the ball would go away from his left hand and he would take a catch. It was the same for Roy Fredericks. When Sobers left, Fredericks took that position for me in the field. If the ball is turning into a right-handed batsman, the only place where the ball could end up is going down to leg slip. If the ball goes straight on it will go to an off slip. The leg slip ball is the one that turns across. If your right hand is high, your arms must nearly touch your ear. From up there you get bounce off the pitch and turn. So, when the ball bounces it hits higher up on the bat, and on the blade, and not on the meaty part. Therefore, it will go to leg slip and that's how I took those wickets and Sobers took those catches. If you bowl as if your arm is right out, as if you're throwing the ball in, you're not really going to get that bounce, which you get from high up.

Sobers total of six catches in the innings equalled the Test record. At 176 for six, the heart of England's batting resistance had now been ripped out. After Sobers caught Illingworth off Gibbs, the West Indians in the crowd were in raptures of excitement and created a crescendo of noise around the ground. A group of about 50 to 60 spectators, many of them West Indian, encroached on the playing area. They were encouraged to go back to the stands by some of the West Indian players. Kanhai had to gently restrain an over-enthusiastic spectator on the edge of the pitch. Sobers, with his first innings century and magnificent fielding, delivered his final Test performance in England with typical skill, style and panache.

After a short period of play after lunch, with Arnold and Willis at the crease and Gibbs preparing to bowl another delivery, there was a dramatic interruption to proceedings. Billy Griffiths, the Secretary of the MCC, made a request on the public address system for all players and spectators to evacuate the ground because of a telephoned bomb threat.

The possibility of a bomb device at Lord's led many in the ground, and watching on television, to suspect that this was the work of the Irish Republican Army (IRA). Earlier in 1973, the IRA began to conduct a violent bombing campaign in England. This included two bombs which exploded in London on the same day. One car bomb exploded near the Central Criminal Court of England and Wales building (The Old Bailey). The other bomb exploded at the Ministry of Agriculture. As a result of these two explosions, one person died and over 200 people were injured.

Two other bombs, which were timed to go off at the same time on the same day, at around 3pm, were planted in cars outside buildings. Both bombs were detected and safely defused by police and army experts. On the first day of the Test at Lord's, a bomb was discovered in a bag in the nearby Baker Street underground station ticket area. On the same day as the bomb scare at Lord's, a security officer at the Bank of England had a hand blown off. A letter bomb exploded as he checked mailbags in a basement sorting office.

Understandably, no risks could be taken after the bomb attacks in London. So, the police and the authorities at Lord's treated the bomb threat with extreme seriousness. The England team assembled in a tent behind the Lord's pavilion. Meanwhile, the West Indian players walked out of the ground and returned to their hotel in nearby Maida Vale. The police then searched the stands.

In response to the announcement made by Billy Griffiths, many of the spectators filtered slowly out of the ground. Some spectators decided to give up and go home. Others waited outside Lord's in the surrounding roads in the hope that play might re-start. However, thousands of spectators ignored the requests and instructions issued and decided to stay in the ground. A mass of spectators moved in waves across the boundary ropes, congregated on the grass, and waited for the match to re-start. 'It came over on the loudspeaker in the ground that they were calling the game off for a while, because the security people had to do a check', remembers Gibbs.

I was bowling at the time, and after the announcement was made we had to go back to the hotel, which was not too far from the ground. We were having some fun in the hotel and then, shortly afterwards, the announcement came that they were ready to resume the game. So we walked back to the ground. I remember some of the West Indian spectators shouting to me, 'Lance, there's no big bomb scare here, man. The bomb is in your hands!' [2]

Deryck Murray was preparing to keep wicket for the next delivery from Gibbs when play was interrupted.

We were in the field and England were batting, and we were asked to stay on the field as it was the safest place for the players to be, because they were going to clear the stands. I remember all the players, including the England players, coming out on to the field as well. Some of the players from both sides were saying that we should give a signal for our wives, families and friends to also come out, because if you're out there on the field and you think there might be a bomb in the stands, you're then concerned about the safety of those closest to you. Before you knew it, the fans followed the instructions to empty the stands, but many of them came on to the field, and some of the West Indians were saying to us that, well, if you're staying out here and a bomb goes off, we're all staying with you! It was their way of showing solidarity with us.

Many of the spectators at Lord's, including the large contingent of West Indian supporters, appeared to be unperturbed by this unique emergency. One of them was Andrew Carnegie's father. Andrew, and our family in south London, in our respective homes, watched this extraordinary sequence of events unfold on television. Andrew's father shared his story with his family when he returned home from Lord's.

My father went to Lord's with three of his friends and two of his friends decided to follow the instructions given and leave the ground. The suspicion was that somebody from the IRA had planted a bomb in the ground. But my father immediately thought it was a hoax and stayed in the ground, walked on to the pitch, and wandered around with one of his friends, while his two other friends walked out. And then, when the all clear was given, my father's two friends came back in the ground

217

and found that their two seats had been taken. Some fans, who had not bought tickets for the match, had come in the ground and sat in their seats to watch the rest of the match.

Tim Bowler and his father were two other spectators who left the ground. Tim, who is now a BBC business news reporter, recalls his expectations and experiences (some of them culinary!) before his earlier than planned departure from Lord's.

We were living in Harrow in north west London, so I always felt that Lord's was 'my' home ground. Before the big day I was most excited about seeing Garry Sobers play. Dad had told me about his amazing six sixes in an over. It seemed a superhuman feat, and he had to be the best cricketer in the world. I still hoped my England heroes, Ray Illingworth, Alan Knott and Bob Willis would save the day, but as we walked to the ground from the tube station that morning several West Indian supporters began to good-naturedly josh us, saying, 'Oh you're gonna lose!' So, I began to reflect that those boyish hopes might be misplaced. After the bomb threat came through, we went home rather than stay for a resumption of play. Which, given England's performance, was probably best for a disappointed 10-year-old. I had my hopes dashed the year before at Lord's when we saw England lose to Australia. I also remember some England supporters, rather resignedly, leaving the stands. They clustered in dispirited groups outside Lord's and listened to the latest updates about the Test on radios, while many of the West Indian supporters stayed on the pitch. One of my other enduring memories of that day is culinary rather than cricket based. Two Italians in the seats in front of us had bought a magnificent hamper of food, which they proceeded to eat from throughout the day. Mum made us some sandwiches which, while they were fine, just simply couldn't compete against this kind of continental competition. And we finished them far too quickly!

Some of the more impatient and vocal spectators on the Lord's outfield produced a chorus of, 'We want cricket!' These included thousands of spectators who had surged across the outfield towards the playing area. Jim Fairbrother and his ground staff team managed to move the protective covers across the turf. They covered the Test pitch just in time before the crowd surged towards it. Umpires Bird and Elliott stayed in the middle. Bird decided to sit on the covers, watch, and wait for the all clear.

> I had the pitch covered because I didn't want it to get damaged as thousands of spectators came on to the field, and I thought the covers would be the safest place to sit. Thousands of West Indies supporters were all around the covers, but it was harmless, and they were in tremendous spirits. The supporters were absolutely wonderful, and not the slightest bit worried about the situation, and one of them said to me, 'Don't worry about the bomb Mr Dickie Bird. Just look at that scoreboard man, and worry about that, 652!'

Tim Cooke, who in the 1950s was a young schoolboy watching Rohan Kanhai play for Ashington Cricket Club in the Northumberland County League, was at the 1973 Lord's Test on day three with his brother. Tim and his brother were two of the many spectators who found sanctuary by sitting on the edge of the pitch covers on the square. 'In 1973, those were the days when the Caribbean community turned out on mass to watch cricket matches when the West Indies were playing, and the atmosphere at Lord's that day was utterly amazing', Tim remembers with an air of nostalgic satisfaction.

> The atmosphere in 1973 at Lord's was similar to the (England v West Indies) Old Trafford Test match I was at in 1976, and it was unforgettable. We heard the message on the public address system asking everyone to evacuate the ground and leave calmly and everything, and what will happen next. My brother and I thought, 'We're not going out!' We could see other people strolling out to the middle, so we just did the same thing and basically sat on the covers. You would probably get arrested and banned if you tried to do that these days. The average cricket crowds in England back then were pretty phlegmatic, and everyone calmly walked out on to the grass or just milled around outside the ground. I don't remember anyone being scared and

there was never any real sense of panic, so I guess these were calmer times. I have a memory of one person who was sitting in one of the big stands at Lord's by himself in glorious isolation and refusing to move until the cricket started again! To walk on the turf at Lord's is a dream for so many people and we did it. I've been back there since but that was in different circumstances. After about half an hour or so, people just milled back in again and we went back to our seats. It was also the first time I can remember in this country that they added extra time on at the end of the day. And that, of course, was when the West Indies got Geoff Boycott out.

As the police continued their search in and around the ground for an explosive device, it was confirmed that the bomb scare was a hoax. England resumed their first innings on 206 for eight at around 4.30pm. There were some empty seats around the ground vacated by spectators who left and not returned. But there were still a substantial number of the original 28,000 spectators on the playing area. They happily returned to their seats determined to watch more cricket. The spectators in the ground were rewarded by an announcement that extra time would be added to make up for lost time. Due to the ongoing security threat, the scheduled Monday/fourth day visit to Lord's by the Queen was cancelled.

England added 27 runs after the interruption before losing their last first innings wicket at 233. Kanhai asked England to follow on 419 runs behind the West Indies first innings total of 652. It appeared to be a lost cause. England's prospects of second innings survival and progress were doomed after Boycott's dramatic dismissal. After surviving a caught behind appeal after the previous delivery by Boyce, Boycott was caught by Alvin Kallicharan at deep square leg off a short-pitched delivery. Boycott had, uncharacteristically, played a hook shot in murky conditions on, what turned out to be, the last ball of the day. Boyce had now claimed England's first three wickets, Amiss, Knott, and Boycott, towards the end of four consecutive overs. England finished day three on 42 for three.

According to Boycott, the hook shot was a suicide stroke played in anger. Boycott suggested that Brian Luckhurst, his batting partner, wanted to avoid Boyce's bowling. Therefore, Luckhurst had refused to run a single called by Boycott. Over 40 years later, during a chat I had with Dickie Bird about Boycott's dismissal at Lord's in 1973, he was still in a state of surprise. 'I'd never seen Boycott play a shot like that in all my life', insists Bird. *Wisden* wrote of the episode, that it was a stroke of remarkable ill judgement by a player of such class and experience. However, it is also worth remembering, that Boycott brilliantly hooked a bouncer from Boyce for six in England's first innings v West Indies at The Oval.

Brian Luckhurst was brought back into the England team at Edgbaston to bat at number three, behind the now established opening pair of Amiss and Boycott. The match at Lord's would be Luckhurst's final Test appearance for England on home soil. Luckhurst was caught behind off Boyce for just a single in England's first innings. In his autobiography, *Boot boy to President*, Luckhurst shared his version of events which led to Boycott's second innings dismissal.

It was murky light, too, and in a subsequent little mid-pitch conference I asked Geoffrey if he wouldn't mind trying to see out the final over from Boyce as I was struggling to adjust to the light, having just come in and faced only two balls. He muttered something, but then got down to the task of seeing out the last over with what looked from my end to be comparative ease. From the final ball of the day, however, Boyce tempted Geoff into a rash hook – and shockingly for all concerned, our number one batsman was caught at long leg. As he walked off past me, his face like thunder, Geoff said to me, 'Happy now, are you?' And he was still chuntering away in the dressing room afterwards until Illy (Illingworth) told him to be quiet! [3]

In the dressing room after the close of play, Illingworth stepped in to cool the rising temperature between Boycott and Luckhurst. Illingworth also brought in Brian Taylor, one of the England selectors, to witness the fact that he was handling a very fraught situation. Boycott was still finding it very difficult to calm down.

What also upset Boycott was the reaction and behaviour of some spectators as he left the field. Another crowd invasion immediately followed after Kallicharan had taken the catch. The race was now on.

Boycott, Luckhurst, Kallicharan, the other West Indian players and the umpires – Bird and Elliott – sprinted to the safety of the dressing room to avoid the onrushing spectators.

Alvin Kallicharan describes taking the catch in front of the invading crowd.

> I felt there were about 500 West Indians trying to catch the ball with me. 500 fellas on the field with me taking the same catch! It was a good thing that I caught the ball in front of them. I fell over and when I got up the ball was gone. And to this day, I don't know who got the ball off me.

Ecstatic after seeing Boycott dismissed on the final ball of the day, and in their over zealousness to celebrate, a few of the West Indian supporters on the field jostled Boycott on his way back to the dressing room. In the later stages of this unfortunate end of play drama, Boycott required the assistance of a few police officers, and used his bat to ward off further physical contact from the crowd.

'In those days, there was a practice that some spectators would run on to the field to congratulate a player who had taken a wicket, or a batsman who had reached a landmark, like a hundred', recalls Deryck Murray.

> When a figure like Boycott, who was not known as a batsman who hooked bouncers, hooks a ball directly to a fielder who was placed there for a hook shot, and goes totally against character. Well, for some of the West Indian and English spectators, they were overcome by that dismissal at such a crucial time. So, you had both sets of spectators on the field, with a handful of them jostling and ridiculing Boycott, and some cheering Kallicharan who took the catch. It didn't escalate into anything more than some jostling, but it was certainly a bit over exuberant, and led to stricter controls about spectators on the field.

Boycott later received an apology from Esmond Kentish, the West Indies tour manager. As a reaction to this sequence of events, and despite the prospect of a loss of revenue, the authorities at Lord's refused to let spectators sit on the grass, or inside the barrier wall, for the fourth day of the Test. Although, the ban did not apply to the rest of the county and Gillette Cup matches scheduled to be played at Lord's.

The fourth day at Lord's was the final day's play in the 1973 series. It was a Bank Holiday Monday – a non-working day. This enabled a healthy crowd of West Indian supporters at Lord's to witness a West Indies victory as the inevitable conclusion to the Test. England were bowled out in their second innings for just 193.

Once again, Keith Fletcher top scored with a defiant 86 not out after three hours. Fletcher was the shining light with the bat for England in the third Test. He was the only batsman to occasionally wrestle the initiative from the West Indian bowlers. Fletcher finished the series with England's best batting average of 66.50. *Wisden* declared that Fletcher was the only English batsman who faced the West Indian bowlers with any real conviction. In England's previous home series v New Zealand, Fletcher hit a match saving second innings score of 178 in the second Test at Lord's. Fletcher played in all six home Tests in 1973 and considers this period as his most successful for England.

Fletcher attributed his performances v West Indies in 1973 to having an advantage over the other English batsmen. He was much more familiar with Keith Boyce's bowling and, rather modestly, suggests he had a considerable slice of fortune.

I played with Boycey (Keith Boyce) for about 10 years at Essex, and I could tell what he was going to bowl at me because of the different ways he ran up to bowl. That was a big advantage for me because we played together at Essex for a long time, and I knew his bowling inside out. I also played a lot of cricket against the likes of Sobers, Vanburn (Holder) and Lance Gibbs. So, they didn't come as any surprise to me at all and, yeah, it all went well for me v the West Indies in '73 and, obviously, I was pleased. I'm not saying I was a better batter than, say, Dennis Amiss or Tony Greig. But in some Test series you play well, you get runs, and you perform. In another series you might be unlucky and get knocked over with some good deliveries. And if you get them in your first ten balls or so, you can be out for a duck and gone.

Frank Hayes, who scored England's only century during the series, finished at Lord's with a disappointing eight and 0 in each innings. After an attempted hook shot off Boyce was easily caught by Holder at square leg, Hayes finished the series without scoring. Boyce claimed a total of eight wickets in the match. He finished the 1973 series as the leading Test wicket taker for the West Indies with 19 wickets. Boyce was also the highest wicket taker (41 wickets) in all first-class tour matches. He could have had more Test wickets if he hadn't suffered an injury before England's second innings at Edgbaston.

After the first Test at The Oval, Inshan Ali was disillusioned after not being selected for the second Test at Edgbaston. After sharing his frustration, Inshan was encouraged by his close friends in the West Indies team, including Keith Boyce and Alvin Kallicharan, to stay on tour and continue taking wickets. Inshan bowled more overs in first-class matches than any other West Indies player during the 1973 tour, and took 38 first-class wickets. Only three behind Keith Boyce.

During the Glamorgan v West Indies tour match, Inshan's wife gave birth to their first child, a boy, back home in Trinidad. The Ali family named their son Darrell Swansea Inshan Ali because the Glamorgan v West Indies match was played in Swansea. Tragically, Inshan's baby son died when he was just four months old.

In 1971 at the Sydney Cricket Ground, in a Test which was plagued by English dissatisfaction with the umpires and crowd disturbances, Illingworth's leadership and player management skills inspired England to beat Australia. He was applauded, cheered, chaired and carried off the ground by his delighted players. As a result, England reclaimed the Ashes back from Australia after 12 years.

Two years later, after a home defeat by the West Indies, Illingworth was relieved of his duties as England captain. Mike Denness, who had only played 10 Tests, was yet to score a Test century, and was not selected for the 1973 Tests v New Zealand and West Indies, was appointed captain for England's tour of the West Indies. The first Test in Trinidad was just under six months away.

The England captaincy was a job that Boycott wanted. When Illingworth was dropped as captain, Boycott considered himself in pole position to replace him. It was Illingworth, by phone, who confirmed to a disappointed Boycott that Denness was his replacement. In June 1974, Boycott asked the England selectors to leave him out of the team.

The pressure and disillusionment of being deprived of the England captaincy, and passed over for Denness, who he struggled to play for and with, was one of the reasons for Boycott's decision. Boycott's self-imposed exile lasted for three years. Denness passed his first captaincy challenge when he led England to a one wicket victory, with only three balls to spare, in the first 1973 ODI v West Indies at Headingley.

Many years later, Frank Hayes shared his thoughts with me about Illingworth's impact as a Test captain.

I rated Illingworth as a fantastic guy, a very fine captain, and one of the best I played under including (Mike) Brearley. Illingworth was a bit more negative that Brearley, but he was a fantastic captain, tactically astute and a good man manager of players.

'I didn't quite understand why Illy (Illingworth) lost the captaincy after that series', says Keith Fletcher. Fletcher shared his thoughts with me on Illingworth's forced departure from Test cricket.

We were all very disappointed to lose the 1973 series but also disappointed that Illy got blamed for the failure of the team. In my opinion, Illy was a far better Test match captain than Mike (Denness) was, but Mike was a very good one day captain. Illy was a very good cricketer and worth his place in the Test side, whether you liked him or not. So, why did the establishment decide to take the captaincy away from him and leave him out of the side? To this day I really have no idea.

'In 1973 in England, I really thought we had a chance', says Vanburn Holder.

It's not that I didn't think we weren't good enough, but I didn't think we'd win the series as convincingly as we did. At the time, in my opinion, there was still a quite a lot of politics involved in West Indies cricket, which continued even up to 1976. And sometimes the best guys were not always picked for the team. But in '73 we did it and, for me, that was the stage when as players we really started to gel as a team.

'1973 was a turning point for West Indies cricket', suggests Maurice Foster.

Because after that series in England there was, at last, a feeling that we were on an upward trend and that we had the players to maintain that level. You can't replace players like Garry Sobers and Rohan Kanhai, but we had players like Kallicharan and others who came in and maintained the level that we needed to keep going on a victorious path.

'That tour was a turning point for me and the team', Clive Lloyd reflected in *Supercat*, his autobiography published in 2007. 'I was confident again and felt that I was established at last. That was so important. And the side won after so many mishaps. It felt like the worst was ever'.[4]

According to Reds Perreira, the late inclusion of Garry Sobers to the West Indies team made a major impact. Sobers was the difference between the two sides. Back in the team after an enforced rest during the home series v Australia, Sobers provided an inspirational supporting role as a former captain, combined with his all-round displays with bat, ball and in the field.

'There had been this frustration of not being able to deliver a knock-out punch in their previous Tests, and many people felt the West Indies wouldn't be able to do it in 1973', summarises Clayton Goodwin.

So, from a West Indian point of view, this tour was a shot in the arm, which helped to lay down the foundations for 1976 onwards. Boyce, in the first Test, immediately showed the ability to deliver a knock-out blow. At Birmingham, Fredericks played that long innings to score his hundred, which was out of character and frustrated the English press, because the West Indies weren't playing 'Calypso cricket'. But that also showed that West Indian batsmen were not just all about 'Calypso cricket', and they all now had the ability to stick around.

My *1974 Playfair Cricket Annual* didn't mince its words. It produced a damning, *West Indies Give England a Caning,* headline for its report on the West Indies innings and 226 runs win at Lord's, and their 2-0 series victory. In the *Daily Telegraph,* EW Swanton ascribed West Indian victory to the specific impact of three players, and the luck of the toss.

> Fielding apart, I would ascribe the rejuvenation of the West Indies to three factors, the emergence of Julien, the sudden and unexpected elevation of Boyce to new, undreamt of heights of achievement, and not least to the glorious Indian summer of Sobers. Again, though they were so incontestably the better side, things were clearly made easier for them by Kanhai's success three times running with the toss.[5]

The West Indies victory in 1973 helped to ease the disappointment of their 1969 tour, which ended in a 2-0 series defeat. Kanhai received the Wisden Trophy, awarded to the winner of each England v West Indies Test series, from Aidan Crawley, the President of the MCC. The joy was shared by West Indian supporters at Lord's and at home, like me, watching on television. This was in sharp contrast, earlier in the year, after the West Indies v Australia series in the Caribbean. Only a few hundred spectators stayed in the Queen's Park Oval, Trinidad, to watch Lady Worrell present the Worrell trophy to Ian Chappell, the winning Australian captain.

The police and stewards at Lord's made very little effort to stem the flow of thousands of jubilant West Indian spectators. After Gibbs bowled Underwood to claim the final wicket of the series, many of them immediately vacated their seats and dashed across the field to celebrate victory. Kanhai marked his first (and only) Test series win as captain by dropping a bottle of champagne from the Lord's balcony. The champagne was eagerly caught, gathered, and sipped by some of the cheering West Indian supporters gathered below on the hallowed Lord's turf.

For Alvin Kallicharan, representing West Indian supporters in England was an essential source of motivation for the 1973 team.

During our interview chat for this book, Kallicharan delivered a heartfelt explanation about why the team played for people like me and my family.

> We were playing for the West Indian people in England. We played for them and what they went through. We understood their struggles and wanted to give them some pride. That was the only thing that gave them some recognition in England. And I experienced this first-hand, talking with West Indians, being with them, and playing for Warwickshire also. It was a sense of wellbeing for all of us players that we were important people for them. Sir Frank Worrell, Clyde Walcott, Everton Weekes, Garry Sobers, Wes Hall, Lance Gibbs, Rohan Kanhai. These greats gave people in England like you and your parents an identity. And then we came along and were asked to maintain it. In any business, you need success and if you can't maintain that – you will fail. All those great people asked us to do was to maintain what we gave to West Indian people in England, and that's all we tried to do.

Stanley Sunich, our neighbour across the road, remembers arranging a drinking session in our local pub to celebrate with some of his West Indian friends. It was a West Indies series victory led by Kanhai, who once lived near Stanley's family home in Berbice, Guyana. 'It was a perfect excuse for us all to go to the pub for a drink', Stanley cheerfully recalls. At our home, the immense feeling of satisfaction after watching West Indian victory in England, live on glorious colour television, was shared by all.

Keith Boyce in action for West Indies in a tour match v Nottinghamshire at Trent Bridge, 30 June 1973 (*Photo by Ken Kelly/Popperfoto/Getty Images*)

Frank Hayes is congratulated on reaching his century by spectators on the final day of the first 1973 England v West Indies Test at The Oval, 31 July 1973 (*Photo by Ken Kelly/Popperfoto/Getty Images*)

Vanburn Holder preparing to bowl for West Indies during the second 1973 England v West Indies Test at Edgbaston, 10 August 1973 (*Photo by Patrick Eagar/ Popperfoto/Getty Images*)

Garry Sobers batting for West Indies during his innings of 150 in the third 1973 England v West Indies Test at Lord's, 24 August 1973. Alan Knott is the wicketkeeper for England and Geoff Arnold is the fielder (*Photo by Patrick Eagar/ Popperfoto/Getty Images*)

Umpire Dickie Bird talks with the crowd while sitting on the covers at Lord's protecting the wicket as the stands are evacuated due to a bomb scare during the third 1973 England v West Indies Test, 25 August 1973 (*Photo by Ken Kelly/ Popperfoto/Getty Images*)

Above: Plaques in the University of West Indies (UWI) Cave Hill campus grounds, Barbados, commemorating four of the West Indian century makers during the 1973 England v West Indies Test series (*Photo by Marisa Huque*)

Above: West Indies captain, Rohan Kanhai, with the Wisden Trophy at Lord's after the West Indies beat England 2-0 in the 1973 Test series (*Photo by Ken Kelly/Popperfoto/Getty Images*)

Below: The Rohan Kanhai pub in Ashington, Northumberland. Kanhai played for Ashington Cricket Club in the Northumberland County League. The pub was named after Kanhai in honour of his service to the club

Right: Mike Denness, Kent captain, proudly holds the Benson and Hedges Cup won by the county in 1973. Kent also won the John Player League in the same year. Denness was appointed to replace Ray Illingworth as England captain after the 1973 England v West Indies Test series *(Photo used with kind permission from Kent CCC)*

Below: Entrance to Inshan Ali Park in Preysal, Trinidad. Named after the bowler who took 38 first-class wickets for the West Indies during the 1973 West Indies tour in England *(Photo by Reza Abasali)*

Postscript, final thoughts and recollections

Part One

In 1973, Rohan Kanhai, working closely with Lance Gibbs, his vice-captain and Garry Sobers, his former captain, led the West Indies to their first Test series win since a 1966/67 2-0 series win in India. The 2-0 victory in England stemmed the flow of a period of frustrating Test series draws and defeats for the West Indies. The success in England was Kanhai's only series win during his three series as captain.

It was the 1973 West Indies tour of England and the major domestic one-day competitions, and especially the John Player League, which confirmed my developing interest in cricket. It was my starting point. 1973 was all about the three Test matches. This is why the ODIs, including the first ever England v West Indies ODI at Headingley, only appear in the results summary in the appendix pages in this book.

As my interest in West Indies cricket increased, I became fascinated with the origins of the game in the Caribbean and the history of West Indies tours in England up to 1973. As a result, both of these historical perspectives are included in this book. One of my most memorable experiences as a writer was talking with Basil Butcher at his home in Wakatoo, Guyana in 2014. We sat in his living room and I was completely absorbed. Basil shared his life and times as a cricketer for the West Indies with me. Some of the highlights included his thoughts on using cricket as a way of experiencing life away from Port Mourant, Berbice and his experiences on tour in England during the 1960s.

Kanhai was retained as captain for the home Test series v England in 1974, which finished in a 1-1 draw. This was also Mike Denness' first series as England captain. As a Scot, Denness completed a British cycle of England captaincy which included Tony Lewis from Wales captaining England in India and Pakistan in 1972/1973, and Ray Illingworth captaining England during the two 1973 home series v New Zealand and West Indies.

The 1974 series in the Caribbean was Kanhai's third and final series as West Indies captain. His 13-match captaincy record was three wins, seven draws and three defeats. Kanhai's considerable attempts to manufacture a credible professional team ethic, despite the frustration and disappointment of a home series defeat v Australia and a home series draw v England, had steadied a faltering West Indies ship. However, Kanhai's role as captain was always scheduled to be temporary rather than long-term, as he progressed towards the end of his career.

Kanhai captained the West Indies from February 1973 to April 1974. He was captain for the first time at the age of 37 and the last time at 38. Alternative options were pursued by the West Indies board. Clive Lloyd was appointed as captain for the 1974/1975 tour of India where he made his Test debut eight years earlier. It was the first of his 74 Tests as captain. Lloyd hit the ground running as captain by scoring a century in the first Test at Bangalore and led the West Indies to a 3-2 series win.

Kanhai's method of leadership was strikingly different in approach and style to Sobers – who he followed and Lloyd – who followed him. In 1973, the West Indies responded to Kanhai's leadership, played some inspired cricket and earned their victory. During my chat with Ron Headley about Kanhai's captaincy during the 1973 tour, Ron was keen to highlight Kanhai's leadership skills.

Rohan was a super captain who knew the game inside out, was very astute, and should have captained the team a lot more. Rohan not only knew the game, but during that (1973) tour he knew the England team's strengths and weaknesses. He was a bit of a fiery character when he was younger, but he had a passion and enthusiasm for the game which always came bubbling through.

'There was quite a contrast between Garry Sobers and Rohan', says Vanburn Holder as he thoughtfully recalled the elation of victory in 1973.

Rohan could be a little harsh at times, and most of the lads in the team were quite young at the time and not quite used to it. But that was Rohan's way of getting the best out of the players. You really had to pull your finger out and in 1973 in England we got the job done and the guys were ecstatic to win. With Sobers it was different as he didn't say much to you to get you to do the right things. He had a different style to Rohan, but he was also a good captain. Sobers liked good cricket and always played to win. But, of course, when you do that you can sometimes lose games.

Clyde Walcott considered Kanhai to be a sound captain, a good tactician and knowledgeable about the game. Walcott appreciated Kanhai's field placing as being studied and usually correct but recognised that Lloyd would prove to be more popular with his players. In Walcott's view, Kanhai somehow lacked that rapport and his mood could also suddenly change.

Lonsdale Skinner, who played for Surrey and Guyana, retired from professional cricketer in 1977. One of his appearances for Guyana was against an England representative team at Bourda, Georgetown during their 1974 West Indies tour. In this tour fixture, Skinner played with and against some of the players who represented West Indies and England during the 1973 series, including Fredericks, Kallicharan, Lloyd, Boycott, Hayes and Underwood.

Skinner is now the chairman of the African Caribbean Cricket Association. This organisation aims to inspire young British people of African and Caribbean heritage to play and excel at cricket. According to Skinner, Kanhai's captaincy methods also made an impact on the Guyana national cricket team.

Kanhai was a professional captain operating in an amateur game in Guyana, and the problem with Guyana around then is that most of the non-professional players in the team, who were resident in Guyana, were club cricketers. They were some of the very best club cricketers in Guyana, but that hard-nosed professionalism was something that they didn't always quite have, and Kanhai acquired that from being up here (playing in England). He carried this on in Guyana but it didn't matter to me, and I didn't think there was anything wrong with it, because I grew up with that here (in England). But some of the guys in the Guyana team at the time didn't have that experience and, therefore, didn't always quite take to it.

Leaving the variety of opinions on Kanhai's leadership style aside, one of the enduring legacies of the 1973 series in England is that the West Indies emerged as a stronger and more competitive team. The rebuilding process, which bore fruit during the 1973 series win in England, provided West Indies cricket with much needed stability. This helped to secure the foundations for future teams led by Clive Lloyd and Viv Richards to dominate England in England.

Lloyd's new vision of West Indies cricket was driven by a disciplined and professional ideal, which left very little room for carefree abandonment. This enhanced sense of professionalism and togetherness was further developed by Lloyd and his players in response to the 1975/1976 5-1 series defeat in Australia and by participating in the breakaway World Series Cricket tournaments in Australia.

In 1975, Lloyd and Kanhai represented the West Indies together for the last time in the inaugural World Cup final v Australia at Lord's. The West Indies won the match by 17 runs with Lloyd as captain. I watched the final on television in our flat and with our Jamaican neighbours in the flat downstairs, in Mr Hibbert's living room. Towards the end of the Australian innings, and with excitement reaching fever pitch in each flat – upstairs and downstairs, Viv Richards spectacularly ran out three Australian batsmen.

Dennis Lillee and Jeff Thomson's defiant last-wicket stand was temporarily halted by the chaos caused by a pitch invasion by spectators who, at one stage, thought the match was over. Throughout this unfolding dramatic climax, and with West Indies supporters at Lord's and in Mr Hibbert's living room unable to suppress their joy, I struggled to get a clear view of the television with all the 'big people' gathered in front of me.

Lloyd, who described the atmosphere during the 1975 final as 'boiling over with West Indians' shared a match-winning all Guyanese 149-run partnership with Kanhai. Lloyd hit a century and Kanhai scored a half-century. One of John Arlott's most memorable commentary moments featuring the West Indies occurred during Lloyd's innings.

Arlott evocatively described one of Lloyd's boundaries as 'the stroke of a man knocking a thistle top off with a walking stick'.

Set against the backdrop of a relentless cycle of political and social distrust, division and tension between the two main ethnic communities in Guyana. The Lloyd and Kanhai partnership in 1975 at Lord's illustrated another vibrant public example of African-Guyanese and Indian-Guyanese collaborative skill and effort, which contributed to a positive result on the cricket field. Similar to the impact and symbolism of the Lloyd and Kallicharan first innings partnership at The Oval, which anchored West Indian domination of the first Test in the 1973 series v England.

Keith Boyce won the Prudential-Wisden player of the series award. In the Caribbean v Australia, Boyce's form revealed little evidence of the exhilarating performances to come in England later in the summer. Boyce played the last four out of the five Tests v Australia and recorded his best bowling figures of three for 68 in Barbados, his home island. His best performance with the bat was a score of 31 in the fifth and final Test in Trinidad.

Boyce, Keith Fletcher and Roy Fredericks were announced in 1974 as three out of the five *Wisden* cricketers of the year. Partly due to their impressive displays during the 1973 England v West Indies series. For 12 seasons, Boyce was also a star performer on the English county cricket circuit for Essex. Keith Fletcher insists that Boyce never bowled as quickly as he did in 1973.

Fletcher described Kanhai, Lloyd, Kallicharan and Sobers as one of the most powerful middle order batting line-ups he faced in Test cricket but, in his opinion, the all-round contribution of Boyce was the main difference between the teams.

'I played with Boycey for about 10 years at Essex and he was a good all-rounder, but I thought he was a better bowler than batter', says Fletcher, Boyce's Essex colleague and England rival in 1973.

He was a bowling all-rounder, and also a very dangerous batsman coming in down the order at number seven or eight. Boycey was also a top fielder, up close or in the deep, and was very popular at Essex because he was the absolute of what every spectator should love. He was a fast bowler and an exciting batsman who could hit the ball out of the ground.

When I spoke to Fletcher about Boyce, he was looking after the Essex under 15s team, watching over the Essex second team and the Academy, advising on the Essex first team, and involved in coaching and development work. 'I'm 74 and still working but only because I enjoy it!' Fletcher told me, with a chuckle, on his way to the Cloudfm County Ground in Chelmsford, the home of Essex cricket – where the West Indies played their first tour match in 1973.

During a phone chat with Brenda Boyce, Keith Boyce's second wife, I casually discovered that she knew some of the Babb family in Barbados, including an aunt, uncle and cousin of mine. So, in addition to the fact that my father had attended the same high school as Keith Boyce, another Boyce and Babb family link in Barbados was revealed as part of my research for this book. As with Inshan Ali, Keith Boyce tragically died at a very young age, 53, in Barbados.

Ron Headley's final international appearance for the West Indies was the second 1973 ODI v England at The Oval. In 1997 at Old Trafford, Dean Headley became the first Test cricketer to be the son (of Ron Headley) and grandson (of George Headley – who at 44 was the oldest player to represent the West Indies) of Test cricketers, when he made his debut for England v Australia.

Stephen Camacho worked for the West Indies Cricket Board as a secretary and chief executive for 18 years after his playing career ended. In those years, he was also a West Indies team manager, assistant manager and selector. The incident at Southampton in 1973 did not affect the friendship which developed between Camacho and Andy Roberts in later years. There was always a lot of mutual respect between them, and they met each other on many occasions at West Indies events, including end of year presentations and awards ceremonies. Camacho and Roberts both lived in Antigua until Camacho died in 2015.

Frank Hayes, the only English centurion during the 1973 series v West Indies, played a total of nine Tests. All Hayes' Tests were v West Indies. 1973 and 1976 in England and 1974 on tour in the Caribbean. His brilliant century at The Oval in 1973 was the only Test innings where he scored more than 50 runs. After retiring from professional cricket, Hayes taught chemistry and physics, and was a cricket organiser and coach at Oakham School in Rutland for 15 years. He is now a part-time physics teacher at the school. Stuart Broad, the England fast-bowler, was one of his students at Oakham. 'I threw balls at Stuart from the age of 12 and I taught him physics as well', Hayes recalls with an air of satisfaction.

Summarising his England career, and being critical of how cricket was organised in the 1970s, 'I don't think I achieved what I should have done in Test cricket', insists Hayes.

> You have your chances in life and there are some things you do well and there are some things you don't. That's how life is. I should have made more of my talent and didn't for all sorts of reasons. I wrote a book which I didn't publish in the 1980s at some time or other. It was a 'piss take' about how the powers that be, who have very little idea on what cricket is all about, administer the game very badly and mess young talent up. I wasn't necessarily referring to myself, but it was about young guys I knew who had been ruined by the system. Some of my colleagues told me I was this kind of player and as good as so and so. David Lloyd once said on television that Joe Root reminded him of me which is quite an extraordinary thing. So, I appreciate now that I was quite a good player and just didn't make the most of what I had.

From 1980 to 1995, the West Indies dominated Test cricket by playing 29 matches without losing a series. From 1975 to 1988, the Caribbean diaspora in Britain were able to witness a total of six West Indies Test and World Cup tours in England. The West Indies won two World Cups in 1975 and 1979 and were victorious in the 1976, 1980, 1984, and 1988 Test series in England.

During this period, the only major setback in England was the shock defeat by India in the 1983 World Cup final at Lord's. Errol Young was born in Britain to parents from Jamaica. Errol's father always talked about the great West Indian players, including Rohan Kanhai, and encouraged him to watch and play cricket. Errol played club cricket, attended Alf Gover's cricket school in Wandsworth, and had trials at Lord's to be a member of the MCC ground staff. He watched the 1983 World Cup final at home in south London.

After the West Indies lost the 1983 Prudential World Cup final I cried, because I was totally gutted, and my heart was just broken. It was just too painful to watch. I thought we had it in the bag and the way the Indians just wiped through our middle order just pained me.

This was also a devastating blow to my assumption of West Indian cricket invincibility. But remembering the shock result of the 1973 Leeds v Sunderland FA Cup final, should have prepared me to always expect the unexpected in professional competitive sport.

In 1984, which was Clive Lloyd's final series in England, the West Indies won all five Tests in Birmingham, Manchester, Leeds, and at Lord's and The Oval in London, in what has become known as the 'Blackwash' series. Television cameras captured a West Indian at the final Test at The Oval proudly waving a white banner with 'Blackwash' (as opposed to the term 'Whitewash') written in thick black ink. This was a sign that projected the triumphant euphoria of some West Indians in Britain. Especially those who viewed West Indies cricket victories in England as a righteous example of vibrant black success and dominance. This sequence of achievements in England continued to deepen the relationship between West Indies cricket and the diaspora in Britain, which included British-born descendants of migrants from the Caribbean.

Roland Butcher played for Middlesex until his retirement from first – class cricket in 1990. Mike Brearley, his captain at Middlesex, and captain of England, claimed that Butcher was one of the most exciting cricketers he had the pleasure of playing with. Basil Butcher was one of Roland's distant cousins in Guyana. Basil offered Roland some encouragement and advice when they eventually met towards the end of Roland's career.

Butcher created history by becoming the first black player to play Test cricket for England. He made his debut in Barbados, where he was born and where he watched his first Test as a young boy, in the third Test in England's 1981 Caribbean tour. After Butcher's landmark appearance, Clive Lloyd remarked that his selection for England was a positive move.

Many young lads from the West Indies have made their mark in soccer in this country (Britain) and I am delighted a young cricketer has come through as well. I think that those back home will be glad. We have so much talent out there that England are not taking anything from us. [1]

In 1988, Butcher became the first black player to captain Middlesex in a county fixture away v Leicestershire at Grace Road. Following his retirement from first-class cricket, Butcher worked as a coach in Bermuda, and returned to Barbados to become the Director of Sports at the University of the West Indies, Cave Hill Campus.

From 1973 onwards, I continued to fail what has been commonly known as the cricket Test or the Tebbit Test. In 1990, Norman Tebbit, a British Conservative party politician and former party Chairman, suggested that Caribbean and Asian people in Britain, and especially those who were born and raised in Britain, should demonstrate their loyalty to Britain by supporting the England cricket team. Tebbit argued that they should always choose to support England at cricket and not their country of birth or immediate heritage – West Indies, India or Pakistan.

In 2016, I was one of the guest speakers at a cricket-themed event at the Guyana High Commission in London. The event was organised to celebrate the nation's 50th year of independence from Britain. Towards the end of the evening, I was asked whether Tebbit's remarks, made all those years ago, had angered me. To be honest, whatever my thoughts about the ideology and politics which dominated the Conservative party during the 1980s, Tebbit's words did not anger me. I did not explode with indignant rage. I just ignored Tebbit's Test and did what I liked. I continued to support West Indies at cricket, Wales at rugby union and, later, England at football. However, I had no serious problems with Tebbit saying what he wanted to say.

On reflection, the whole Tebbit Test saga and discussions I've had with various people about it over the years, always remind me of two separate stories. The first was at my primary school in 1976 and the other at The Oval in 1991. During a morning break-time period in the summer of 1976 at my primary school, Mr Wallis (a teacher who had never previously expressed an interest in any sport) wheeled a colour television into our classroom. He then announced that he would show the morning session of the England v West Indies Test at Old Trafford for us all to see.

My main memory of watching the morning session at Old Trafford was Mike Selvey, on debut, claiming the first three prized West Indies wickets – Fredericks, Richards and Kallicharan. This left the West Indies first innings in a precarious position of 19 for three. On his first Test match tour in England, after the disappointment of missing out in 1973, Gordon Greenidge provided the sheet anchor run scoring role to rescue the West Indies with a century. The West Indies were bowled out in their first innings for only 211.

Only a handful of children in my class stayed in the room to watch the drama unfold at Old Trafford. Much later, a few children from some of the younger year groups drifted in to make up the numbers. These included a boy with Jamaican heritage called Derek. As the match progressed during the morning session up to lunch, some of us began to shout out in joy or agony as West Indian wickets continued to tumble, or when Greenidge struck a ball to the boundary. It soon became obvious that Derek was supporting England.

I remember feeling astonished at this. I had not met anyone from the Caribbean, or of Caribbean heritage in Britain, who supported the England cricket team when they played against the West Indies. In addition to this, Andy, one of the English lads in my class, was supporting the West Indies and proudly wearing a West Indies 1970s football style silk scarf. Therefore, I was introduced to a couple of new social experiences. I was in the presence of a lad of West Indian heritage in Britain who supported England v West Indies at cricket. Derek had passed the Tebbit Test with first-class honours. On the other side of the room was an English lad who proudly supported West Indies v England.

Let's now fast forward to The Oval in 1991. This was the fifth and final Test in the England v West Indies series that year. England won the match by five wickets to draw the series 2-2. This was the first home series since 1969 that England had avoided defeat v West Indies. Malcolm Marshall and Viv Richards made their final Test appearances. Richards left the field after being dismissed for 60 in the West Indies second innings to a tremendous, nerve-tingling ovation from The Oval crowd.

On the final day of the Test, I sat in a stand behind two young black lads with mini curly-permed afro hairstyles. They both appeared to be in their mid to late 20s. As England closed in on victory it was clear, due to their reactions to the action on the field, they were supporting England.

Unlike the bewildering situation I had experienced at my primary school with Derek and Andy in 1976, I was completely relaxed about this. I was 15 years older and my views on personal identity and sporting team choices had altered. These two lads had passed the Tebbit Test. They were supporting an England team at The Oval which had four players born in the Caribbean or born in Britain with Caribbean heritage: Phil DeFreitas (born in Dominica), David 'Syd' Lawrence (born in Britain – Jamaican parents), Chris Lewis (born in Guyana) and Mark Ramprakash (born in Britain – Guyanese father).

A Barbadian woman who was sitting next to me at The Oval completely disapproved of their support for England. For her, this was a severe form of identity treachery. She gave both lads a loud and severe verbal scolding which lasted for about 30 seconds. The two lads quietly accepted their telling off and continued to support England, but in a more subdued and less vocal manner.

Alongside my commitment to playing competitive cricket for my Boys' Brigade team, I also played for my south London secondary school team. Our school team didn't play in any league or cup competitions, but we did play a few matches a year against local rival schools. These were usually competitive after-school late afternoon friendly matches. Our results, as I recall, were an even mixture of wins and defeats.

I opened the batting for my secondary school from the first year to sixth form. I approached my responsibilities as an opening batsman in my usual steady and unspectacular manner. Only once did I release my Viv Richards inner-self and aggressively take on a bowling attack from start to finish. That was against a local rival Catholic school, when I hit a rapid 20 or 30 to set up a winning run chase. I was only in a hurry to help my team win because I had a train to catch.

After I was out, caught after attempting another lofted hit over mid-wicket, I quickly packed my bag and trotted to a nearby train station. I had to catch a train to my next match, which was a Boys' Brigade fixture somewhere in Surrey. I missed the team meeting time at the station, caught a later train and arrived at the ground minutes after the match had started. As a punishment for my lateness, I was called to be the 12th man. I sat on a bench by myself, beyond the boundary, hot, sweaty, frustrated, and in a major sulk.

A few days later, during a morning assembly, I was surprised, bemused and faintly proud to be called out in the front of the entire school. For the first and only time, I received a certificate from our head teacher followed by a ripple of applause. This certificate was awarded in recognition for my quick-fire innings which propelled our team to victory. All because of a sustained adrenalin rush, which forced me to score quickly because I had a train to catch.

Richard, my opening batting partner at secondary school, and fellow left-handed batsman, was our school's genuine class act cricketer. He had a very correct stance and a decent range of strokes. Richard also opened the bowling with his right-arm medium pace. His initial interest in cricket happened a year before me. Richard was captivated by watching the BBC television coverage of the 1972 England v Australia series, which ended in a 2-2 draw. He was influenced by the personalities of Geoffrey Boycott, Dennis Lillee, John Snow and Keith Stackpole. Richard quickly became a big fan of Yorkshire because of Geoffrey Boycott, who was his batting idol, and wore a long-sleeve Yorkshire cricket jumper when he played for the school team.

Our school had no access to nearby playing fields. So, for cricket matches against other schools, we hired cricket pitches in local public parks. The other option was to travel on hired buses, supplied by the local education authority, to play at schools in the more refined and affluent neighbourhoods in North Surrey. We usually appeared as the poorer relations compared with some of these schools we competed against. Through cricket, I slowly widened my social experience by meeting young people from fee-paying schools for the first time.

Our collection of players, English and those with Caribbean and Irish heritage, were wide-eyed, mildly envious and slightly intimidated (although some of us didn't want to show it) by our well-healed, well-scrubbed and better organised opposition. But it didn't hinder our determination to beat them.

We were usually dressed in a roughly assembled array of white, cream, light-brown, beige and pale yellow. Our shared school cricket kitbag looked like a collection of equipment purchased at a Saturday morning, small town church hall jumble sale. Especially, when compared to the pristine equipment paraded by our private school opponents. At one school we visited, I was astonished to discover that they had a mini-pavilion and organised dressing rooms.

Therefore, victory against these schools, as and when they happened, always tasted a bit sweeter. After one of our victories, some of us invaded the playing area to celebrate with the batsmen who scored the winning runs with only a few balls left. In our innocent schoolboy minds, we were excitedly mimicking celebratory crowd invasions we'd been involved in or watched on television. Especially during the 1973 and 1976 England v West Indies Test series. The school we defeated were furious about the way we behaved after the match. They complained to Mr Josephs, our PE teacher. As a result, we were forced to concede the game due to our, perceived, unreasonable behaviour.

Mr Josephs gave us an almighty telling off during our bus journey back to school. None of us wanted to accept responsibility for leading the invasion of the field. However, many of us felt the response to our post-match celebrations from our opposition was an unnecessary overreaction and sour grapes after being defeated.

Part Two

T he legacy and impact of the 1973 Leeds United v Sunderland FA Cup final, one of the biggest shock results in the history of the competition, continues to this day. When Leeds travelled to play Sunderland in a Championship (second tier of English league football) fixture in 2017, *The Sunday Times* newspaper reminded its readers that, 'This remains one of the most evocative fixtures in English football'.

> Especially on Wearside, of course, where the famous FA Cup win under the Twin Towers at Wembley almost 45 years ago is stamped into the DNA of everyone connected with Sunderland. The images of a trillbied Bob Stokoe striding across the turf to embrace double-save hero Jim Montgomery is still folklore after the second-tier outsiders upstaged Don Revie's much-heralded Leeds United to lift the famous trophy way back in 1973. Indeed, Stokoe's statue outside the Stadium of Light (Sunderland's home ground) is still a point of pilgrimage. [1]

The current trend for many football clubs in the English Premier League is to disregard the FA Cup as a low priority domestic knock-out competition. Especially in comparison with winning the Premier League, finishing in the top four of the Premier League to ensure qualification for the following season's European-wide Champions League, or avoiding relegation from the Premier League to maintain the substantial revenue stream available from each club's share of television and broadcasting rights income.

After suffering two cup final defeats in May 1973 at Wembley v Sunderland, and v Inter Milan in Greece, Leeds had an impressive start to the 1973/1974 First Division season. They started their 1973/

1974 campaign with a record-breaking run of 29 games unbeaten before losing at Stoke City in February 1974.

At the end of the 1973/1974 season, Leeds were crowned First Division champions for the first time in five years. Don Revie moved on to accept the England manager's job. Brian Clough, a high-profile critic of Revie for many years, was (surprisingly in the opinion of many) appointed by Leeds to replace Revie as manager. Soon after Clough arrived at Elland Road, he told the Leeds players to throw their winner's medals and international caps in the bin. According to Clough, they didn't deserve them as they were won by cheating. Clough's reign at Leeds infamously lasted for a short and turbulent period of 44 days before he was dismissed by the club.

By 1978, Charlie Williams, who was still performing regularly on stage as a comedian, was now a member of the Board of Directors at Barnsley Football Club. Barnsley was his home town club. Therefore, Williams became one of the first non-white members of a board at a professional football club in England. One of his first major decisions was to help bring Allan Clarke, my number one football hero, from Leeds to join Barnsley as a player-manager.

During the 1970s/1980s, despite the increase in raw racism in and around football stadiums on match days, attempts by far-right political groups to recruit white supporters, and organised recreational hooligan violence, my support for Leeds United continued. In addition to this, a minority of supporters with Caribbean heritage also developed a prominent reputation for football-related violence. The football hooligan gangs, known as 'firms', involved in this violent subculture attached themselves to various clubs.

Some of the firms with high profile members with Caribbean heritage included Danny Brown from Aston Villa's C-Crew, Barrington 'One-eyed Baz' Patterson from the Birmingham City Zulus, Ian 'Tiny' Garwood at Millwall, and Carol 'Cass' Pennant at West Ham United. Pennant was one of the leaders of West Ham's notorious Inter City Firm (ICF). He was born in Britain to parents from Jamaica and adopted by a white English family in Kent. Pennant later wrote a book, also adapted as a feature film, which detailed his upbringing and violent exploits at football matches with the ICF.

As far as I was concerned, I decided to support Leeds and I was standing up for my right to do so. Being a black boy living outside

Leeds was not going to stand in my way. From 1973, it took another 12 years before I made my first visit to Leeds in 1985.

Towards the end of the 1980s, Leeds Fans United Against Racism and Fascism, one of the first organised groups created to remove racism from football, began to challenge racist activity at Leeds United. Their campaign was spearheaded by their *Marching Altogether* fanzine. I still have a collection of these fanzines, alongside my collection of football programmes, under my desk at home. All of them neatly packed together in a plastic storage box.

During the 2015 Arsenal v Aston Villa FA Cup final at Wembley, the FA commemorated the 50th year of Albert Johanneson's pioneering achievement in 1965 as the first black African footballer to play in a Cup final. One of Johanneson's daughters and a grand-daughter travelled from the US to be guests of honour in the Wembley Stadium Royal Box. A couple of days before the 2015 final, Johanneson's family took part in a ceremony to donate his medals, including his 1965 FA Cup runners-up medal, to the National Football Museum in Manchester.

In 2019, a special Leeds Civic Trust Blue Plaque to commemorate Johanneson's life was unveiled by one of his grand-daughters and Brian Deane – a former Leeds player with family roots in Nevis, and two Leeds Councillors. The Leeds United Supporters' Trust also helped to sponsor the plaque.

When I last spoke to Paul Eubanks, he was still determined to keep Johanneson's memory alive and widen the recognition of his life and football career.

People in the African and Caribbean community in Leeds were very proud of what Albert achieved at the football club, and Leeds United supporters loved him. After I heard that Albert died, I was determined to commemorate his achievements, and over 20 years later, I'm still doing it.

It was through my support for Leeds United that I discovered the pleasure of listening to BBC World Service radio. In 1989 in Hong Kong, during a stint as a teacher in a language school, and an unsuccessful attempt to work as a model and film extra, I stumbled across a West Ham United v Leeds match on a radio. I tuned in to the match on a borrowed radio, owned by an English guy who lived in the same residential block as me. For the record, Leeds won 1-0 with a goal scored by Vinnie Jones. Twenty years on from my first short-term stay in Hong Kong, I began working for the BBC World Service in the English language teaching by radio department.

Clyde Best left West Ham in 1976 to play professional football in the US. During his lengthy stint in the US, which was briefly interrupted by a spell playing for Feyenoord in Holland, Best occasionally played against Ade Coker, the young Nigerian lad he took under his wing at West Ham. During his time in the early 1980s in the US, Best rekindled his passion for cricket by playing for a couple of teams in Florida. One was a British team and the other was a team with mainly Barbadian players. Remembering how watching the 1973 West Indies team had inspired him during his time playing football in England, Best told me that:

> Moving over to England and watching the West Indies play cricket made me feel proud that I could see people of colour from the Caribbean doing so well, and the guys put on a tremendous show – Garfield Sobers, Rohan Kanhai, Keith Boyce, Alvin Kallicharan and all of them. It was great for me to be in England at that time watching the West Indies win cricket matches left, right and centre, and it was great for all of us here (in England), you know, watching the team being at the top of the world, because it made you feel better. The West Indies cricket team was so powerful for me. I tell people this all the time, and I really appreciated all those guys and what they did. Because once I saw them doing well it made me step up and feel that I could do well too.

Many of my childhood memories from our flat in south London, where I lived until the end of the 1970s, are centred on the shared experience of vibrant social gatherings of family and friends from across the Caribbean. This included sharing Caribbean food and drink, playing cards and dominoes in a raucous fashion, intrigued by listening to stories about past experiences back in the Caribbean and living in Britain, and opinionated views on politics and cricket in the Caribbean and Britain. All of this was accompanied by a musical backdrop of calypso, funk, Motown, reggae, soca and soul.

Then, of course, there was the ultimate domestic and national collective experience. Watching my/our favourite weekly and annual television shows at scheduled times from a choice of three available terrestrial channels in Britain. BBC1, BBC2 and a regional independent television channel. This was an integral part of my 1970s childhood.

As families in British households, increasingly and individually, watch unscheduled 'on demand' television shows, video-sharing channels, satellite and subscription broadcasting services with multi-channel options, on demand online services, portable video streaming devices – including phones and tablets, and play video games. The idea of millions of families regularly watching scheduled terrestrial television programmes from start to finish (with no start, stop, pause and rewind) will continue to be a rare shared experience.

In 2016, following a national referendum, Britain narrowly voted by 51.9% to 48.1% to leave the European Union (EU), which it joined in 1973 as the European Economic Community (EEC), also popularly known as the Common Market. In March 2017, Theresa May, the British Prime Minister, signed a letter which notified the EU that Britain intended to give up its membership and leave the EU. The letter triggered a period of pain-staking formal negotiations between the British government and the EU on the terms of the departure permitted under Article 50 of the Lisbon treaty. As this book went to press, negotiations between the British government and the EU on the terms of departure were ongoing.

Meanwhile, CARICOM, created in 1973, continues to face the ongoing challenges of continued regional cooperation. As well as being forced to analyse the future impact of Brexit on its long-term political, trade, investment and development relationships with Britain and the EU.

CARICOM has also increased its attempts to reform the organisation, structure and development of cricket in the Caribbean. In 2015, CARICOM commissioned a report on the governance of West Indies cricket. The main mandate of the cricket Review Panel was to review the administrative and governance structure of the West Indies Cricket Board (WICB). It submitted its recommendations through Dr. the Right Honourable Keith Mitchell, Prime Minister of Grenada and CARICOM Secretary-General to the Chairman of the Cricket Governance Committee. One of the Panel's major recommendations in their final report was the immediate dissolution of the WICB (re-branded in 2017 as Cricket West Indies) to be replaced with the appointment of an interim board. This recommendation was resisted by the WICB.

Deryck Murray was a member of the cricket review panel that met and produced the report for CARICOM. Two of the former West Indies players interviewed by the panel, Lance Gibbs and Alvin Kallicharan, also played in the 1973 Test series in England.

When I reflect on my life as a young boy in 1973, when Prime Minister Edward Heath, during his last full year in office, led Britain to membership of the EEC, I would describe my personal and cultural identity then as West Indian or just black, or sometimes both. Some days I just felt connected to my immediate countries of heritage. Especially Guyana, as most of my family in Britain during the 1970s were Guyanese.

Regardless of my opinions on the outcome of the 2016 EU membership referendum, I have never felt European, or called myself European, at any stage in my life. Even as I approach late middle-age, the thought of living and working again in different parts of the world still has its attractions. However, I would not consider moving with my British, Caribbean, South American, west Balkan mixed-race family to live in another country in Europe.

Over the last 20 to 30 years, during my years of growing adulthood, I have also become more comfortable about the idea of being British, if not English. This has been a long personal journey of identifying with my immediate Caribbean heritage, combined with an increasing sense of Britishness and a firm sense of a two-fold identity. I support the West Indies in cricket and England at football. Without feeling in any way unique in making these choices.

This experience was also shaped by my attempt to travel around the country, as much as possible, after I left secondary school in London in the early 80s. I wanted to find out more about the country I lived in. For work, study, music, photography, football, cricket, holiday, adventure, curiosity, and visiting friends, family and acquaintances who lived in a different British cities and towns. This included some areas in and around London that I rarely travelled to.

In the autumn of 1992, I travelled to Coventry and Wolverhampton. I stayed in each place for a few days, simply because

I had not been to these cities before. I increased my familiarity with different Caribbean communities who lived in significant numbers in various British cities and towns. These included Dominicans in Bradford, Kittitians and Nevisians in Leeds, Vincentians in High Wycombe and Luton, and Barbadians in Reading. On the many trips I made to Reading during the mid-1990s, I enjoyed several visits to the Reading Caribbean club. I was always made welcome by the many Barbadians who, whenever I was there, were most of the Caribbean members in the club. I also developed relationships with West Indian cricket clubs in various parts of Britain, including clubs based in Birmingham, Bristol, Leeds and Leicester.

Much of my time in the 1980s outside London in Britain was spent in Manchester, in the 1990s in Leeds, and in the 2000s in Coventry. Alongside this experience of discovering Britain, my West Indian connections continued to take root and flourish, and were underpinned by family, work, publicity, investigative travel, pleasure and leisure trips to the Caribbean, and my life long relationship with West Indies cricket.

These included 'pilgrimages' to the Bourda ground in Georgetown, the Kensington Oval and the Cricket Museum – Home of the Cricket Legends – in Barbados, the Darren Sammy National Cricket Stadium in St. Lucia, the Arnos Vale ground in St. Vincent, and the West Indies Cricket Heritage Centre at Spice Basket, Grenada – where I donated a copy of *They Gave the Crowd Plenty Fun* to the Centre's library collection. I also made a rash attempt to take a closer look at the Providence cricket ground in Guyana during construction. Understandably, I was denied entry to the site by a security official. One of my family connections to cricket in the Caribbean was through a cousin, Renee Babb, who was the Honorary Secretary for the Pickwick Cricket Club in Barbados.

For some in the Caribbean community in Britain, their assumption of Britishness, nationality, and identity was shattered during celebrations commemorating the 70th anniversary of the arrival of the *Windrush*. In 2018, British immigration officials believed they wrongly detained or removed over 160 Caribbean-born people, incorrectly identified as illegal migrants, who had been living in Britain for many years.

Many of those who faced harassment from Home Office officials, and who were unable to produce documents to prove their right to remain in Britain, were Commonwealth citizens who arrived before January 1973. This followed the 1971 Immigration Act, which amended and replaced the existing laws, including changes in the law regarding citizenship.

I have used cricket as a way of explaining my identity during work and travel experiences in different countries. During a trip to New Zealand, when some people expressed curiosity about my West Indian heritage, I repeatedly used West Indian cricket as a way of making quick and easy references to the Caribbean to establish a sense of familiarity.

Observing West Indies cricket and West Indian cricketers is still one of the very few ways that non-Caribbean people in Britain, and around the world, can gain an insight into the cosmopolitan nature of Caribbean society. I often use West Indian cricketers to illustrate this to non-Caribbean people, whether they are cricket fans or not.

I remind people about the 1973 West Indies team, the first West Indies team I forged a connection with, which had a collective African-Caribbean, Indian-Caribbean and European-Caribbean presence. This included Garry Sobers, Keith Boyce, Roy Fredericks, Clive Lloyd, Inshan Ali, Rohan Kanhai, Alvin Kallicharan, Deryck Murray and Stephen Camacho. If necessary, I also drift back and refer to the 1950 West Indies team in England with John Goddard, Sonny Ramadhin, Jeffrey Stollmeyer and the three Ws.

I often refer to Tony Cozier, the Barbadian journalist, author and commentator, who I had the pleasure of interviewing for *They Gave the Crowd Plenty Fun*. I was also delighted to share a BBC radio commentary box with Cozier at The Oval in 2013, during my first stint as a Test Match Special (TMS) lunchtime guest. When Cozier appeared on television, he often shocked and surprised people I met in Britain from a wide variety of backgrounds. They assumed, after listening to Cozier's Barbadian accent on BBC radio, that he was black and not white.

An article written by Jim Jinkoo, an Indian-Trinidadian in London, commemorating Indian Arrival Day 2000, made specific references to the role cricket played in increasing the profile of Indian-Caribbean people in 1970s Britain.

To illustrate our position in this country, I shall try to relate a short story. In 1970, I started work in the finance department of a local authority and was probably the only Indo-Caribbean person amongst over 3000 employees. Five years later, I filled in an application form for another position and entered 'Indo-Caribbean' as my race. I was summoned to Personnel and confronted by two female officers, one white and the other black. They told me I could not put 'Indo-Caribbean' on the form because there is no such thing, and in any case, they did not have that category in their Equal Opportunities monitoring programme. I was told I should change it to Indian, Pakstani or even Afro-Caribbean since I was from the West Indies. At one stage a senior personnel officer entered the room and after some discussions about race and migration she agreed that there were 'Indians' in the Caribbean because she had heard about Sonny Ramadhin, believed Rohan Kanhai was one of the best batsmen she had seen and thought Alvin Kallicharan was a cute little thing. The conclusion was that I could list myself as Indo-Caribbean – thanks to cricket.[2]

Since 1973, I've also used cricket as a way of explaining the relationship between Guyana and the English-speaking Caribbean islands, through their shared, economic, political and social history of British colonial rule. This is one of my default methods of answering a question that I often receive. How and why does a country in South America produce cricketers qualified to represent the West Indies?

The 1973 West Indies tour of England was the catalyst, which triggered my life-long interest in cricket from a British-resident Caribbean perspective. I also don't think my interest would have immediately ended if the West Indies lost the series. Alongside the John Player League on BBC television this was my starting point. This happened in a year which was, for me, and many of the contributors and people mentioned in this book, a significant one for a wide variety of memorable reasons.

The decline of West Indies cricket since the mid-1990s, and the continuous pattern of poor results and disappointing performances, has been well documented, analysed, commented on and furiously debated by all concerned with the past, present and future of cricket in the Caribbean. According to the ICC rankings, just before the publication of this book, West Indies were ranked eighth in Test cricket, ninth in ODIs, and ninth in T20Is. Many reasons have been produced to explain this downward spiral. With various levels of optimism expressed for future improvement and progress.

These include criticism of the management, organisation and structure of cricket controlled by CWI. The financial restraints which prevent significant levels of investment in cricket in the Caribbean. The size of the economies in the Caribbean which prevent investment in cricket rising above a fraction of the levels spent in other countries, including Australia, England and India. The questionable standards of first-class cricket, facilities and pitches in the Caribbean. The conflicts and lack of trust between players, CWI and WIPA over salaries, conditions, management and selection policies, and the persistent challenge of wielding cricketers, coaches and administrators from several independent nations and six territorial cricket boards into a cohesive regional force. Then there is the criticism of the approach and attitude of some players when they represent the West Indies.

The preference of some West Indian players is to play in the lucrative global franchise T20 tournaments. These tournaments offer them far higher levels of remuneration, compared with the money on offer to represent the West Indies. The rapid development of unregulated T20 tournaments, often played during the Caribbean domestic season, has had a greater impact on the West Indies compared with the other Test playing nations. In addition to the above, there is the ongoing concern that the Caribbean is being left behind with international cricket's administrative, financial and political power held by India, England and Australia. It has been argued that this development could affect the long-term competitive balance of international cricket.

In 2014, the West Indies tour of India came to a premature end after three out of the five ODIs were completed. The intensity of another very public contract and pay dispute between the players, WIPA and the WICB, had been an unfortunate backdrop and distraction from the start of the tour. This resulted in the tour being cancelled and the West Indies players returning home. The rest of the tour's fixture list included a one day international, a T20 match, and three Tests still to play.

In response, India announced a series of games with Sri Lanka to replace the matches with the West Indies. Following this, there was a strained relationship between CWI and the Board of Control for Cricket

India (BCCI). The BCCI, arguably the most powerful board in world cricket, demanded damages from CWI amounting to $US 42m following the dissolution of the 2014 tour.

Another consideration, which should not be overlooked, is how the format and structure of international cricket has been completely reshaped over the last 45 years. In 1973, the West Indies faced international competition in one format of the game, Test cricket. There were six nations who played international cricket with Test status: Australia, England, India, New Zealand, Pakistan and West Indies. After the 1973 Test series, the West Indies played their first two ODIs at Headingley and The Oval. The inaugural ODI Cricket World cup in England was still just under two years away.

Over 45 years later, the number of Test playing nations has risen to 12. In 1992, South Africa returned to Test cricket after an absence of 22 years v West Indies in Barbados. Following the release of Nelson Mandela in South Africa, progress made in dismantling the apartheid system, and two years ahead of the nation's first national elections in which all races were permitted to vote. The most recent teams to join the international family of Test playing nations were Afghanistan and Ireland. Both were granted Test status by the International Cricket Council (ICC) in 2017.

Put simply, from a West Indies perspective, there is more international competition from more countries across more formats. For all international teams, it's a near impossible task to claim long-term dominance across all three formats at the same time. The West Indies have won two T20 World Cups. The 2012 T20 World Cup in Sri Lanka, and 2016 in India. In 2016, the West Indies women won the Women's T20 World Cup in India. In the same year, the young men representing the West Indies won the Under-19s ODI World Cup in Bangladesh. Michael Vaughan, the former England captain, now a cricket broadcaster, was inspired to tweet that the West Indies Under-19s triumph was 'the best cricket news in years'.

2016 was a year full of West Indian cricket achievement and promise. But in the following year, the men's team, which was ranked ninth in the ICC ODI rankings by the qualification deadline in September 2015, did not qualify for the 2017 Champions Trophy tournament in England. Later in 2017, the West Indies suffered a 2-1 defeat in England in a three Test series. Since 1976, this was the first West Indies tour to

England where I did not attend any matches – Tests, ODIs or T20Is. This was due to family, travel, work commitments and wavering levels of interest.

Lance Gibbs, during the first 2017 Test at Edgbaston, which was the first day-night Test in England, on a visit to a ground where he played for Warwickshire with distinction for many years, was introduced to players from both teams. England comfortably won this Test by an innings and 209 runs within three days. During this Test the West Indies lost 19 wickets in one day.

In the second Test at Headingley, the West Indies famously fought back to win by five wickets. The series was now level at 1-1 with one Test remaining. This was the first West Indies Test victory in England since 2000. Shai Hope, one of seven players from Barbados, produced one of the most outstanding individual West Indian Test batting performances in England for many years. Hope hit a century in each innings.

Hope (please excuse the pun) was now in the hearts of many West Indian cricket followers in Britain. They were thrilled to see their team have an unlikely opportunity to win the series at Lord's. Unfortunately, this morale boosting flicker of optimism was quickly dampened. The West Indies lost the final Test at Lord's by nine wickets in a low-scoring match which finished in three days.

Brenda Boyce was sitting in one of the small groups of West Indian spectators who witnessed Test victory at Headingley. For the last 15 years or so, Brenda has combined coming to watch the West Indies in England with visiting her mother, siblings, aunts and friends she has met following the team. In the 2017 tour, in addition to the Test at Headingley, Brenda also watched the drawn West Indies v Kent tour match at Canterbury and met John Shepherd. She has also followed the West Indies on tour in New Zealand and South Africa. Brenda remains loyal to the cause of West Indies cricket.

> The support for the West Indies is not there like it used to be in England, because we keep losing. So, some people in Barbados ask me when I come over to watch the West Indies (in England), why are you still going behind them? But I just tell them that I'm West Indian and I'm with the team through thick and thin. And that's why I'm still there with them.

Another dedicated West Indian supporter at Headingley was Keith 'Pipeman' van Anderson, who migrated from Guyana to Britain as a 13-year-old schoolboy in 1964. The first match he attended was the 1973 England v West Indies Test at Lord's. From that day on, Pipeman attended every Test at Lord's and, throughout the special highs and devastating lows of West Indies cricket, he also regularly followed the team on overseas tours. He earned the Pipeman nickname because he was very rarely seen without a pipe stylishly positioned in the corner of his mouth. Sadly, Keith 'Pipeman' van Anderson passed away in 2019.

The relationship between West Indies cricket and the Caribbean diaspora in Britain continues to face serious challenges. The increased detachment from cricket has coincided with the West Indies team having limited value as an estimation of community self-worth. I reflected on reasons expressed for the decline in the relationship between West Indies cricket and the Caribbean diaspora in Britain in *They Gave the Crowd Plenty Fun.*

Some of the reasons include the dismal sequence of performances and results produced by the West Indies in England. The West Indies have not won a Test series in England since a 4-0 victory in 1988. Following the two (2-2) drawn series in England in 1991 and 1995, the West Indies completed six tours up to 2017. In 2000, England won the series 3-1. This was the first England Test series win over the West Indies at home since 1969. In 2004, England beat West Indies 4-0; in 2007, England beat West Indies 3-0; in 2009, England beat West Indies 2-0; in 2012, England beat West Indies 2-0; in 2017, England beat West Indies 2-1.

During this period, there was one significant highlight. As the darkness descended across The Oval in the 2004 ICC Champions Trophy final v England, Ian Bradshaw and Courtney Browne – a British-born Barbadian and a future CWI Chairman of selectors – steered the West Indies towards an unlikely but thrilling victory.

At home in the Caribbean, the West Indies have always been a difficult team for England to beat. Since 1968, the West Indies have only lost one Test series v England in the Caribbean. A 3-0 series defeat by England in 2004. In 2019 in the Caribbean, with England widely regarded as favourites, the West Indies won the Test series 2-1. The ODI series was drawn 2-2. England convincingly won the T2OI series 3-0. During the Test series, the West Indies displayed an encouraging sense of further developed talent, determination, resilience, and an increased belief in each other. The team was impressively captained by Jason Holder, who led from the front with a double hundred in the first Test 381 run win in Barbados.

Months later, the West Indies finished in a disappointing 9th place in the league table of 10 teams – after the group stage of the 2019 Cricket World Cup in England and Wales. With only two wins, they failed to qualify for the semi-final knockout phase by six points and finished five points clear of bottom of the table Afghanistan. 2019 marked forty years since the West Indies won their second and last World Cup final at Lord's in 1979.

Whether the West Indies can produce a lengthy sequence of improved results against the top international teams, across all formats of the game, home and away from the Caribbean, remains to be seen. Some Caribbean people in Britain, who are committed to the cause of West Indies cricket, still feel an intense longing for a collection of moral boosting performances by the team in England, the Caribbean and beyond.

The relentless cycle of West Indies Test defeats in England has had a serious impact on the numbers of West Indians attending matches. Although, more West Indian spectators attend England v West Indies ODI and T20I matches compared with Tests. As Neville Carberry explains, some of the older generation of West Indies supporters have had enough of watching the team deliver poor performances in England.

The standard of cricket the West Indies play when they come here is not exciting enough or good enough for us to pay money to go and watch them. The standard of cricket is nowhere near the level that it used to be. In my day in the 1960s and '70s (in England) we had to queue up from 1 or 2 o'clock in the morning to get into the grounds to watch them. Then from 3 and 4 in the morning, the queues just got longer. There were some great cricketers putting their heart and soul into the game when they came here (to England), and they were proud to represent the West Indies and give us some pride. So, I will not go out of my way to watch them play here until the standard of cricket improves. It's as simple as that.

Ian Bradshaw played five Tests for the West Indies. All of them in 2006. In 2004, he won the ICC Champions Trophy final player of the match award. His late rescue batting partnership with Courtney Browne helped the West Indies beat England in the final at The Oval by two wickets. Bradshaw insists, while the large numbers of Caribbean people in Britain have distanced themselves from West Indies cricket, the recent generation of West Indian players still appreciate and respect the support from the diaspora in Britain:

> The numbers of supporters and the interest in England amongst a lot of the West Indian communities is nowhere near the same as it used to be, and the generations coming through now in England don't necessarily see themselves as being West Indian. They may have an appreciation of that part of their legacy or heritage, but not necessarily that they are part of it. By that fact, and the other reasons why less West Indians came to watch the games, you will find that as professional sportsmen you may not have the same connection with these communities. But what I can say, with certainty, is that every cricketer that comes to play in England from the West Indies still has an appreciation of the fact that there are still some people there who very much connect with the team. On the occasions when we got to interact with the West Indian fans that came to support us, I know that these occasions were thoroughly enjoyed by all the players. But it is a shame that we don't get the numbers in the grounds to watch the games as we did in the past.[3]

Other reasons for the rapidly declining interest include dissatisfaction with international ground regulations in England, which restrict bringing in your own food, drink and instruments. The ticket allocation systems and unaffordable prices have kept older members of the Caribbean community away from grounds. Older generations of West Indian people in Britain, with intimate connections to the Caribbean and West Indies cricket, have either passed away or returned to live in the Caribbean. Migration from the Caribbean to Britain gradually petered out from the 1970s onwards, as migration from the Caribbean to the US and Canada increased. So, in very basic terms, the Caribbean population in Britain is not being 'refilled'.

Robert Bradford grew up in Trinidad with his English father and Trinidadian mother. Learie Constantine was a family friend and Charlie Davis, another former West Indies Test cricketer, was a close neighbour. As a young schoolboy, Robert attended every day of the 1974 West Indies v England Test in Port of Spain with his English grandmother. He was in the crowd on the final day when Kanhai and Sobers ended their Test careers.

Robert and his family migrated to England two weeks after that 1974 Test. His family flew to England on the same plane as Bernard Julien, who was resuming his contract as a player for Kent. Sixteen years later, Robert was living in south London and witnessed the steadily decreasing support from the Caribbean diaspora in Britain.

'When Sky televised the 1990 West Indies v England series in the Caribbean, which was the first England cricket tour they showed live, I used to go to a pub in Clapham Park Road and watch the matches on the television with some older West Indian guys, who would be there having a drink and watching with me', says Robert.

But their sons, who were in the pub with us, had no interest in what was going on. I remember when the West Indies won the Test in Barbados, we were all jumping up and down hugging each other and celebrating but their sons were not interested. They could talk about football all day long but had no interest in West Indies cricket whatsoever. So, I don't think that the interest in cricket has been passed down as much as we think it did. And especially now down the generations through to people who were born here to families from the Caribbean. In all my years living in London, I met very few young West Indians born in Britain who really knew anything about the Caribbean, cricket, wanted to go to the Caribbean, liked it when they went there or, like me, wanted to find out more about their Caribbean family history. Added to that, you've got to look at the results, and our results over the years here (in England) have been terrible. So, who really wants to go and watch the West Indies get mash-up again and again?

Steve Walcott, who saw his first Test at Edgbaston in 1973, observed dwindling levels of West Indian support in England during the 1995 West Indies tour.

I remember going to the England v West Indies Test at Old Trafford where Brian Lara made 140 odd runs in the second innings. I went by myself but, thankfully, I got chatting to another West Indian fan, a guy from Doncaster. We got chatting and I remember that day at Old Trafford very well. He was equally enthusiastic about West Indies cricket as me, but we talked a lot that day about seeing chinks in the armour in the West Indian support in the crowd. There were very few West Indians at Old Trafford that day and that was in 1995.

'Test matches in England are still sold out. So, it's just a different type of person who goes to them', says Simon Lister. 'So, the question you must ask yourself is whether that's a good thing or not'. Lister is a senior BBC TV news producer, journalist and author of *Supercat: The Authorised Biography of Clive Lloyd* and *Fire in Babylon: How the West Indies Cricket Team Brought a People to its Feet.*

I mean, when you talk about the West Indies, the number of West Indian fans who go to Test matches now in England is tiny compared to 1973. But then, for people with Caribbean heritage in Britain, there are so many other reasons why they are not interested in West Indies cricket nowadays. And it's not just about not being able to get tickets for a Test match. There are a dozen reasons why and the availability and prices of tickets are just a couple of them. It's as much about how the Caribbean has changed as much as how Britain has changed. The way the Caribbean has changed has reflected how people of Caribbean heritage in Britain have changed as well. So, if cricket is not front and centre in the Caribbean, it's not going to be front and centre in the consciousness of many people of Caribbean heritage in Britain.

There is a permanent disconnection with cricket experienced by the recent British-born generation with Caribbean heritage. Then there is the relentless domination of other sports, including football, athletics, and basketball. These sports continued to capture the imagination and dedication, watching and playing, of most of the current descendants of the *Windrush* generation. After the successes of Jamaican and other Caribbean athletes during the 2012 Olympics in London, David

Lammy, the Labour Party MP for Tottenham in north London, born and raised in Britain with Guyanese parents, proclaimed on Twitter that, 'We're all Jamaican now! Not felt this good since the West Indian cricket teams of (the) Clive Lloyd and Viv Richards'.

Most young people of Caribbean heritage in Britain attend state schools where cricket, compared with private fee-paying schools, is very rarely played. Compared with English cricket, in terms of national representation, it is far more likely that a Great Britain or England international rugby league or rugby union player would have Caribbean heritage. Danny Cipriani, Jonathan Joseph, Courtney Lawes, Jermaine McGillvary, Leon Pryce, Kyle Sinckler, Anthony Watson and Marland Yarde are all players born in the Caribbean, or with Caribbean heritage, who have represented Great Britain or England at rugby league or union in recent years.

In 2005, England beat Australia 2-1 to win the Ashes for the first time in 18 years. This series was broadcast live on Channel 4 television. The excitement and tension throughout the series, which led to an historic England win, captured the imagination of millions of cricket fans, non-cricket fans, and casual observers alike. The fifth and final Test at The Oval had the highest-ever average ratings for a Test in the seven seasons Channel 4 televised live cricket. There was an average total of three million viewers across all 15 sessions of the Test. Two million viewers watched the morning session on day five, and 4.7 million people tuned in to watch the dramatic final afternoon session.[4] The 2005 Ashes series in England was the last series of live international cricket available on terrestrial television.

Since 2005, live international cricket in Britain has been relocated to the arena of 'pay-TV' sport on satellite television. Despite Sky TV's excellent coverage, this has made cricket more difficult to access, and less visible for a potentially interested audience of casual observers, young people and cricket enthusiasts who can't afford the subscription fees. These include younger and older people with Caribbean heritage. If I was a primary schoolboy in Britain today, with limited or no access to Sky TV, I would not be able to easily develop an interest in cricket. As I did in 1973 stimulated by watching live international Test and domestic one day cricket on BBC television.

'You just have to look at the climaxes of two very exciting series. Against India in 2018 and against Australia in 2005', says Simon Lister.

At the end of the Ashes series in 2005, the nation came to a standstill but in 2018 against India, the series was probably only watched by an audience in the tens of thousands. So, in the space of a dozen years, that's a very stark illustration of how much young people are missing cricket on free to air television nowadays.

This broadcasting trend was briefly interrupted in 2019, when Sky agreed to share its exclusive live rights to home England men's cricket – for one match only. The England v New Zealand World Cup final at Lord's. The final was shown on terrestrial free-to-air television on Channel 4, with a move to More 4 during the British Grand Prix at Silverstone, and back to Channel 4 later in the afternoon.

An estimated combined audience of eight million television viewers, via free-to-air and Sky, were treated to a dramatic tied match after the regulation 50 overs each. England won their first World Cup after a nail-biting sudden-death super over, which produced one of the most thrilling finishes to an international match in British televised cricket history. However, just before this book was published, there was no indication of any long-term agreements in Britain to broadcast live international cricket matches on free-to-air television.

Since 1973, there is also the reality that the Caribbean diaspora in Britain has moved on, evolved and been reshaped. For most people born in Britain with Caribbean heritage, a West Indies team on tour in England has very little or no impact on their lives. A British Labour Force survey reported that by 1998, among the black Caribbean population in Britain, 48% of Caribbean men and 34% of women were in an inter-ethnic relationship.[5]

For 55% of Caribbean men living with a partner and children under 16, and 40% of Caribbean women, that partner was from a different ethnic group.[6] This evolving trend has resulted in an increasing number of people with mixed identities, of which Caribbean heritage only forms a part. In turn, for those born in Britain in the last 15 to 20 years who have some Caribbean heritage, and a serious interest in cricket, there is no guarantee they would support the West Indies over England.

In years to come, sustaining Caribbean community and cultural institutions in Britain, including West Indian cricket, sports and social clubs, will continue to be a difficult task. The declining numbers of people in Britain with a direct and intimate connection to the Caribbean, and a sense of Caribbean family history, will continue to present a serious challenge to families attempting to transmit values and practices associated with Caribbean heritage. As the years have rolled on, decreasing numbers of young people in Britain with Caribbean heritage look back to the homelands of their parents or grandparents.

Without being overtly nostalgic, when I reflect on the 1973 tour from a West Indian perspective, with its compelling stories and cast of characters – both West Indian and English, and the individual achievements and memorable events which took place on the field and beyond the boundary, I also recognise how this series revitalised West Indies cricket. The momentum which 1973 developed was an essential building block. It helped to secure a solid platform and create a winning formula. This led to the West Indies becoming a vital force in international cricket, with years of dominance on tours in England during the 1970s and 1980s.

The steady stream of West Indian cricket achievement in England during this period, and the muscularity, rhythm and style in the way the West Indies played the game, continued to consolidate the cultural, political and social impact of cricket, and strengthen the relationship between cricket and the Caribbean diaspora. It delivered a rich source of collective self-esteem, inspiration and pride. It also supplied unmeasurable amounts of pleasure for many Caribbean and some non-Caribbean people in Britain. For these reasons alone, the impact, legacy and memory of the 1973 West Indies tour of England should not be casually underestimated or easily forgotten.

England v West Indies 1973 Test and ODI results summary

First Test match at The Oval, London: July 26, 27, 28, 30, 31

West Indies won the toss and decided to bat first. Umpires: David Constant and Tom Spencer.

West Indies first innings: 415 (Lloyd 132, Kallicharan 80, Boyce 72. Arnold 5 for 113).

England first innings: 257 (Boycott 97. Boyce 5 for 70).

West Indies second innings: 255 (Kallicharan 80, Sobers 51. Arnold 3 for 49, Illingworth 3 for 50, Snow 3 for 62).

England second innings: 255 (Hayes 106 no. Boyce 6 for 77).

West Indies won by 158 runs.

Second Test match at Edgbaston, Birmingham: August 9, 10, 11, 13, 14

West Indies won the toss and decided to bat first. Umpires: Dickie Bird and Arthur Fagg.

West Indies first innings: 327 (Fredericks 150, Julien 54. Underwood 3 for 40, Arnold 3 for 74, Old 3 for 86).

England first innings: 305 (Boycott 56, Amiss 56, Fletcher 52 no. Sobers 3 for 62, Holder 3 for 83).

West Indies second innings: 302 (Lloyd 94, Sobers 74, Kanhai 54. Arnold 4 for 43).

England second innings: 182 for 2 (Amiss 86 no).

Match drawn.

Third Test match at Lord's, London: August 23, 24, 25, 27

West Indies won the toss and decided to bat first. Umpires: Dickie Bird and Charlie Elliott.

West Indies first innings: 652 for 8 declared (Kanhai 157, Sobers 150 no, Julien 121, Lloyd 63, Fredericks 51. Willis 4 for 118).

England first innings: 233 (Fletcher 68. Boyce 4 for 50, Holder 4 for 56).

England second innings: 193 (Fletcher 86 no. Boyce 4 for 49).

West Indies won by an innings and 226 runs.

Keith Boyce won the Prudential-Wisden player of the series award.

First Prudential Trophy ODI match at Headingley, Leeds: September 5 – 55 overs a-side

West Indies won the toss and decided to bat first. Umpires: Charlie Elliott and Arthur Fagg.

West Indies: 181 all out from 54 overs (Kanhai 55. Old 3 for 43).

England: 182 for 9 from 54.3 overs (Denness 66).

England won by one wicket.

Second Prudential Trophy ODI match at The Oval, London: September 7 – 55 overs a-side

England won the toss and decided to bat first. Umpires: Dusty Rhodes and Tom Spencer.

England: 189 for 9 from 55 overs (Fletcher 63).

West Indies: 190 for 2 from 42.2 overs (Fredericks 105, Kallicharan 53).

West Indies won by eight wickets.

Author Q&A with Harold 'Dickie' Bird

Harold 'Dickie' Bird made his international debut as a Test match umpire in 1973. His first match was the third Test of the England v New Zealand series at Headingley. As a Yorkshireman who played for Yorkshire, Headingley was an appropriate venue to start his Test career. Later in the summer of 1973, Bird umpired two Test matches in the England v West Indies series. The second Test at Edgbaston and the third Test at Lord's.

'Dickie was quite a nervous character, but he always umpired well and kept things right', says Vanburn Holder. 'People liked that, respected that, and it was always quite fun when he was on the field. Even when he was getting on a bit and, maybe, getting one or two things wrong, he was still loved by everyone, everywhere he went'. Holder also worked as an umpire in England after his retirement from playing professional cricket.

Bird's total career appearances as an international umpire included 66 Tests, the first three World Cup finals at Lord's, and 92 ODIs. In the 2011 New Year's honours list, Bird received an OBE for his services to cricket and charity. The Dickie Bird Foundation was set up in 1998 to help less privileged young people in Britain to play sport. In 2017, an exhibition entitled 'Dickie Bird: My Life in Cricket' was open to the public for three months at the Experience Barnsley Museum and Discovery Centre.

As a Test match umpire, who was the best cricketer you saw on the field?

Garry Sobers was the greatest cricketer that ever lived. And I'm telling you, you will not see anyone as good in your lifetime or anybody else's lifetime. Sobers was a tremendous player and there will never be another one like him. At Lord's (in 1973) he tore his muscle in the field and got that score on one leg. It was a magnificent knock of 150 and one of the best innings I've ever seen.

How did you cope with crowd invasions when you umpired? There were several crowd invasions during the 1973 England v West Indies series, especially at The Oval and Lord's?

Dickie Bird *(Photo kindly supplied by Ted Cowley)*

When the supporters came on the field after a wicket had gone down, or at the close of play, they were harmless because they didn't really cause any problems. I just made sure they got off the pitch quickly. When the West Indian supporters came on to the field, they used to have a chat, a joke and a laugh with me, and give me pats on the back before running off back to their seats! I thought the West Indian supporters were wonderful and they brought so much pleasure to the game. I had a really good relationship with them and when I meet some West Indians now, including supporters and former players, they always remember me, and that for me is a real compliment. I also loved what the Pakistan and Indian fans brought to the game. I was in hospital recently with a nosebleed and I had to see one of the specialists to get it checked out. The specialist was Indian and after 20 minutes I asked him, 'Sir, can you tell me, how's my nose?' But he just wanted to talk about cricket and all the great Indian players he could think of for another 20 minutes!

What was the best bowling performance you saw as an umpire?

Dennis Lillee at Edgbaston in 1975 when the Australians came to England (Dickie Bird umpired the match with Arthur Fagg). Mike Denness put the Australians into bat on a beautiful day and, of course, once we started the Test match it was left to the elements. Australia batted first and got out just around lunch on the second day for 300 odd and the heavens opened. Just before the Australians were all out, John Edrich told me, standing next to me at square leg, 'I think we're going to get caught on a sticky (wicket) one here, Dickie'. Well, he was right. The heavens opened, it rained, and the ground was flooded. The ground staff at Edgbaston went to work and did a magnificent job to get it fit to play at quarter to five. England went out to bat, were 83 for 7 at the close of play and Lillee got three wickets (5 for 15 for the innings after England were all out the next day for 101). It was one of the best pieces of bowling I have seen while umpiring a Test match.

Who was the best captain you saw on the field while umpiring?

Ray Illingworth was one of the greatest captains I've seen. Illingworth was a great thinker and he really understood the game. During my time, I rated Illingworth, Michael Brearley, Imran Khan, Ian Chappell, Steve Waugh, Kapil Dev and Clive Lloyd – what a player he was! That's seven great captains there. But if I was in a real battle on the field, I'd want Ian Chappell on one side and Steve Waugh on the other side, and I'm sure I'd win some matches.

What was your most memorable match as an umpire?

There have been so many but the 1975 World Cup final, West Indies and Australia, will always stand out for me as it was the first ever World Cup final. I was also the first English umpire to go abroad, and one of the best Test matches I umpired was Pakistan v Australia in Karachi in 1994. It was towards the end of my career when I umpired quite a few matches abroad. When I did the Pakistan v Australia match in Karachi, I saw one of the best Test innings ever by Inzamam-ul-Haq. He scored 58 not out on a pitch that was turning square. He was facing Shane Warne and Tim May in Pakistan's second innings, the ball was taking spin, and he won the match for Pakistan. It was a wonderful knock.

How would you have coped with using video technology and the Decision Review System (DRS)?

I think I would have found it very easy because the technology helps you to get out of any problems doesn't it? I used to go to Barnsley

Football Club when I was umpiring and trained with the professional players. I used to do 50-yard and 100-yard sprints, so I could be in a good position to judge run outs. I always said to myself that if I was physically fit I'd be mentally fit. Now, umpires don't have to always run into position to call a run out. They go straight to the third umpire for a lot of run outs now, and that's the difference. I'm all for helping umpires out and technology has certainly done that. So, I don't necessarily see it as a bad thing, because if they get into any problems, they go to the third umpire. However, in my day, we always made our own decisions, rightly or wrongly. And, you see, we were open to criticism all the time if we made wrong decisions. Now, I don't think umpires are criticised as much because of the third umpire. All umpires make mistakes but if I made a good decision, I got a lot of satisfaction from that. You've got to get the big decisions right, just like the referees try to do in football, and that's the most important thing.

Who was the best umpire you umpired with in international cricket?

In my era we had a very good panel of Test umpires, Barrie Meyer, Ken Palmer, David Constant, Tommy Spencer and Charlie Elliott. They were all good umpires and I enjoyed umpiring with every one of them. And, as I said earlier, we made our own decisions because we didn't have the technology. The technology today means that a lot of the authority is being taken away from umpires and that is sad because in my era the umpire was part of the game. It was very rare that any of the lads on that panel made a mistake, but if they did make a mistake people talked about it. The press talked about it, and they talked about it in the pubs and the clubs. It was just part of the game.

Did you give Michael Holding his Whispering Death nickname?

Yes, that was me! I gave him that name because when he ran up to the wicket to bowl you couldn't hear anything. He was so light footed and that was amazing for a fast bowler.

What kept you going so long as an umpire?

I just tried to enjoy it. I did 25 years as a Test cricket umpire which is a long time. There are so many Test matches played now, that somebody worked out that if I was a Test umpire for 25 years today, I would have done 500 Tests. Unbelievable! These days there is a Test match every week somewhere in the world. Dennis Lillee once said that, 'Dickie had the knack of, if there was any trouble on the field, to be in straight away. He'd have it all sorted out and then he'd have a joke and a laugh with all of us. But when it came down to decision making, he always got them right'. The other thing is, that I can honestly say, I never had any problems with any professional cricketers throughout my career across the cricketing world, and I think that is because of my honesty and being fair.

What advice would you give to someone who was thinking of taking up a career as a cricket umpire?

Number one – enjoy it. Relax, use your common sense and have plenty of application, dedication and concentration.

Do you have any career regrets?

I just have one regret in my career and that was leaving Yorkshire to join Leicestershire. Yorkshire didn't want me to go and Herbert Sutcliffe said, 'I want this man to stay here'. I was playing my best cricket at Yorkshire at the time I left. I got 180-odd not out at Bradford Park (Avenue) against Glamorgan, and nobody else got any runs that day apart from Gilbert Parkhouse for Glamorgan. I was dropped for the next match but got a lot of runs that season, even though I was in and out of the Yorkshire side. We had a great side at Yorkshire then and it was very difficult for me to break in. If I could turn the clock back which, of course, I can't, I would have stayed at Yorkshire.

How thrilled were you to launch your My Life in Cricket exhibition in Barnsley, your home town?

I had everything there, including all my medals and quotes from all the great players across the world that played the game and, even, Prime Ministers. It was marvellous. I was at the opening ceremony and a lot of the Yorkshire team were there, and people from all over the country came to see it, which I'm very proud of. I was very surprised because, you know, when you get on in life you think people might have forgotten all about you. But after about three months about 25,000 people went through the exhibition. There was a quote on the wall of the exhibition about me from the great Viv Richards that said, 'The best Test umpire I have ever seen. There will never be another to touch him'. That gave me a lump in my throat and, do you know, I broke down in tears. Amazing that, isn't it?

Deryck Murray on Inshan Ali

Inshan Ali, who played in the first 1973 Test at The Oval, was the only player in the 1973 West Indies team who, some years later, I still had limited knowledge of. While researching and writing this book, I made it one of my priorities to find out more about Inshan's life and career. This is why I've included notes about his contribution to the 1973 tour in this book.

Inshan, also known as 'The Pride of Preysal', made his debut for Trinidad at the age of 16 and was the first cricketer from central Trinidad to play for the West Indies. He played 12 Tests and took 34 wickets at a cost of just under 48 runs each. But Inshan's other legacy is that he created a path for other players from Preysal, a remote village in central Trinidad just over 40 miles south of the capital, Port of Spain, to play Test cricket. These included Rangy Nanan, Denesh Ramdin and Ravi Rampaul.

Inshan sadly passed away in Trinidad at the young age of 45. In 1988, a recreational park and playing field in Preysal was named after him. Inshan's daughter, Aneesa, married Narsingh Deonarine who played for Guyana and 18 Tests for the West Indies.

Deryck Murray captained Inshan during their time playing together for Trinidad and Tobago. Murray also kept wicket to Inshan's bowling for Trinidad and Tobago, and the West Indies.

Inshan was a unique type of bowler and these mystery spinners come up every generation – somebody who comes along and is different. But they sometimes need special treatment, in the way they are not always sure what they are doing, and they need to be nursed and nurtured along during a Test match – almost session by session.

Inshan Ali batting (*Photo kindly supplied by Shafeeza Ali-Motilal*)

It's always very difficult to manage somebody like that within the team. So, with Inshan's Test career he tended to play in one game, then get left out, then play a few Test matches later in a series, or in the next series. So, Inshan didn't really have a continuous run in the West Indies team, and you can find players like that in every Test team in any generation throughout the world. For example, Johnny Gleeson in Australia and Paul Adams in South Africa.

You always get these types of players, and Inshan was really a mystery spinner in a sense that he could bowl Chinamen and googlies and, I suppose, part of the attraction of bowlers like Inshan is that they are not necessarily consistent. So, you're not sure what you're going to get and it's the same for the opposition. They are not sure what they are coming up against.

During his time playing for the Trinidad and Tobago team he was very successful. But he was not managed in the same way as he was when he played for the West Indies team, and so I don't think the West Indies truly saw the best of Inshan.

Author Q&A with Colin Grant on The Wailers in Britain 1973

In September 1972, Bob Marley, Peter Tosh and Bunny Wailer from The Wailers met Chris Blackwell at Basing Street in West London and signed for Island Records, Blackwell's record label. Blackwell gave The Wailers £4,000 to make the album *Catch A Fire*. A month later, the band returned to Jamaica to record the tracks for the album. In early 1973, Blackwell listened to recording session master tapes in Jamaica. He was mightily impressed, arranged for The Wailers to return to Britain for a tour, and booked Benjamin Foot to be their tour manager.

In 1973, The Wailers completed their first major tour of Britain on the back of *Catch A Fire*. By the end of the tour their popularity in Britain had significantly increased. Colin Grant, historian, author and broadcaster, is the author of *I & I – The Natural Mystics: Marley, Tosh, and Wailer*, *Negro with a Hat: The Rise and Fall of Marcus Garvey and His Dream of Mother Africa*, and *Homecoming: Voices of the Windrush Generation*.

When The Wailers first arrived in Britain in 1973, they were unknown. I think Bob Marley may have come through Britain briefly by his own, but this was the first time they came here to tour as a group. They lived hand to mouth in North London near Willesden and had a small beaten-up Mercedes van, which they used to do their mini-tours bombing up and down the M1 motorway. Their road manager was a guy called Benjamin Foot who was the son of Hugh Foot, one of the governors of Jamaica. Benjamin was only in his early 20s then.

What was very interesting was, even though The Wailers were not well known here, they soon started to get some attention and the rock critics were immediately enthralled by them. I think what was

Bob Marley and the Wailers (left to right - Peter McIntosh 'Tosh', Aston 'Family Man' Barrett, Bob Marley, Earl 'Wire' Lindo, Carlton 'Carly' Barrett and Neville 'Bunny' Livingston) pose for a portrait in 1973 in London (*Photo by Michael Ochs Archives/Getty Images*)

interesting about The Wailers, and some of the early reggae musicians, was their sincerity and their adherence to Rastafari and the Bible.

For example, Benjamin Foot talks about when they were in the tour bus going up and down the motorway, The Wailers would be arguing non-stop. But they weren't arguing about who was going to write all the songs or about girls. They would argue about scripture and Benjamin Foot says it was more like being in a seminary than being with a band.

Why were The Wailers so keen to meet Chris Blackwell, owner of Island Records?

The Wailers realised that if they came to England, they would have a chance to meet Chris Blackwell. They heard a lot about Chris Blackwell in Jamaica and really wanted to meet him. By this time, The Wailers had ten years together and they made a lot of records in Jamaica. By 1973, Bob Marley had written around several hundred songs, but they were really struggling to make a living out of it. The market in Jamaica was very small but in England there was an explosion of Blue Beat Records and reggae music.

Some of The Wailers' records were also being sold here, so they wanted to come to England and find out if they were getting the right royalties and payments for the records they made. Some of their records were being sold out of the back of vans by Chris Blackwell and Esther Anderson at Island, and they were not sure whether they were being properly paid. So, they came to England to see whether this was true or not.

Also, they recognised that other Jamaican artistes had done well here. For example, Millie Small had done well and half a dozen others, including Desmond Decker, and Bob (Andy) and Marcia (Griffiths) with *Young, Gifted and Black*. So, these kinds of things were very encouraging for them.

What type of audiences came to see The Wailers on tour in 1973 in Britain?

They mostly played to student audiences in polytechnics and universities, and Bunny Wailer says they played in freak show clubs and striptease clubs and that's what really annoyed him. So, he headed back home to Jamaica before the rest of the band. The Wailers played in venues which could only hold around 60 to 100 people maximum. But they got a major break in May 1973 when they appeared on the BBC's *Old Grey Whistle Test,* and if you watch that performance you will see how unusual they were, and how tight they were as musicians. They'd been playing together for about 10 years, so they were very well rehearsed and blew the socks off the people who saw that show on television.

How and why did their popularity develop during and after the 1973 tour?

What also enthralled people in Britain about The Wailers was the music and the way they presented themselves was so serious, because this was not throw-away pop music. These were songs which were like musical biographies. So, when Bob Marley sings, *Cold ground was my bed last night, and rock was my pillow too*, that's a real-life experience he is articulating. It's not made up. So, people began to get a real sense of their sincerity. There is something about the Caribbean voice which has a lot of gravitas and that is especially true in the Caribbean singing voice. I think there was something unique, modern and vibrant back then about the sounds of reggae and the sound of The Wailers as well.

Can you summarise why 1973 was such a crucial year for The Wailers and their overall impact as a group?

1973 was a pivotal year for The Wailers because, after being signed by Chris Blackwell, they produced *Catch a Fire*, an amazing album promoted by Blackwell at Island records. They then toured Britain for the first time and got some rave reviews for the album. The Wailers made about eight albums in Jamaica before they came to England. But if they hadn't met Chris Blackwell, we wouldn't be talking about them in the same way today. So, 1973 was their breakout year without a shadow of doubt.

Author's Acknowledgements

Special thanks to: Arif Ali and Kash Ali at Hansib Publications for all your support and help in publishing this book.

Many thanks to: Reza Abasali, Devon Aitchison, Renee Babb, Robert Bradford, Lloyd Bradley, Dougie Brimson, Ted Cowley at The Dickie Bird Foundation, Emily at The Rohan Kanhai Pub – Ashington, Jack Gordon-Brown at deCoubertin Books, Peter and Sheila Hicks, Marisa Huque, Simon Lister, Alia McKellar at Profile Books, Derek Marshall, Clifford Narinesingh at Royards Publishing Company – Trinidad, Suresh Rambaran, Angela Ramcharan, David Robertson – Honorary Curator at Kent County Cricket Club, Charles and Lucy Robinson at Printique, Earle Robinson, and John Stevenson for helping me with contacts, copyright and permissions, inspiration, interviews, research material and website design/production.

Many thanks to: Ruby Ali-Strayton and Karen Manser for creative support and editorial recommendations.

Additional photography: Reza Abasali, Marisa Huque and Majlinda Zeqiri-Babb.

Many thanks again to all who kindly agreed to be interviewed and share their experiences, opinions, reflections and stories which were essential to the development of *1973*:

Reza Abasali, Shafeeza Ali-Motilal, Dennis Amiss, Nzingha Assata, Mark Babb, Mavis Babb, Clyde Best, Harold 'Dickie' Bird, Tim Bowler, Robert Bradford, Ian Bradshaw, Basil Butcher, Brian Camacho, Neville Carberry, Andrew Carnegie, Tim Cooke, Mark Cripps, Desree Dinsdale, Vasbert Drakes, Graham Dransfield, Nick Finch, Keith Fletcher, Maurice Foster, Lance Gibbs, Clayton Goodwin, Colin Grant, Frank Hayes, Beryl 'Bobby' Haynes, Richard Hayward, Ron Headley, Russell Holden, Vanburn Holder, Karen Hunte, Muriel

Hunte, *Bernard Julien, Alvin Kallicharan, Thelma Lewis, Simon Lister, Lainy Malkani, Patrick Manning, Eric McClymont, Professor Joe Moran, Deryck Murray, Brian Osborne, Joseph 'Reds' Perreira, Susan Price, Earle Robinson, Professor Clem Seecharan, Neil Sillett, Lonsdale Skinner, Steve Stephenson, Dwight Stevens, Stanley and Theresa Sunich, David Thorpe, Steve Walcott, Rod Westmaas, Errol Young.

*Bernard Julien was interviewed for *1973* by Reza Abasali in Trinidad.

New and previously used content from interviews with Tony Cozier, Paul Eubanks, Sam King and Cyrille Regis was included in the production of *1973*. Sadly, Tony Cozier, Paul Eubanks, Sam King and Cyrille Regis have passed away since I interviewed them in the years leading up to the publishing of this book. *1973* is also dedicated to the life, spirit and work of Tony Cozier, Paul Eubanks, Sam King and Cyrille Regis.

* * *

Some names and identifying details in this book have been changed to protect the privacy of individuals.

Endnotes

CHAPTER 1

1. Conrad Hunte, *Playing to Win* (London, 1971), p.44-45.
2. Ann Kramer, *Many rivers to cross: The History of the Caribbean Contribution to the NHS 1948-69* (Norwich, 2006), p.20.
3. John La Guerre, *Calcutta to Caroni: The East Indians of Trinidad* (London, 1974), preface.
4. Edward Heath, *The Course of My Life: My Autobiography* (London, 1998), p.394.
5. '1973: Britain joins the EEC', BBC website: news.bbc.co.uk/ onthisday/hi/dates/stories/january/1/newsid_2459000/ 2459167.stm

CHAPTER 2

1. Clem Seecharan, *Muscular Learning: Cricket and Education in the Making of the British West Indies at the End of the 19th Century* (Jamaica, 2006), p.5.
2. C.L.R James, *Beyond a Boundary* (London, 2005), p.66.
3. Hilary McD Beckles, *The Development of West Indies Cricket: The Age of Nationalism, Vol. 1* (Jamaica, 1998), p.26.
4. Michael Manley, *A History of West Indian Cricket* (London, 1988), p.21.
5. Arif Ali (Ed), *Guyana at 50: Reflection, Celebration and Inspiration* (Hertford, 1988), p.41.

CHAPTER 3

1. 'Caribbean workers arriving in Panama, on board the Cristobal', BBC website, 17 February 2011: www.bbc.co.uk/history/british/ victorians/panama_gallery_04.shtml

2. Colin Babb, *They Gave the Crowd Plenty Fun: West Indies Cricket and its Relationship with the British-Resident Caribbean Diaspora* (Hertford, 2015), p.34.
3. Lloyd Bradley, *Sounds Like London: 100 Years of Black Music in the Capital* (London, 2013), pp.31-32.
4. David Dabydeen, John Gilmore and Cecily Jones, *The Oxford Companion to Black British History* (Oxford, 2007), p.219.
5. Gordon Ross (Ed), *Great Moments in Cricket: a Cricketer Special* (London, 1975), p.37.
6. David Dabydeen, John Gilmore and Cecily Jones, *The Oxford Companion to Black British History* (Oxford, 2007), p.219.
7. Geoff Armstrong, *The 100 Greatest Cricketers* (London, Sydney, Auckland, 2015), p.26.
8. Geoffrey Boycott, *The Autobiography* (London, 1987), p.110.

CHAPTER 4
1. Rob Bagchi and Paul Rogerson, *The Unforgiven: The Story of Don Revie's Leeds United* (London, 2009), p.4.
2. Ibid., p4.
3. The Times newspaper, 'The Cup final', The Times, 4 May 1973, p.12.
4. Roger Hermiston, *Clough and Revie – The Rivals Who Changed the Face of England Football* (Edinburgh, 2011), p.150.
5. Ken Jones (Ed), *Football Champions* (London, 1973), p.47.
6. Oliver Owen, 'The 10 coolest items of sportswear ever', Guardian newspaper website, 6 April 2003: www.theguardian.com/sport/2003/apr/06/features.sportmonthly3
7. Ken Jones (Ed), *Football Champions* (London, 1973), pp.35-36.
8. Paul Harrison, *The Black Flash: The Albert Johanneson Story* (Skipton, 2012), p. 202.
9. Dougie Brimson, *Kicking Off* (London, 2006), p.141.

CHAPTER 5
1. Colin Babb, 'The kick-off for black footballers – Cyrille Regis', Caribbean Intelligence website, 3 May 2016: www.caribbeanintelligence.com/content/kick-black-footballers-cyrille-regis
2. Dan Lucas, 'The forgotten history of the 1973 Five Nations championship', Guardian newspaper website, 5 March 2014:

www.theguardian.com/sport/blog/2014/mar/05/1973-five-nations-forgotten-story

3. David 'Bumble' Lloyd, *Last in the Tin Bath: The Autobiography* (London, 2016), p.108.

4. Jo Moran, *Armchair Nation: An intimate history of Britain in front of the TV* (London, 2014), p.164.

5. Richard Wagner, 'Colour TV switch-on tomorrow', The Times, 30 June 1967, p.20.

6. The Times Newspaper, Obituaries, 10 November 2000, p.25.

7. James Allan, 'Miss World loses title because of 'adverse publicity'', The Daily Telegraph, 8 March 1974, p.17.

CHAPTER 6

1. David Frith (Ed), *The Cricketer. Volume 54 No.4 April (Spring Annual)* (1973), Inside back cover.

2. Richard H Thomas, 'The John Player League and the Bat-Swinging Sixties', All Out Cricket website, 17 January 2014: www.alloutcricket.com/features/the-john-player-league-and-the-bat-swinging-sixties

3. Gordon Ross (Ed), *Playfair Cricket Annual 1973* (London, 1973), p.5.

4. Edward Baugh, 'A Toast to Cricket', in Mervyn Morris and Jimmy Carnegie (eds), *Lunchtime Medley: Writings on West Indies Cricket* (Kingston, 2008), pp. 3-4.

5. Adrian Milledge, 'Paper Talk', *Backspin Magazine*, Issue 11, Winter 2015-16, p.48.

6. Gordon Greenidge, *Gordon Greenidge: The Man in the Middle* (Newton Abbot, 1980), p.10.

7. Barry Richards, *The Barry Richards Story* (Newton Abbot, 1978), p.125.

8. David Frith (Ed), *The Cricketer. Volume 54 No.4 April (Spring Annual)* (1973), p.6.

9. David 'Bumble' Lloyd, *Last in the Tin Bath: The Autobiography* (London, 2016), pp.92-93.

10. David Frith (Ed), *The Cricketer. Volume 54 No.4 April (Spring Annual)* (1973), pp.27-31.

11. Norman Preston (Ed), *Wisden Cricketers Almanak 1974* (London, 1974), p.484.

12. Adrian Milledge, 'Paper Talk', *Backspin Magazine*, Issue 11, Winter 2015-16, p.49.
13. Roland Butcher and Brigette Lawrence, *Rising to the Challenge* (London, 1989), p.32.
14. David Frith (Ed), *The Cricketer. Volume 54 No.4 April (Spring Annual)* (1973), p.29.
15. Colin Babb, *They Gave the Crowd Plenty Fun: West Indies Cricket and its Relationship with the British-Resident Caribbean Diaspora* (Hertford, 2015), p.146.

CHAPTER 7
1. Martin Williamson, 'Clive Radley', ESPN Cricinfo website: www.espncricinfo.com/england/content/player/19316.html

CHAPTER 8
1. David Frith (Ed), *The Cricketer. Volume 54 No.4 April (Spring Annual)* (1973), p.7.
2. Clyde Walcott with Brian Scovell, *Sixty Years on the Back Foot: The Cricketing Life of Sir Clyde Walcott* (London, 1999), p.65.
3. Peter Gillman, 'Cricket, lovely, cricket', *Radio Times* magazine, 26 July 1973, p.48.

CHAPTER 9
1. EW Swanton, 'Greig fit to bowl so Hayes may get big chance', The Daily Telegraph, 26 July 1973, p.34.

CHAPTER 10
1. Conrad Hunte, *Playing to Win* (London, 1971), p.89.

CHAPTER 11
1. John Woodcock, 'Illingworth turns screw and silences calypsos', The Times, 10 August 1973, p.8.
2. Gerry Cotter, *England versus West Indies: A History of the Tests and Other Matches* (Swindon, 1991), p.173.

CHAPTER 12
1. Norman Preston (Ed), *Wisden Cricketers Almanak 1974* (London, 1974), p.349.

2. Colin Babb, *They Gave the Crowd Plenty Fun: West Indies Cricket and its Relationship with the British-Resident Caribbean Diaspora* (Hertford, 2015), p.61.
3. Brian Luckhurst, *Boot boy to President* (Kent, 2004), p.66.
4. Simon Lister, *Supercat – The Authorised biography of Clive Lloyd* (Bath, 2007), p.83.
5. EW Swanton, 'England crushed by West Indies all-round skills', The Daily Telegraph, 28 August 1973, p.24.

POSTSCRIPT – PART 1
1. Roland Butcher and Brigette Lawrence, *Rising to the Challenge* (London, 1989), p.65.

POSTSCRIPT – PART 2
1. Ron Clarke, 'Sorry Sunderland are still learning the hard way', The Sunday Times – Sport, 20 August 2017, p.4.
2. Jim Jinkoo, 'Indo Caribbeans in the UK', in Jim Jinkoo (Ed), *Chutney Village magazine – Souvenir Edition: Commemoration of Indian Arrival Day 2000* (2000), p.9.
3. Colin Babb, *They Gave the Crowd Plenty Fun: West Indies Cricket and its Relationship with the British-Resident Caribbean Diaspora* (Hertford, 2015), pp.159-160.
4. Channel 4, 'England's Ashes victory helps Channel 4 to best ever day', Channel 4 website: www.channel4.com/info/press/news/englands-ashes-victory-helps-channel-4-to-best-ever-day
5. Lucinda Platt, *Ethnicity and Family. Relationships within and between ethnic groups: An analysis using the Labour Force Survey* (Essex, 1998), p.7.
6. Ibid., p.7.

Bibliography

PRIMARY SOURCES

Ahmed, Maryam and Rodgers, Lucy, Windrush: Who exactly was on board? BBC website, 27 April 2018: www.bbc.com/news/uk-43808007

Allan, James, 'Miss World loses title because of 'adverse publicity'', *The Daily Telegraph*, 8 March 1974.

Babb, Colin, The kick-off for black footballers – Cyrille Regis, Caribbean Intelligence website, 2016: www.caribbeanintelligence.com/content/kick-black-footballers-cyrille-regis

Bourne, Stephen, Obituary: Charlie Williams, *Guardian* newspaper website, 4 September 2006: www.theguardian.com/media/2006/sep/04/obituaries.guardianobituaries

Caribbean workers arriving in Panama, on board the Cristobal, BBC website, 17 February 2011: www.bbc.co.uk/history/british/victorians/panama_gallery_04.shtml

Channel 4, England's Ashes victory helps Channel 4 to best ever day, Channel 4 website, 13 September 2005: www.channel4.com/info/press/news/englands-ashes-victory-helps-channel-4-to-best-ever-day

Clarke, Ron, Sorry Sunderland are still learning the hard way, *The Sunday Times* newspaper – Sport, 20 August 2017.

England v The West Indies. 1950 to 1976. (BBC Radio Collection audio cassette set) 1990.

Gillman, Peter, 'Cricket, lovely, cricket', *Radio Times* magazine, 26 July 1973.

Lucas, Dan, The forgotten history of the 1973 Five Nations championship, *Guardian* newspaper website, 5 March 2014: www.theguardian.com/sport/blog/2014/mar/05/1973-five-nations-forgotten-story

Milledge, Adrian, Paper Talk, *Backspin* Magazine, Issue 11, Winter 2015-16.

Murray, Deryck, interviewed on British Broadcasting Corporation (BBC) radio programme, '*Windies Wonders.*' Broadcast on BBC World Service, August 2013.

1973: Britain joins the EEC, BBC website: news.bbc.co.uk/onthisday/hi/dates/stories/january/1/newsid_2459000/2459167.stm

Owen, Oliver, The 10 coolest items of sportswear ever, *Guardian* newspaper website, 2003: www.theguardian.com/sport/2003/apr/06/features.sportmonthly3

Shuster, Alvin, London is shaken by two bombings laid to the IRA, *New York Times* website, 9 March 1973: www.nytimes.com/1973/03/09/archives/london-is-shaken-by-two-bombings-laid-to-the-ira-one-dead-and-243.html

Staff Reporter, 'Miss World stripped of title by Mecca', *The Times* newspaper, 8 March 1974.

Swanton, EW, 'England crushed by West Indies all-round skills', *The Daily Telegraph*, 28 August 1973.

Swanton, EW, 'Greig fit to bowl so Hayes may get big chance', *The Daily Telegraph*, 26 July 1973.

The Cup final, *The Times* newspaper, 4 May 1973.

Thomas, Richard H, The John Player League and the Bat-Swinging Sixties, All Out Cricket website, 2014: www.alloutcricket.com/features/the-john-player-league-and-the-bat-swinging-sixties

Wagner, Richard, Colour TV switch-on tomorrow, *The Times* newspaper, 30 June 1967.

Williamson, Martin, Clive Radley, *ESPN Cricinfo website*: www.espncricinfo.com/england/content/player/19316.html

Woodcock, John, 'Illingworth turns screw and silences calypsos', *The Times* newspaper, 10 August 1973.

SECONDARY PUBLISHED SOURCES

Ali, Arif (Ed), *Guyana at 50: Reflection, Celebration and Inspiration*, (Hansib) 2016.

Ali-Motilal, Shafeeza, *The Pride of Preysal: The Inshan Ali Story*, (Royards Publishing Company) 2014.

Armstrong, Geoff, *The 100 Greatest Cricketers*, (New Holland Publishers) 2015.

Babb, Colin, *They Gave the Crowd Plenty Fun: West Indies Cricket and its Relationship with the British-Resident Caribbean Diaspora*, (Hansib) 2015.

Bagchi, Rob and Rogerson, Paul, *The Unforgiven: The Story of Don Revie's Leeds United*, (Aurum Press) 2009.

Baskcomb, Julian (Ed), *Leeds United FC – The Official Millennium Handbook*, 1999.

Baugh, Edward, A Toast to Cricket, in *Lunchtime Medley: Writings on West Indies Cricket*, edited by Mervyn Morris and Jimmy Carnegie, (Ian Randle Publishers) 2008.

Beckles, Hilary McD, *The Development of West Indies Cricket: The Age of Nationalism, Vol. 1*, (The Press University of the West Indies) 1998.

Benaud, Richie, *Anything but...An Autobiography*, (Hodder and Stoughton) 1998.

Berry, Scyld, *Cricket: The Game of Life: Every reason to celebrate*, (Hodder and Stoughton) 2016.

Best, Clyde, *The Acid Test – The Autobiography of Clyde Best*, (deCoubertin Books) 2016.

Birbalsingh, Frank, *Indian-Caribbean Test Cricketers and the Quest for Identity*, (Hansib) 2014.

Bird, Dickie, *80 Not Out: My Favourite Cricket Memories*, (Hodder and Stoughton) 2014.

Bird, Dickie, *My Autobiography*, (Hodder and Stoughton) 1997.

Boycott, Geoffrey, *The Autobiography,* (Macmillan) 1987.

Bradley, Lloyd, *Sounds Like London: 100 Years of Black Music in the Capital*, (Serpent's Tail) 2013.

Brimson, Dougie, *Kicking Off,* (Headline) 2006.

Butcher, Roland and Lawrence, Brigette, *Rising to the Challenge*, (Pelham Books/Stephen Greene Press) 1989.

CARICOM, *Final Report of the Review Panel on the Governance of Cricket* – October 2015, (2015).

Claypole, William and Robottom, John, *Caribbean Story: Book 2*, (Longman) 2001.

Cotter, Gerry, *England versus West Indies: A History of the Tests and Other Matches*, (The Crowood Press) 1991.

Dabydeen, David, Gilmore, John and Jones, Cecily, *The Oxford Companion to Black British History*, (Oxford University Press) 2007.

Fletcher, Keith, *Captain's Innings: an autobiography*, (Stanley Paul and Co. Ltd) 1983.

Frith, David (Ed), *The Cricketer. Volume 54 No.4 April (Spring Annual)*, 1973.

Gambaccini, Paul, Rice, Tim, Rice, Jonathan and Brown, Tony, *The Complete Eurovision Song Contest Companion*, (Pavilion Books Limited) 1998.

Goodwin, Clayton, *Caribbean Cricketers: From the Pioneers to Packer*, (George G. Harrap and Co. Ltd) 1980.

Greenidge, Gordon, *Gordon Greenidge: The Man in the Middle*, (David and Charles) 1980.

Harrison, Paul, *The Black Flash: The Albert Johanneson Story*, (Vertical) 2012.

Heath, Edward, *The Course of My Life: My Autobiography*, (Hodder and Stoughton) 1998.

Hermiston, Roger, *Clough and Revie – The Rivals Who Changed the Face of England Football*, (Mainstream) 2011.

Hewitt, Guy, *Fathering a Nation: Barbados and the Legacy of Errol Walton Barrow*, (Hansib) 2016.

Hunte, Conrad, *Playing to Win*, (Hodder and Stoughton) 1971.

Hunter, Norman, *Biting Talk: My autobiography*, (Hodder and Stoughton) 2004.

James, C.L.R, *Beyond A Boundary*, (Yellow Jersey Press) 2005.

Jones, Ken (Ed), *Football Champions,* (Purnell) 1973.

Kramer, Ann, *Many rivers to cross: The History of the Caribbean Contribution to the NHS 1948-69*, (The Stationery Office) 2006.

Kumar, Vijay P, *Cricket, Lovely, Cricket. West Indies v England 1950. 50th Anniversary Tribute*, (Vijay P. Kumar) 2000.

La Guerre, John, *Calcutta to Caroni: The East Indians of Trinidad*, (Longman Caribbean) 1974.

Lister, Simon, *Supercat – The Authorised biography of Clive Lloyd*, (Fairfield Books) 2007.

Lloyd, Clive, *Living for Cricket,* (Stanley Paul) 1980.

Lloyd, David 'Bumble', *Last in the Tin Bath: The Autobiography,* (Simon and Schuster) 2016.

Luckhurst, Brian, *Boot boy to President*, (KOS Media Publishing Limited) 2004.

Malkani, Lainy, *Sugar, Sugar: Bitter-sweet Tales of Indian Migrant Workers*, (Hope Road publishing) 2017.

Manley, Michael, *A History of West Indian Cricket*, (André Deutsch) 1988.

Martin-Jenkins, Christopher, *Cricket – A Way of Life: The Cricketer Illustrated History of Cricket*, (St. Michael) 1986.

Milledge, Adrian, *Paper Talk*, in Backspin Magazine, Issue 11, Winter 2015.

Moran, Joe, *Armchair Nation: An intimate history of Britain in front of the TV,* (Profile Books Ltd) 2014.

Nakhuda, Sabir, *Bengal to Barbados: A 100 year history of East Indians in Barbados*, (Sabir Nakhuda) 2013.

Platt, Lucinda, *Ethnicity and Family. Relationships within and between ethnic groups: An analysis using the Labour Force Survey*, (Institute for Social and Economic Research, University of Essex) 1998.

Preston, Norman (Ed), *Wisden Cricketers Almanak 1974,* (Sporting Handbooks Limited) 1974.

Regis, Cyrille, *My Story: The Autobiography of the First Black Icon of British Football*, (André Deutsch) 2010.

Richard, Cliff, *My Life, My Way*, (Headline) 2009.

Richards, Barry, *The Barry Richards Story*, (Faber and Faber) 1978.

Richards, Sir Vivian, *Viv Richards: The Definitive Autobiography*, (Penguin) 2001.

Ross, Gordon (Ed), *Great Moments in Cricket: a Cricketer Special*, (The Cricketer Ltd), 1975.

Ross, Gordon (Ed), *Playfair Cricket Annual 1973*, (The Dickens Press) 1973.

Ross, Gordon (Ed), *Playfair Cricket Annual 1974*, (The Queen Anne Press) 1973.

Seecharan, Clem, *Hand-In-Hand: History of Cricket in Guyana, 1865-1897. Volume 1: The Foundation*, (Hansib) 2015.

Seecharan, Clem, *Muscular Learning: Cricket and Education in the Making of the British West Indies at the End of the 19th Century*, (Ian Randle) 2000.

Smith, Stephen, *Charlie: The Charlie Williams Story*, (Neville-Douglas Publishing Ltd) 1998.

The Topical Times Football Book 1972-3, (D.C. Thomson and Co. Ltd) 1973.

Walcott, Clyde with Scovell, Brian, *Sixty Years on the Back Foot: The Cricketing Life of Sir Clyde Walcott*, (Victor Gollancz) 1999.

Williams, Jack, *Entertaining the Nation: A Social History of British Television*, (Sutton Publishing Limited) 2004.